The Java™ Native Interface

Programmer's Guide and Specification

The Java™ Series

Lisa Friendly, Series Editor

Tim Lindholm, Technical Editor

Please see our web site (http://www.awl.com /cseng/javaseries) for more information on these titles.

Ken Arnold and James Gosling, *The Java™ Programming Language, Second Edition*
ISBN 0-201-31006-6

Mary Campione and Kathy Walrath, *The Java™ Tutorial, Second Edition: Object-Oriented Programming for the Internet* (Book/CD)
ISBN 0-201-31007-4

Mary Campione, Kathy Walrath, Alison Huml, and the Tutorial Team, *The Java™ Tutorial Continued: The Rest of the JDK™* (Book/CD)
ISBN 0-201-48558-3

Patrick Chan, *The Java™ Developers Almanac 1999*
ISBN 0-201-43298-6

Patrick Chan and Rosanna Lee, *The Java™ Class Libraries, Second Edition, Volume 2: java.applet, java.awt, java.beans*
ISBN 0-201-31003-1

Patrick Chan, Rosanna Lee, and Doug Kramer, *The Java™ Class Libraries, Second Edition, Volume 1: java.io, java.lang, java.math, java.net, java.text, java.util*
ISBN 0-201-31002-3

Patrick Chan, Rosanna Lee, and Doug Kramer, *The Java™ Class Libraries, Second Edition, Volume 1: Supplement for the Java™ 2 Platform, Standard Edition, v1.2*
ISBN 0-201-48552-4

Li Gong, *Inside Java™ 2 Platform Security: Architecture, API Design, and Implementation*
ISBN 0-201-31000-7

James Gosling, Bill Joy, and Guy Steele, *The Java™ Language Specification*
ISBN 0-201-63451-1

James Gosling, Frank Yellin, and The Java Team, *The Java™ Application Programming Interface, Volume 1: Core Packages*
ISBN 0-201-63453-8

James Gosling, Frank Yellin, and The Java Team, *The Java™ Application Programming Interface, Volume 2: Window Toolkit and Applets*
ISBN 0-201-63459-7

Jonni Kanerva, *The Java™ FAQ*
ISBN 0-201-63456-2

Doug Lea, *Concurrent Programming in Java™, Second Edition: Design Principles and Patterns*
ISBN 0-201-31009-0

Sheng Liang, *The Java™ Native Interface: Programmer's Guide and Specification*
ISBN 0-201-32577-2

Tim Lindholm and Frank Yellin, *The Java™ Virtual Machine Specification, Second Edition*
ISBN 0-201-43294-3

Henry Sowizral, Kevin Rushforth, and Michael Deering, *The Java™ 3D API Specification*
ISBN 0-201-32576-4

Kathy Walrath and Mary Campione, *The JFC Swing Tutorial: A Guide to Constructing GUIs*
ISBN 0-201-43321-4

Seth White, Maydene Fisher, Rick Cattell, Graham Hamilton, and Mark Hapner, *JDBC™ API Tutorial and Reference, Second Edition: Universal Data Access for the Java™ 2 Platform*
ISBN 0-201-43328-1

The Java™ Native Interface

Interface

Programmer's Guide and Specification

Sheng Liang

ADDISON-WESLEY

An imprint of Addison Wesley Longman, Inc.

Reading, Massachusetts • Harlow, England • Menlo Park, California
Berkeley, California • Don Mills, Ontario • Sydney
Bonn • Amsterdam • Tokyo • Mexico City

The publisher offers discounts on this book when ordered in quantity for special sales. For more information, please contact the Corporate, Government, and Special Sales Group, CEPUB, Addison Wesley Longman, Inc., One Jacob Way, Reading, Massachusetts 01867.

Text printed on recycled and acid-free paper.

ISBN 0201325772

3 4 5 6 7 8   MA   02 01 00 99

3rd Printing December 1999

To the VM Teams

Contents

Part Three: Specification

Preface

THIS book covers the Java™ Native Interface (JNI). It will be useful to you if you are interested in any of the following:

- integrating a Java application with legacy code written in languages such as C or C++
- incorporating a Java virtual machine implementation into an existing application written in languages such as C or C++
- implementing a Java virtual machine
- understanding the technical issues in language interoperability, in particular how to handle features such as garbage collection and multithreading

First and foremost, the book is written for developers. You will find easy steps to get started with the JNI, informative discussions on various JNI features, and helpful tips on how to use the JNI effectively. The JNI was initially released in early 1997. The book summarizes two years of collective experience gained by engineers at Sun Microsystems as well as the vast number of developers in the Java technology community.

Second, the book presents the design rationale of various JNI features. Not only is this of interest to the academic community, but a thorough understanding of the design is also a prerequisite to using the JNI effectively.

Third, a part of the book is the definitive JNI specification for the Java 2 platform. JNI programmers may use the specification as a reference manual. Java virtual machine implementors must follow the specification to achieve conformance.

Send comments on this specification or questions about JNI to our electronic mail address: jni@java.sun.com. For the latest on the Java 2 platform, or to get the latest Java 2 SDK release, visit our web site at http://java.sun.com. For updated information about The Java™ Series, including errata for this book, and previews of forthcoming books, visit http://java.sun.com/Series.

The JNI was designed following a series of discussions between Sun Microsystems and Java technology licensees. The JNI partly evolved from Netscape's Java Runtime Interface (JRI), which was designed by Warren Harris. Many people from Java technology licensee companies actively participated in the design discussions. They include Russ Arun (Microsoft), Patrick Beard (Apple), Simon Nash (IBM), Ken Root (Intel), Ian Ellison-Taylor (Microsoft), and Mike Toutonghi (Microsoft).

The JNI design also benefited greatly from Sun internal design reviews conducted by Dave Bowen, James Gosling, Peter Kessler, Tim Lindholm, Mark Reinhold, Derek White, and Frank Yellin. Dave Brown, Dave Connelly, James McIlree, Benjamin Renaud, and Tom Rodriguez made significant contributions to the JNI enhancements in Java 2 SDK 1.2. Carla Schroer's team of compatibility testers in Novosibirsk, Russia, wrote compatibility tests for the JNI. In the process they uncovered places where the original specification was unclear or incomplete.

The JNI technology would not have been developed and deployed without the management support of Dave Bowen, Larry Abrahams, Dick Neiss, Jon Kannegaard, and Alan Baratz. I received full support and encouragement to work on this book from my manager Dave Bowen.

Tim Lindholm, author of *The Java™ Virtual Machine Specification*, led the Java virtual machine development effort at the time when the JNI was being designed. Tim did pioneering work on the virtual machine and native interfaces, advocated the use of the JNI, and added rigor and clarity to this book. He also provided the initial sketch for this book's "kitchen and dining room" cover art design.

This book benefited from the help of many colleagues. Anand Palaniswamy wrote a portion of Chapter 10 on common traps and pitfalls. Janet Koenig carefully reviewed a preliminary draft and contributed many useful ideas. Beth Stearns wrote a draft of Chapter 2 based on the online JNI tutorial.

I received valuable comments on a draft of this book from Craig J. Bordelon, Michael Brundage, Mary Dageforde, Joshua Engel, and Elliott Hughes.

Lisa Friendly, editor of The Java™ Series, was instrumental in getting this book written and published. Ken Arnold, author of *The Java™ Programming Language*, first suggested that a JNI book be written. I am indebted to Mike Hendrikson and Marina Lang at Addison-Wesley for their help and their patience throughout the process. Diane Freed oversaw the production process from copy editing to final printing.

In the past several years I have had the privilege of working with a group of talented and dedicated people in Java Software at Sun Microsystems, in particular members of the original, HotSpot, and Sun Labs virtual machine teams. This book is dedicated to them.

Sheng Liang
May 1999

Part One: Introduction and Tutorial

CHAPTER 1

Introduction

THE Java™ Native Interface (JNI) is a powerful feature of the Java platform. Applications that use the JNI can incorporate *native code* written in programming languages such as C and C++, as well as code written in the Java programming language. The JNI allows programmers to take advantage of the power of the Java platform, without having to abandon their investments in legacy code. Because the JNI is a part of the Java platform, programmers can address interoperability issues once, and expect their solution to work with all implementations of the Java platform.

This book is both a programming guide and a reference manual for the JNI. The book consists of three parts:

- Chapter 2 introduces the JNI through a simple example. It is a tutorial intended for the beginning users who are unfamiliar with the JNI.

- Chapters 3 to 10 constitute a programmer's guide that gives a broad overview of a number of JNI features. We will go though a series of short but descriptive examples to highlight various JNI features and to present the techniques that have proven to be useful in JNI programming.

- Chapters 11 to 13 present the definitive specification for all JNI types and functions. These chapters are also organized to serve as a reference manual.

This book tries to appeal to a wide audience with different needs for the JNI. The tutorial and programming guide are targeted toward beginning programmers, whereas experienced developers and JNI implementors may find the reference sections more useful. The majority of readers will likely be developers who use the JNI to write applications. The term "you" in this book will implicitly denote developers who program with the JNI, as opposed to JNI implementors or end-users of applications written using the JNI.

The book assumes that you have basic knowledge of the Java, C, and C++ programming languages. If not, you may refer to one of the many excellent books that are available: *The Java™ Programming Language, Second Edition*, by Ken Arnold and James Gosling (Addison-Wesley, 1998), *The C Programming Language, Second Edition*, by Brian Kernighan and Dennis Ritchie (Prentice Hall,

1988), and *The C++ Programming Language, Third Edition*, by Bjarne Stroustrup (Addison-Wesley, 1997).

The remainder of this chapter introduces the background, role, and evolution of the JNI.

1.1 The Java Platform and Host Environment

Because this book covers applications written in the Java programming language as well as in native (C, C++, etc.) programming languages, let us first clarify the exact scope of the programming environments for these languages.

The Java platform is a programming environment consisting of the Java virtual machine (VM) and the Java Application Programming Interface (API).[1] Java applications are written in the Java programming language, and compiled into a machine-independent binary class format. A class can be executed on any Java virtual machine implementation. The Java API consists of a set of predefined classes. Any implementation of the Java platform is guaranteed to support the Java programming language, virtual machine, and API.

The term *host environment* represents the host operating system, a set of native libraries, and the CPU instruction set. *Native applications* are written in *native programming languages* such as C and C++, compiled into host-specific binary code, and linked with native libraries. Native applications and native libraries are typically dependent on a particular host environment. A C application built for one operating system, for example, typically does not work on other operating systems.

Java platforms are commonly deployed on top of a host environment. For example, the Java Runtime Environment (JRE) is a Sun product that supports the Java platform on existing operating systems such as Solaris and Windows. The Java platform offers a set of features that applications can rely on independent of the underlying host environment.

1.2 Role of the JNI

When the Java platform is deployed on top of host environments, it may become desirable or necessary to allow Java applications to work closely with native code written in other languages. Programmers have begun to adopt the Java platform to build applications that were traditionally written in C and C++. Because of the

---

[1.] As used herein, the phrases "Java virtual machine" or "Java VM" mean a virtual machine for the Java platform. Similarly, the phrase "Java API" means the API for the Java platform.

existing investment in legacy code, however, Java applications will coexist with C
and C++ code for many years to come.

The JNI is a powerful feature that allows you to take advantage of the Java
platform, but still utilize code written in other languages. As a part of the Java virtual machine implementation, the JNI is a *two-way* interface that allows Java
applications to invoke native code and vice versa. Figure 1.1 illustrates the role of
the JNI.

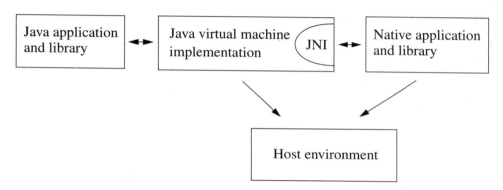

Figure 1.1   Role of the JNI

The JNI is designed to handle situations where you need to combine Java
applications with native code. As a two-way interface, the JNI can support two
types of native code: native *libraries* and native *applications*.

- You can use the JNI to write *native methods* that allow Java applications to
  call functions implemented in native libraries. Java applications call native
  methods in the same way that they call methods implemented in the Java programming language. Behind the scenes, however, native methods are implemented in another language and reside in native libraries.

- The JNI supports an *invocation interface* that allows you to embed a Java virtual machine implementation into native applications. Native applications can
  link with a native library that implements the Java virtual machine, and then
  use the invocation interface to execute software components written in the
  Java programming language. For example, a web browser written in C can
  execute downloaded applets in an embedded Java virtual machine implemen-
  tion.

1.3   Implications of Using the JNI

Remember that once an application uses the JNI, it risks losing two benefits of the Java platform.

First, Java applications that depend on the JNI can no longer readily run on multiple host environments. Even though the part of an application written in the Java programming language is portable to multiple host environments, it will be necessary to recompile the part of the application written in native programming languages.

Second, while the Java programming language is type-safe and secure, native languages such as C or C++ are not. As a result, you must use extra care when writing applications using the JNI. A misbehaving native method can corrupt the entire application. For this reason Java applications are subject to security checks before invoking JNI features.

As a general rule, you should architect the application so that native methods are defined in as few classes as possible. This entails a cleaner isolation between native code and the rest of the application.

1.4   When to Use the JNI

Before you embark on a project using the JNI, it is worth taking a step back to investigate whether there are alternative solutions that are more appropriate. As mentioned in the last section, applications that use the JNI have inherent disadvantages when compared with applications written strictly in the Java programming language. For example, you lose the type-safety guarantee of the Java programming language.

A number of alternative approaches also allow Java applications to interoperate with code written in other languages. For example:

- A Java application may communicate with a native application through a TCP/IP connection or through other inter-process communication (IPC) mechanisms.

- A Java application may connect to a legacy database through the JDBC™ API.

- A Java application may take advantage of distributed object technologies such as the Java IDL API.

A common characteristic of these alternative solutions is that the Java application and native code reside in different processes (and in some cases on different machines). Process separation offers an important benefit. The address space protection supported by processes enables a high degree of fault isolation—a crashed native application does not immediately terminate the Java application with which it communicates over TCP/IP.

Sometimes, however, you may find it necessary for a Java application to communicate with native code *that resides in the same process*. This is when the JNI becomes useful. Consider, for example, the following scenarios:

- The Java API might not support certain host-dependent features needed by an application. An application may want to perform, for example, special file operations that are not supported by the Java API, yet it is both cumbersome and inefficient to manipulate files through another process.

- You may want to access an existing native library and are not willing to pay for the overhead of copying and transmitting data across different processes. Loading the native library in the same process is much more efficient.

- Having an application span multiple processes could result in unacceptable memory footprint. This is typically true if these processes need to reside on the same client machine. Loading a native library into the existing process hosting the application requires less system resources than starting a new process and loading the library into that process.

- You may want to implement a small portion of time-critical code in a lower-level language, such as assembly. If a 3D-intensive application spends most of its time in graphics rendering, you may find it necessary to write the core portion of a graphics library in assembly code to achieve maximum performance.

In summary, use the JNI if your Java application must interoperate with native code that resides in the same process.

1.5 Evolution of the JNI

The need for Java applications to interoperate with native code has been recognized since the very early days of the Java platform. The first release of the Java platform, Java Development Kit (JDK™) release 1.0, included a native method interface that allowed Java applications to call functions written in other languages such as C and C++. Many third-party applications, as well as the implementation of the Java class libraries (including, for example, `java.lang`, `java.io`, and `java.net`), relied on the native method interface to access the features in the underlying host environment.

Unfortunately, the native method interface in JDK release 1.0 had two major problems:

- First, the native code accesses fields in objects as members of C structures. However, the Java virtual machine specification does not define how objects are laid out in memory. If a given Java virtual machine implementation lays out objects in a way other than that assumed by the native method interface, then you have to recompile the native method libraries.

- Second, the native method interface in JDK release 1.0 relies on a conservative garbage collector because native methods can get hold of direct pointers to objects in the virtual machine. Any virtual machine implementation that uses more advanced garbage collection algorithms cannot support the native method interface in JDK release 1.0.

The JNI was designed to overcome these problems. It is an interface that can be supported by all Java virtual machine implementations on a wide variety of host environments. With the JNI:

- Each virtual machine implementor can support a larger body of native code.

- Development tool vendors do not have to deal with different kinds of native method interfaces.

- Most importantly, application programmers are able to write one version of their native code and this version will run on different implementations of the Java virtual machine.

The JNI was first supported in JDK release 1.1. Internally, however, JDK release 1.1 still uses old-style native methods (as in JDK release 1.0) to implement the Java APIs. This is no longer the case in Java 2 SDK release 1.2 (formerly known as JDK release 1.2). Native methods have been rewritten so that they conform to the JNI standard.

The JNI is the native interface supported by all Java virtual machine implementations. From JDK release 1.1 on, you should program to the JNI. The old-style native method interface is still supported in Java 2 SDK release 1.2, but will not (and cannot) be supported in advanced Java virtual machine implementations in the future.

Java 2 SDK release 1.2 contains a number of JNI enhancements. The enhancements are backward compatible. All future evolutions of JNI will maintain complete binary compatibility.

1.6   Example Programs

This book contains numerous example programs that demonstrate JNI features. The example programs typically consist of multiple code segments written in the

Java programming language as well as C or C++ native code. Sometimes the native code refers to host-specific features in Solaris and Win32. We also show how to build JNI programs using the command line tools (such as javah) shipped with JDK and Java 2 SDK releases.

Keep in mind that the use of the JNI is not limited to specific host environments or specific application development tools. The book focuses on writing the code, not on the tools used to build and run the code. The command line tools bundled with JDK and Java 2 SDK releases are rather primitive. Third-party tools may offer an improved way to build applications that use the JNI. We encourage you to consult the JNI-related documentation bundled with the development tools of your choice.

You can download the source code of the examples in this book, as well as the latest updates to this book, from the following web address:

```
http://java.sun.com/docs/books/jni/
```

CHAPTER 2

Getting Started

THIS chapter walks you through a simple example of using the Java Native Interface. We will write a Java application that calls a C function to print "Hello World!".

2.1 Overview

Figure 2.1 illustrates the process for using JDK or Java 2 SDK releases to write a simple Java application that calls a C function to print "Hello World!". The process consists of the following steps:

1. Create a class (HelloWorld.java) that declares the native method.

2. Use javac to compile the HelloWorld source file, resulting in the class file HelloWorld.class. The javac compiler is supplied with JDK or Java 2 SDK releases.

3. Use javah -jni to generate a C header file (HelloWorld.h) containing the function prototype for the native method implementation. The javah tool is provided with JDK or Java 2 SDK releases.

4. Write the C implementation (HelloWorld.c) of the native method.

5. Compile the C implementation into a native library, creating HelloWorld.dll or libHelloWorld.so. Use the C compiler and linker available on the host environment.

6. Run the HelloWorld program using the java runtime interpreter. Both the class file (HelloWorld.class) and the native library (HelloWorld.dll or libHelloWorld.so) are loaded at runtime.

The remainder of this chapter explains these steps in detail.

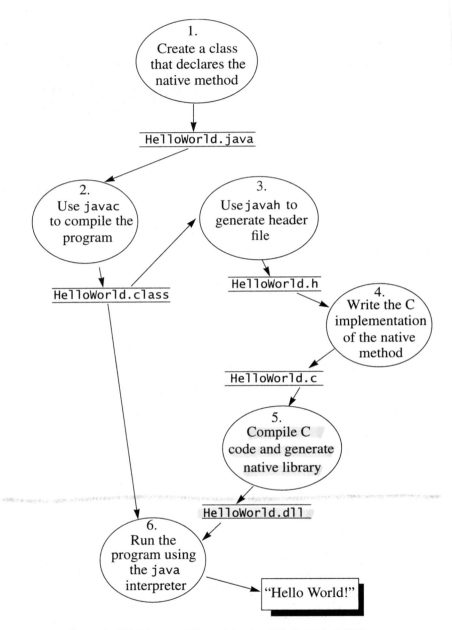

Figure 2.1   Steps in Writing and Running the "Hello World" Program

2.2 Declare the Native Method

You begin by writing the following program in the Java programming language. The program defines a class named HelloWorld that contains a native method, print.

```
class HelloWorld {
    private native void print();
    public static void main(String[] args) {
        new HelloWorld().print();
    }
    static {
        System.loadLibrary("HelloWorld");
    }
}
```

The HelloWorld class definition begins with the declaration of the print native method. This is followed by a main method that instantiates the HelloWorld class and invokes the print native method for this instance. The last part of the class definition is a static initializer that loads the native library containing the implementation of the print native method.

There are two differences between the declaration of a native method such as print and the declaration of regular methods in the Java programming language. A native method declaration must contain the native modifier. The native modifier indicates that this method is implemented in another language. Also, the native method declaration is terminated with a semicolon, the statement terminator symbol, because there is no implementation for native methods in the class itself. We will implement the print method in a separate C file.

Before the native method print can be called, the native library that implements print must be loaded. In this case, we load the native library in the static initializer of the HelloWorld class. The Java virtual machine automatically runs the static initializer before invoking any methods in the HelloWorld class, thus ensuring that the native library is loaded before the print native method is called.

We define a main method to be able to run the HelloWorld class. HelloWorld.main calls the native method print in the same manner as it would call a regular method.

System.loadLibrary takes a library name, locates a native library that corresponds to that name, and loads the native library into the application. We will discuss the exact loading process later in the book. For now simply remember that in order for System.loadLibrary("HelloWorld") to succeed, we need to create a native library called HelloWorld.dll on Win32, or libHelloWorld.so on Solaris.

2.3 Compile the `HelloWorld` Class

After you have defined the `HelloWorld` class, save the source code in a file called `HelloWorld.java`. Then compile the source file using the `javac` compiler that comes with the JDK or Java 2 SDK release:

```
javac HelloWorld.java
```

This command will generate a `HelloWorld.class` file in the current directory.

2.4 Create the Native Method Header File

Next we will use the `javah` tool to generate a JNI-style header file that is useful when implementing the native method in C. You can run `javah` on the `HelloWorld` class as follows:

```
javah -jni HelloWorld
```

The name of the header file is the class name with a ".h" appended to the end of it. The command shown above generates a file named `HelloWorld.h`. We will not list the generated header file in its entirety here. The most important part of the header file is the function prototype for `Java_HelloWorld_print`, which is the C function that implements the `HelloWorld.print` method:

```
JNIEXPORT void JNICALL
Java_HelloWorld_print (JNIEnv *, jobject);
```

Ignore the `JNIEXPORT` and `JNICALL` macros for now. You may have noticed that the C implementation of the native method accepts two arguments even though the corresponding declaration of the native method accepts no arguments. The first argument for every native method implementation is a `JNIEnv` interface pointer. The second argument is a reference to the `HelloWorld` object itself (sort of like the "this" pointer in C++). We will discuss how to use the `JNIEnv` interface pointer and the `jobject` arguments later in this book, but this simple example ignores both arguments.

2.5   Write the Native Method Implementation

The JNI-style header file generated by `javah` helps you to write C or C++ implementations for the native method. The function that you write must follow the prototype specified in the generated header file. You can implement the `Hello-World.print` method in a C file `HelloWorld.c` as follows:

```
#include <jni.h>
#include <stdio.h>
#include "HelloWorld.h"

JNIEXPORT void JNICALL
Java_HelloWorld_print(JNIEnv *env, jobject obj)
{
    printf("Hello World!\n");
    return;
}
```

The implementation of this native method is straightforward. It uses the `printf` function to display the string "`Hello World!`" and then returns. As mentioned before, both arguments, the `JNIEnv` pointer and the reference to the object, are ignored.

The C program includes three header files:

- `jni.h` — This header file provides information the native code needs to call JNI functions. When writing native methods, you must always include this file in your C or C++ source files.

- `stdio.h` — The code snippet above also includes `stdio.h` because it uses the `printf` function.

- `HelloWorld.h` — The header file that you generated using `javah`. It includes the C/C++ prototype for the `Java_HelloWorld_print` function.

2.6   Compile the C Source and Create a Native Library

Remember that when you created the `HelloWorld` class in the `HelloWorld.java` file, you included a line of code that loaded a native library into the program:

```
System.loadLibrary("HelloWorld");
```

Now that all the necessary C code is written, you need to compile `Hello-World.c` and build this native library.

Different operating systems support different ways to build native libraries. On Solaris, the following command builds a shared library called `libHello-World.so`:

```
cc -G -I/java/include -I/java/include/solaris
     HelloWorld.c -o libHelloWorld.so
```

The -G option instructs the C compiler to generate a shared library instead of a regular Solaris executable file. Because of the limitation of page width in this book, we break the command line into two lines. You need to type the command in a single line, or place the command in a script file. On Win32, the following command builds a dynamic link library (DLL) `HelloWorld.dll` using the Microsoft Visual C++ compiler:

```
cl -Ic:\java\include -Ic:\java\include\win32
     -MD -LD HelloWorld.c -FeHelloWorld.dll
```

The -MD option ensures that `HelloWorld.dll` is linked with the Win32 multi-threaded C library. The -LD option instructs the C compiler to generate a DLL instead of a regular Win32 executable. Of course, on both Solaris and Win32 you need to put in the include paths that reflect the setup on your own machine.

2.7 Run the Program

At this point, you have the two components ready to run the program. The class file (`HelloWorld.class`) calls a native method, and the native library (`Hello-World.dll`) implements the native method.

Because the `HelloWorld` class contains its own `main` method, you can run the program on Solaris or Win32 as follows:

```
java HelloWorld
```

You should see the following output:

```
Hello World!
```

It is important to set your native library path correctly for your program to run. The native library path is a list of directories that the Java virtual machine searches when loading native libraries. If you do not have a native library path set up correctly, then you see an error similar to the following:

```
java.lang.UnsatisfiedLinkError: no HelloWorld in library path
        at java.lang.Runtime.loadLibrary(Runtime.java)
        at java.lang.System.loadLibrary(System.java)
        at HelloWorld.main(HelloWorld.java)
```

Make sure that the native library resides in one of the directories in the native library path. If you are running on a Solaris system, the LD_LIBRARY_PATH environment variable is used to define the native library path. Make sure that it includes the name of the directory that contains the libHelloWorld.so file. If the libHelloWorld.so file is in the current directory, you can issue the following two commands in the standard shell (sh) or KornShell (ksh) to set up the LD_LIBRARY_PATH environment variable properly:

```
LD_LIBRARY_PATH=.
export LD_LIBRARY_PATH
```

The equivalent command in the C shell (csh or tcsh) is as follows:

```
setenv LD_LIBRARY_PATH .
```

If you are running on a Windows 95 or Windows NT machine, make sure that HelloWorld.dll is in the current directory, or in a directory that is listed in the PATH environment variable.

In Java 2 SDK 1.2 release, you can also specify the native library path on the java command line as a system property as follows:

```
java -Djava.library.path=. HelloWorld
```

The "-D" command-line option sets a Java platform system property. Setting the java.library.path property to "." instructs the Java virtual machine to search for native libraries in the current directory.

Part Two: Programmer's Guide

CHAPTER 3

Basic Types, Strings, and Arrays

ONE of the most common questions programmers ask when interfacing Java applications with native code is how data types in the Java programming language map to the data types in native programming languages such as C and C++. In the "Hello World!" example presented in the last chapter, we did not pass any arguments to the native method, nor did the native method return any result. The native method simply printed a message and returned.

In practice, most programs will need to pass arguments to native methods, and receive results from native methods as well. In this chapter, we will describe how to exchange data types between code written in the Java programming language and the native code that implements native methods. We will start with primitive types such as integers and common object types such as strings and arrays. We will defer the full treatment of arbitrary objects to the next chapter, where we will explain how the native code can access fields and make method calls.

3.1 A Simple Native Method

Let us start with a simple example that is not too different from the HelloWorld program in the last chapter. The example program, Prompt.java, contains a native method that prints a string, waits for user input, and then returns the line that the user has typed in. The source code for this program is as follows:

```
class Prompt {
    // native method that prints a prompt and reads a line
    private native String getLine(String prompt);

    public static void main(String args[]) {
        Prompt p = new Prompt();
        String input = p.getLine("Type a line: ");
        System.out.println("User typed: " + input);
    }
    static {
        System.loadLibrary("Prompt");
    }
}
```

Prompt.main calls the native method Prompt.getLine to receive user input. The static initializer calls the System.loadLibrary method to load a native library called Prompt.

3.1.1 C Prototype for Implementing the Native Method

The Prompt.getLine method can be implemented with the following C function:

```
JNIEXPORT jstring JNICALL
Java_Prompt_getLine(JNIEnv *env, jobject this, jstring prompt);
```

You can use the javah tool (§2.4) to generate a header file containing the above function prototype. The JNIEXPORT and JNICALL macros (defined in the jni.h header file) ensure that this function is exported from the native library and C compilers generate code with the correct calling convention for this function. The name of the C function is formed by concatenating the "Java_" prefix, the class name, and the method name. Section 11.3 contains a more precise description of how the C function names are formed.

3.1.2 Native Method Arguments

As briefly discussed in Section 2.4, the native method implementation such as Java_Prompt_getLine accepts two standard parameters, in addition to the arguments declared in the native method. The first parameter, the JNIEnv interface pointer, points to a location that contains a pointer to a function table. Each entry in the function table points to a *JNI function*. Native methods always access data structures in the Java virtual machine through one of the JNI functions. Figure 3.1 illustrates the JNIEnv interface pointer.

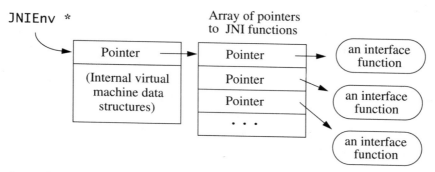

Figure 3.1   The JNIEnv Interface Pointer

The second argument differs depending on whether the native method is a static or an instance method. The second argument to an *instance* native method is a reference to the object on which the method is invoked, similar to the this pointer in C++. The second argument to a *static* native method is a reference to the class in which the method is defined. Our example, Java_Prompt_getLine, implements an instance native method. Thus the jobject parameter is a reference to the object itself.

3.1.3 Mapping of Types

Argument types in the native method declaration have corresponding types in native programming languages. The JNI defines a set of C and C++ types that correspond to types in the Java programming language.

There are two kinds of types in the Java programming language: *primitive types* such as int, float, and char, and *reference types* such as classes, instances, and arrays. In the Java programming language, strings are instances of the java.lang.String class.

The JNI treats primitive types and reference types differently. The mapping of primitive types is straightforward. For example, the type int in the Java programming language maps to the C/C++ type jint (defined in jni.h as a signed 32-bit integer), while the type float in the Java programming language maps to the C and C++ type jfloat (defined in jni.h as a 32-bit floating point number). Section 12.1.1 contains the definition of all primitive types defined in the JNI.

The JNI passes objects to native methods as *opaque references*. Opaque references are C pointer types that refer to internal data structures in the Java virtual machine. The exact layout of the internal data structures, however, is hidden from the programmer. The native code must manipulate the underlying objects via the appropriate JNI functions, which are available through the JNIEnv interface pointer. For example, the corresponding JNI type for java.lang.String is jstring. The exact value of a jstring reference is irrelevant to the native code. The native code calls JNI functions such as GetStringUTFChars (§3.2.1) to access the contents of a string.

All JNI references have type jobject. For convenience and enhanced type safety, the JNI defines a set of reference types that are conceptually "subtypes" of jobject. (*A* is a subtype of *B* of every instance of *A* is also an instance of *B*.) These subtypes correspond to frequently used reference types in the Java programming language. For example, jstring denotes strings; jobjectArray denotes an array of objects. Section 12.1.2 contains a complete listing of the JNI reference types and their subtyping relationships.

3.2 Accessing Strings

The Java_Prompt_getLine function receives the prompt argument as a jstring type. The jstring type represents strings in the Java virtual machine, and is different from the regular C string type (a pointer to characters, char *). You cannot use a jstring as a normal C string. The following code, if run, would not produce the desired results. In fact, it will most likely crash the Java virtual machine.

```
JNIEXPORT jstring JNICALL
Java_Prompt_getLine(JNIEnv *env, jobject obj, jstring prompt)
{
    /* ERROR: incorrect use of jstring as a char* pointer */
    printf("%s", prompt);
    ...
}
```

3.2.1 Converting to Native Strings

Your native method code must use the appropriate JNI functions to convert jstring objects to C/C++ strings. The JNI supports conversion both to and from Unicode and UTF-8 strings. Unicode strings represent characters as 16-bit values, whereas UTF-8 strings (§12.3.1) use an encoding scheme that is upward compatible with 7-bit ASCII strings. UTF-8 strings act like NULL-terminated C strings, even if they contain non-ASCII characters. All 7-bit ASCII characters whose values are between 1 and 127 remain the same in the UTF-8 encoding. A byte with the highest bit set signals the beginning of a multi-byte encoded 16-bit Unicode value.

The `Java_Prompt_getLine` function calls the JNI function `GetStringUTF-Chars` to read the contents of the string. The `GetStringUTFChars` function is available through the `JNIEnv` interface pointer. It converts the `jstring` reference, typically represented by the Java virtual machine implementation as a Unicode sequence, into a C string represented in the UTF-8 format. If you are certain that the original string contains only 7-bit ASCII characters, you may pass the converted string to regular C library functions such as `printf`. (We will discuss how to handle non-ASCII strings in Section 8.2.)

```
JNIEXPORT jstring JNICALL
Java_Prompt_getLine(JNIEnv *env, jobject obj, jstring prompt)
{
    char buf[128];
    const jbyte *str;
    str = (*env)->GetStringUTFChars(env, prompt, NULL);
    if (str == NULL) {
        return NULL; /* OutOfMemoryError already thrown */
    }
    printf("%s", str);
    (*env)->ReleaseStringUTFChars(env, prompt, str);
    /* We assume here that the user does not type more than
     * 127 characters */
    scanf("%s", buf);
    return (*env)->NewStringUTF(env, buf);
}
```

Do not forget to check the return value of `GetStringUTFChars`. Because the Java virtual machine implementation needs to allocate memory to hold the UTF-8 string, there is a chance that memory allocation will fail. When that happens, `Get-StringUTFChars` returns `NULL` and throws an `OutOfMemoryError` exception. As we will learn in Chapter 6, throwing an exception through the JNI is different from throwing an exception in the Java programming language. A pending exception thrown through the JNI does not automatically change control flow in native C code. Instead, we need to issue an explicit `return` statement in order to skip the remaining statements in the C function. After `Java_Prompt_getLine` returns, the exception will be thrown in `Prompt.main`, caller of the `Prompt.getLine` native method.

3.2.2 Freeing Native String Resources

When your native code finishes using the UTF-8 string obtained through `Get-StringUTFChars`, it calls `ReleaseStringUTFChars`. Calling `ReleaseString-UTFChars` indicates that the native method no longer needs the UTF-8 string

Important !

returned by GetStringUTFChars; thus the memory taken by the UTF-8 string can be freed. Failure to call ReleaseStringUTFChars would result in a memory leak, which could ultimately lead to memory exhaustion.

3.2.3 Constructing New Strings

You can construct a new java.lang.String instance in the native method by calling the JNI function NewStringUTF. The NewStringUTF function takes a C string with the UTF-8 format and constructs a java.lang.String instance. The newly constructed java.lang.String instance represents the same sequence of Unicode characters as the given UTF-8 C string.

If the virtual machine cannot allocate the memory needed to construct the java.lang.String instance, NewStringUTF throws an OutOfMemoryError exception and returns NULL. In this example, we do not need to check its return value because the native method returns immediately afterwards. If NewString-UTF fails, the OutOfMemoryError exception will be thrown in the Prompt.main method that issued the native method call. If NewStringUTF succeeds, it returns a JNI reference to the newly constructed java.lang.String instance. The new instance is returned by Prompt.getLine and then assigned to the local variable input in Prompt.main.

3.2.4 Other JNI String Functions

The JNI supports a number of other string-related functions, in addition to the GetStringUTFChars, ReleaseStringUTFChars, and NewStringUTF functions introduced earlier.

GetStringChars and ReleaseStringChars obtain string characters represented in the Unicode format. These functions are useful when, for example, the operating system supports Unicode as the native string format.

UTF-8 strings are always terminated with the '\0' character, whereas Unicode strings are not. To find out the number of Unicode characters in a jstring reference, JNI programmers can call GetStringLength. To find out how many bytes are needed to represent a jstring in the UTF-8 format, JNI programmers can either call the ANSI C function strlen on the result of GetStringUTFChars, or call the JNI function GetStringUTFLength on the jstring reference directly.

The third argument to GetStringChars and GetStringUTFChars requires additional explanation:

```
const jchar *
GetStringChars(JNIEnv *env, jstring str, jboolean *isCopy);
```

Upon returning from GetStringChars, the memory location pointed to by isCopy will be set to JNI_TRUE if the returned string is a *copy* of the characters in the original java.lang.String instance. The memory location pointed to by isCopy will be set to JNI_FALSE if the returned string is a *direct* pointer to the characters in the original java.lang.String instance. *When the location pointed to by isCopy is set to JNI_FALSE, native code must not modify the contents of the returned string.* Violating this rule will cause the original java.lang.String instance to be modified as well. This breaks the invariant that java.lang.String instances are immutable.

Most often you pass NULL as the isCopy argument because you do not care whether the Java virtual machine returns a copy of the characters in the java.lang.String instance or a direct pointer to the original.

It is in general not possible to predict whether the virtual machine will copy the characters in a given java.lang.String instance. Programmers must therefore assume functions such as GetStringChars may take time and space proportional to the number of characters in the java.lang.String instance. In a typical Java virtual machine implementation, the garbage collector relocates objects in the heap. Once a direct pointer to a java.lang.String instance is passed back to the native code, the garbage collector can no longer relocate the java.lang.String instance. To put it another way, the virtual machine must *pin* the java.lang.String instance. Because excessive pinning leads to memory fragmentation, the virtual machine implementation may, at its discretion, decide to either copy the characters or pin the instance for each individual GetString-Chars call.

Do not forget to call ReleaseStringChars when you no longer need access to the string elements returned from GetStringChars. *The ReleaseStringChars call is necessary whether GetStringChars has set *isCopy to JNI_TRUE or JNI_FALSE.* ReleaseStringChars either frees the copy or unpins the instance, depending upon whether GetStringChars has returned a copy or not.

3.2.5 New JNI String Functions in Java 2 SDK Release 1.2

To increase the possibility that the virtual machine is able to return a direct pointer to the characters in a java.lang.String instance, Java 2 SDK release 1.2 introduces a new pair of functions, Get/ReleaseStringCritical. On the surface, they appear to be similar to Get/ReleaseStringChars functions in that both return a pointer to the characters if possible; otherwise, a copy is made. *There are, however, significant restrictions on how these functions can be used.*

You must treat the code inside this pair of functions as running in a "critical region." Inside a critical region, native code must not call arbitrary JNI functions, or any native function that may cause the current thread to block and wait for another thread running in the Java virtual machine. For example, the current thread must not wait for input on an I/O stream being written to by another thread.

These restrictions make it possible for the virtual machine to disable garbage collection when the native code is holding a direct pointer to string elements obtained via GetStringCritical. When garbage collection is disabled, any other threads that trigger garbage collection will be blocked as well. *Native code between a Get/ReleaseStringCritical pair must not issue blocking calls or allocate new objects in the Java virtual machine.* Otherwise, the virtual machine may deadlock. Consider the following scenario:

- A garbage collection triggered by another thread cannot make progress until the current thread finishes the blocking call and reenables garbage collection.

- Meanwhile, the current thread cannot make progress because the blocking call needs to obtain a lock already held by the other thread that is waiting to perform the garbage collection.

It is safe to overlap multiple pairs of GetStringCritical and Release-StringCritical functions. For example:

```
jchar *s1, *s2;
s1 = (*env)->GetStringCritical(env, jstr1);
if (s1 == NULL) {
    ... /* error handling */
}
s2 = (*env)->GetStringCritical(env, jstr2);
if (s2 == NULL) {
    (*env)->ReleaseStringCritical(env, jstr1, s1);
    ... /* error handling */
}
...      /* use s1 and s2 */
(*env)->ReleaseStringCritical(env, jstr1, s1);
(*env)->ReleaseStringCritical(env, jstr2, s2);
```

The Get/ReleaseStringCritical pairs need not be strictly nested in a stack order. We must not forget to check its return value against NULL for possible out of memory situations, because *GetStringCritical might still allocate a buffer and make a copy of the array* if the VM internally represents arrays in a different format. For example, the Java virtual machine may not store arrays contiguously. In that case, GetStringCritical must copy all the characters in the jstring instance in order to return a contiguous array of characters to the native code.

To avoid deadlocks, you must make sure that the native code does not call arbitrary JNI functions after it issues a GetStringCritical call and before it makes the corresponding ReleaseStringCritical call. The only JNI functions allowed in the "critical region" are overlapped Get/ReleaseStringCritical and Get/ReleasePrimitiveArrayCritical (§3.3.2) calls.

The JNI does not support GetStringUTFCritical and ReleaseStringUTF-Critical functions. Such functions would likely require the virtual machine to make a copy of the string, because virtual machines implementation almost certainly represent strings internally in the Unicode format.

Other additions to Java 2 SDK release 1.2 are GetStringRegion and GetStringUTFRegion. These functions copy the string elements into a preallocated buffer. The Prompt.getLine method may be reimplemented using Get-StringUTFRegion as follows:

```
JNIEXPORT jstring JNICALL
Java_Prompt_getLine(JNIEnv *env, jobject obj, jstring prompt)
{
    /* assume the prompt string and user input has less than 128
        characters */
    char outbuf[128], inbuf[128];
    int len = (*env)->GetStringLength(env, prompt);
    (*env)->GetStringUTFRegion(env, prompt, 0, len, outbuf);
    printf("%s", outbuf);
    scanf("%s", inbuf);
    return (*env)->NewStringUTF(env, inbuf);
}
```

The GetStringUTFRegion function takes a starting index and length, both counted as number of Unicode characters. The function also performs bounds checking, and raises StringIndexOutOfBoundsException if necessary. In the above code, we obtained the length from the string reference itself, and are thus certain that there will be no index overflow. (The above code, however, lacks the necessary checks to ensure that the prompt string contains less than 128 characters.)

The code is somewhat simpler than using GetStringUTFChars. Because Get-StringUTFRegion performs no memory allocation, we need not check for possible out-of-memory conditions. (Again, the above code lacks the necessary checks to ensure that the user input contains less than 128 characters.)

3.2.6 Summary of JNI String Functions

Table 3.1 summarizes all string-related JNI functions. Java 2 SDK 1.2 release adds a number of new functions that enhance performance for certain string operations. The added functions support no new operations other than bringing performance improvements.

Table 3.1 Summary of JNI String Functions

JNI Function	Description	Since
GetStringChars ReleaseStringChars	Obtains or releases a pointer to the contents of a string in Unicode format. May return a copy of the string.	JDK1.1
GetStringUTFChars ReleaseStringUTFChars	Obtains or releases a pointer to the contents of a string in UTF-8 format. May return a copy of the string.	JDK1.1
GetStringLength	Returns the number of Unicode characters in the string.	JDK1.1
GetStringUTFLength	Returns the number of bytes needed (not including the trailing 0) to represent a string in the UTF-8 format.	JDK1.1
NewString	Creates a java.lang.String instance that contains the same sequence of characters as the given Unicode C string.	JDK1.1
NewStringUTF	Creates a java.lang.String instance that contains the same sequence of characters as the given UTF-8 encoded C string.	JDK1.1
GetStringCritical ReleaseStringCritical	Obtains a pointer to the contents of a string in Unicode format. May return a copy of the string. Native code must not block between a pair of Get/ReleaseStringCritical calls.	Java 2 SDK1.2
GetStringRegion SetStringRegion	Copies the contents of a string to or from a preallocated C buffer in the Unicode format.	Java 2 SDK1.2
GetStringUTFRegion SetStringUTFRegion	Copies the content of a string to or from a preallocated C buffer in the UTF-8 format.	Java 2 SDK1.2

3.2.7 Choosing among the String Functions

Figure 3.2 illustrates how a programmer may choose among the string-related functions in JDK release 1.1 and Java 2 SDK release 1.2:

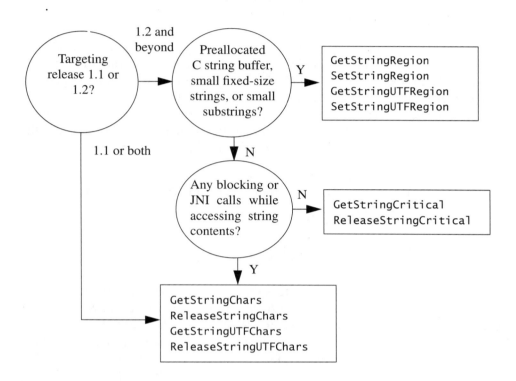

Figure 3.2   Choosing among the JNI String Functions

If you are targeting 1.1 or both 1.1 and 1.2 releases, there is no choice other than `Get/ReleaseStringChars` and `Get/ReleaseStringUTFChars`.

If you are programming in Java 2 SDK release 1.2 and above, and you want to copy the contents of a string into an already-allocated C buffer, use `GetString-Region` or `GetStringUTFRegion`.

For small fixed-size strings, `Get/SetStringRegion` and `Get/SetString-UTFRegion` are almost always the preferred functions because the C buffer can be allocated on the C stack very cheaply. The overhead of copying a small number of characters in the string is negligible.

One advantage of `Get/SetStringRegion` and `Get/SetStringUTFRegion` is that they do not perform memory allocation, and therefore never raise unexpected out-of-memory exceptions. No exception checking is necessary if you make sure that index overflow cannot occur.

Another advantage of Get/SetStringRegion and Get/SetStringUTFRegion is that the you can specify a starting index and the number of characters. These functions are suitable if the native code only needs to access a subset of characters in a long string.

GetStringCritical must be used with extreme care (§3.2.5). You must make sure that while holding a pointer obtained through GetStringCritical, the native code does not allocate new objects in the Java virtual machine or perform other blocking calls that may cause the system to deadlock.

Here is an example that demonstrates the subtle issues in the use of Get-StringCritical. The following code obtains the content of a string and calls the fprintf function to write out the characters to the file handle fd:

```
/* This is not safe! */
const char *c_str = (*env)->GetStringCritical(env, j_str, 0);
if (c_str == NULL) {
    ... /* error handling */
}
fprintf(fd, "%s\n", c_str);
(*env)->ReleaseStringCritical(env, j_str, c_str);
```

The problem with the above code is that it is not always safe to write to a file handle when garbage collection is disabled by the current thread. Suppose, for example, that another thread T is waiting to read from the fd file handle. Let us further assume that the operating system buffering is set up in such a way that the fprintf call waits until the thread T finishes reading all pending data from fd. We have constructed a possible scenario for deadlocks: If thread T cannot allocate enough memory to serve as a buffer for reading from the file handle, it must request a garbage collection. The garbage collection request will be blocked until the current thread executes ReleaseStringCritical, which cannot happen until the fprintf call returns. The fprintf call is waiting, however, for thread T to finish reading from the file handle.

The following code, although similar to the example above, is almost certainly deadlock free:

```
/* This code segment is OK. */
const char *c_str = (*env)->GetStringCritical(env, j_str, 0);
if (c_str == NULL) {
    ... /* error handling */
}
DrawString(c_str);
(*env)->ReleaseStringCritical(env, j_str, c_str);
```

DrawString is a system call that directly writes the string onto the screen. Unless the screen display driver is also a Java application running in the same virtual machine, the DrawString function will not block indefinitely waiting for garbage collection to happen.

In summary, you need to consider all possible blocking behavior between a pair of Get/ReleaseStringCritical calls.

3.3 Accessing Arrays

The JNI treats *primitive arrays* and *object arrays* differently. Primitive arrays contain elements that are of primitive types such as int and boolean. Object arrays contain elements that are of reference types such as class instances and other arrays. For example, in the following code segment written in the Java programming language:

```
int[] iarr;
float[] farr;
Object[] oarr;
int[][] arr2;
```

iarr and farr are primitive arrays, whereas oarr and arr2 are object arrays.

Accessing primitive arrays in a native method requires the use of JNI functions similar to those used for accessing strings. Let us look at a simple example. The following program calls a native method sumArray that adds up the contents of an int array.

```
class IntArray {
    private native int sumArray(int[] arr);
    public static void main(String[] args) {
        IntArray p = new IntArray();
        int arr[] = new int[10];
        for (int i = 0; i < 10; i++) {
            arr[i] = i;
        }
        int sum = p.sumArray(arr);
        System.out.println("sum = " + sum);
    }
    static {
        System.loadLibrary("IntArray");
    }
}
```

3.3.1   Accessing Arrays in C

Arrays are represented by the `jarray` reference type and its "subtypes" such as `jintArray`. Just as `jstring` is not a C string type, neither is `jarray` a C array type. You cannot implement the `Java_IntArray_sumArray` native method by indirecting through a `jarray` reference. The following C code is illegal and would not produce the desired results:

```c
/* This program is illegal! */
JNIEXPORT jint JNICALL
Java_IntArray_sumArray(JNIEnv *env, jobject obj, jintArray arr)
{
    int i, sum = 0;
    for (i = 0; i < 10; i++) {
        sum += arr[i];
    }
}
```

You must instead use the proper JNI functions to access primitive array elements, as shown in the following corrected example:

```c
JNIEXPORT jint JNICALL
Java_IntArray_sumArray(JNIEnv *env, jobject obj, jintArray arr)
{
    jint buf[10];
    jint i, sum = 0;
    (*env)->GetIntArrayRegion(env, arr, 0, 10, buf);
    for (i = 0; i < 10; i++) {
        sum += buf[i];
    }
    return sum;
}
```

3.3.2   Accessing Arrays of Primitive Types

The previous example uses the `GetIntArrayRegion` function to copy all the elements in the integer array into a C buffer (buf). The third argument is the starting index of the elements, and the fourth argument is the number of elements to be copied. Once the elements are in the C buffer, we can access them in native code. No exception checking is necessary because we know that 10 is the length of the array in our example, and thus there cannot be an index overflow.

The JNI supports a corresponding `SetIntArrayRegion` function that allows native code to modify the array elements of type `int`. Arrays of other primitive types (such as `boolean`, `short`, and `float`) are also supported.

The JNI supports a family of *Get/Release<Type>ArrayElements* functions (including, for example, Get/ReleaseIntArrayElements) that allow the native code to obtain a direct pointer to the elements of primitive arrays. Because the underlying garbage collector may not support pinning, the virtual machine may return a pointer to a copy of the original primitive array. We can rewrite the native method implementation in Section 3.3.1 using GetIntArrayElements as follows:

```
JNIEXPORT jint JNICALL
Java_IntArray_sumArray(JNIEnv *env, jobject obj, jintArray arr)
{
    jint *carr;
    jint i, sum = 0;
    carr = (*env)->GetIntArrayElements(env, arr, NULL);
    if (carr == NULL) {
        return 0; /* exception occurred */
    }
    for (i=0; i<10; i++) {
        sum += carr[i];
    }
    (*env)->ReleaseIntArrayElements(env, arr, carr, 0);
    return sum;
}
```

The GetArrayLength function returns the number of elements in primitive or object arrays. The fixed length of an array is determined when the array is first allocated.

Java 2 SDK release 1.2 introduces Get/ReleasePrimitiveArrayCritical functions. These functions allow virtual machines to disable garbage collection while the native code accesses the contents of primitive arrays. Programmers must apply the same kind of care as when using Get/ReleaseStringCritical functions (§3.2.4). Between a pair of Get/ReleasePrimitiveArrayCritical functions, the native code must not call arbitrary JNI functions, or perform any blocking operations that may cause the application to deadlock.

3.3.3 Summary of JNI Primitive Array Functions

Table 3.2 is a summary of all JNI functions related to primitive arrays. Java 2 SDK release 1.2 adds a number of new functions that enhance performance for certain array operations. The added functions do not support new operations other than bringing performance improvements.

Table 3.2   Summary of JNI Primitive Array Functions

JNI Function	Description	Since
`Get<Type>ArrayRegion` `Set<Type>ArrayRegion`	Copies the contents of primitive arrays to or from a pre-allocated C buffer.	JDK1.1
`Get<Type>ArrayElements` `Release<Type>ArrayElements`	Obtains a pointer to the contents of a primitive array. May return a copy of the array.	JDK1.1
`GetArrayLength`	Returns the number of elements in the array.	JDK1.1
`New<Type>Array`	Creates an array with the given length.	JDK1.1
`GetPrimitiveArrayCritical` `ReleasePrimitiveArrayCritical`	Obtains or releases a pointer to the contents of a primitive array. May disable garbage collection, or return a copy of the array.	Java 2 SDK1.2

3.3.4   Choosing among the Primitive Array Functions

Figure 3.3 illustrates how a programmer may choose among JNI functions for accessing primitive arrays in JDK release 1.1 and Java 2 SDK release 1.2:

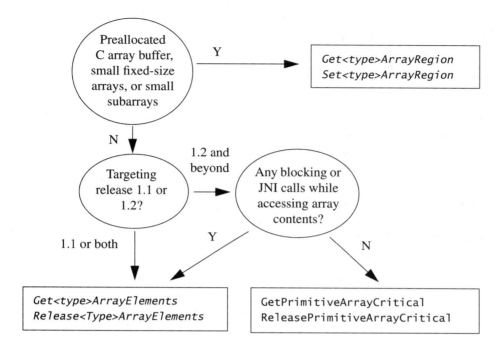

Figure 3.3   Choosing among Primitive Array Functions

If you need to copy to or copy from a preallocated C buffer, use the *Get/Set<Type>ArrayRegion* family of functions. These functions perform bounds checking and raise `ArrayIndexOutOfBoundsException` exceptions when necessary. The native method implementation in Section 3.3.1 uses `GetIntArrayRegion` to copy 10 elements out of a `jarray` reference.

For small, fixed-size arrays, *Get/Set<Type>ArrayRegion* is almost always the preferred function because the C buffer can be allocated on the C stack very cheaply. The overhead of copying a small number of array elements is negligible.

The *Get/Set<Type>ArrayRegion* functions allow you to specify a starting index and number of elements, and are thus the preferred functions if the native code needs to access only a subset of elements in a large array.

If you do not have a preallocated C buffer, the primitive array is of undetermined size and the native code does not issue blocking calls while holding the pointer to array elements, use the Get/ReleasePrimitiveArrayCritical functions in Java 2 SDK release 1.2. Just like the Get/ReleaseStringCritical functions, the Get/ReleasePrimitiveArrayCritical functions must be used with extreme care in order to avoid deadlocks.

It is always safe to use the *Get/Release<type>ArrayElements* family of functions. The virtual machine either returns a direct pointer to the array elements, or returns a buffer that holds a copy of the array elements.

3.3.5   Accessing Arrays of Objects

The JNI provides a separate pair of functions to access objects arrays. GetObjectArrayElement returns the element at a given index, whereas SetObjectArrayElement updates the element at a given index. Unlike the situation with primitive array types, you cannot get all the object elements or copy multiple object elements at once.

Strings and arrays are of reference types. You use Get/SetObjectArray-Element to access arrays of strings and arrays of arrays.

The following example calls a native method to create a two-dimensional array of int and then prints the content of the array.

```
class ObjectArrayTest {
    private static native int[][] initInt2DArray(int size);
    public static void main(String[] args) {
        int[][] i2arr = initInt2DArray(3);
        for (int i = 0; i < 3; i++) {
            for (int j = 0; j < 3; j++) {
                System.out.print(" " + i2arr[i][j]);
            }
            System.out.println();
        }
    }
    static {
        System.loadLibrary("ObjectArrayTest");
    }
}
```

The static native method initInt2DArray creates a two-dimensional array of the given size. The native method that allocates and initializes the two-dimensional array may be written as follows:

```
JNIEXPORT jobjectArray JNICALL
Java_ObjectArrayTest_initInt2DArray(JNIEnv *env,
                                    jclass cls,
                                    int size)
{
    jobjectArray result;
    int i;
    jclass intArrCls = (*env)->FindClass(env, "[I");
    if (intArrCls == NULL) {
        return NULL; /* exception thrown */
    }
    result = (*env)->NewObjectArray(env, size, intArrCls,
                                    NULL);
    if (result == NULL) {
        return NULL; /* out of memory error thrown */
    }
    for (i = 0; i < size; i++) {
        jint tmp[256];  /* make sure it is large enough! */
        int j;
        jintArray iarr = (*env)->NewIntArray(env, size);
        if (iarr == NULL) {
            return NULL; /* out of memory error thrown */
        }
        for (j = 0; j < size; j++) {
            tmp[j] = i + j;
        }
        (*env)->SetIntArrayRegion(env, iarr, 0, size, tmp);
        (*env)->SetObjectArrayElement(env, result, i, iarr);
        (*env)->DeleteLocalRef(env, iarr);
    }
    return result;
}
```

The newInt2DArray method first calls the JNI function FindClass to obtain a reference of the element class of the two-dimensional int array. The "[I" argument to FindClass is the *JNI class descriptor* (§12.3.2) that corresponds to the int[] type in the Java programming language. FindClass returns NULL and throws an exception if class loading fails (due to, for example, a missing class file or an out-of-memory condition).

Next the NewObjectArray function allocates an array whose element type is denoted by the intArrCls class reference. The NewObjectArray function only allocates the first dimension, and we are still left with the task of filling in the array elements that constitute the second dimension. The Java virtual machine has no special data structure for multi-dimensional arrays. A two-dimensional array is simply an array of arrays.

The code that creates the second dimension is quite straightforward. `NewInt-Array` allocates the individual array elements, and `SetIntArrayRegion` copies the contents of the `tmp[]` buffer into the newly allocated one-dimensional arrays. After completing the `SetObjectArrayElement` call, the `j`th element of the `i`th one-dimensional array has value `i+j`.

Running the `ObjectArrayTest.main` method produces the following output:

```
0 1 2
1 2 3
2 3 4
```

The `DeleteLocalRef` call at the end of the loop ensures that the virtual machine does not run out of the memory used to hold JNI references such as `iarr`. Section 5.2.1 explains in detail when and why you need to call `DeleteLocalRef`.

CHAPTER 4

Fields and Methods

NOW that you know how the JNI lets native code access primitive types and reference types such as strings and arrays, the next step will be to learn how to interact with fields and methods in arbitrary objects. In addition to accessing fields, this includes making calls to methods implemented in the Java programming language from native code, commonly known as performing *callbacks* from native code.

We will begin by introducing the JNI functions that support field access and method callbacks. Later in this chapter we will discuss how to make such operations more efficient by using a simple but effective caching technique. In the last section, we will discuss the performance characteristics of calling native methods as well as accessing fields and calling methods from native code.

4.1 Accessing Fields

The Java programming language supports two kinds of fields. Each instance of a class has its own copy of the *instance fields* of the class, whereas all instances of a class share the *static fields* of the class.

The JNI provides functions that native code can use to get and set instance fields in objects and static fields in classes. Let us first look at an example program that illustrates how to access instance fields from a native method implementation.

Note!

```
class InstanceFieldAccess {
    private String s;

    private native void accessField();
    public static void main(String args[]) {
        InstanceFieldAccess c = new InstanceFieldAccess();
        c.s = "abc";
        c.accessField();
        System.out.println("In Java:");
        System.out.println("  c.s = \"" + c.s + "\"");
    }
    static {
        System.loadLibrary("InstanceFieldAccess");
    }
}
```

The InstanceFieldAccess class defines an instance field s. The main method creates an object, sets the instance field, and then calls the native method InstanceFieldAccess.accessField. As we will see shortly, the native method prints out the existing value of the instance field and then sets the field to a new value. The program prints the field value again after the native method returns, demonstrating that the field value has indeed changed.

Here is the implementation of the InstanceFieldAccess.accessField native method.

```
JNIEXPORT void JNICALL
Java_InstanceFieldAccess_accessField(JNIEnv *env, jobject obj)
{
    jfieldID fid;    /* store the field ID */
    jstring jstr;
    const char *str;

    /* Get a reference to obj's class */
    jclass cls = (*env)->GetObjectClass(env, obj);

    printf("In C:\n");

    /* Look for the instance field s in cls */
    fid = (*env)->GetFieldID(env, cls, "s",
                            "Ljava/lang/String;");
    if (fid == NULL) {
        return; /* failed to find the field */
    }
```

```
    /* Read the instance field s */
    jstr = (*env)->GetObjectField(env, obj, fid);
    str = (*env)->GetStringUTFChars(env, jstr, NULL);
    if (str == NULL) {
        return; /* out of memory */
    }
    printf("  c.s = \"%s\"\n", str);
    (*env)->ReleaseStringUTFChars(env, jstr, str);

    /* Create a new string and overwrite the instance field */
    jstr = (*env)->NewStringUTF(env, "123");
    if (jstr == NULL) {
        return; /* out of memory */
    }
    (*env)->SetObjectField(env, obj, fid, jstr);
}
```

Running the InstanceFieldAccess class with the InstanceFieldAccess native library produces the following output:

```
In C:
  c.s = "abc"
In Java:
  c.s = "123"
```

4.1.1 Procedure for Accessing an Instance Field

To access an instance field, the native method follows a two-step process. First, it calls GetFieldID to obtain the *field ID* from the class reference, field name, and field descriptor:

```
fid = (*env)->GetFieldID(env, cls, "s", "Ljava/lang/String;");
```

The example code obtains the class reference cls by calling GetObjectClass on the instance reference obj, which is passed as the second argument to the native method implementation.

Once you have obtained the field ID, you can pass the object reference and the field ID to the appropriate instance field access function:

```
jstr = (*env)->GetObjectField(env, obj, fid);
```

Because strings and arrays are special kinds of objects, we use GetObject-Field to access the instance field that is a string. Besides Get/SetObjectField, the JNI also supports other functions such as GetIntField and SetFloatField for accessing instance fields of primitive types.

4.1.2 Field Descriptors

You might have noticed that in the previous section we used a specially encoded C string `"Ljava/lang/String;"` to represent a field type in the Java programming language. These C strings are called *JNI field descriptors*.

The content of the string is determined by the declared type of the field. For example, you represent an `int` field with `"I"`, a `float` field with `"F"`, a `double` field with `"D"`, a `boolean` field with `"Z"`, and so on.

The descriptor for a reference type, such as `java.lang.String`, begins with the letter L, is followed by the JNI class descriptor (§3.3.5), and is terminated by a semicolon. The "`.`" separators in fully qualified class names are changed to "`/`" in JNI class descriptors. Thus, you form the field descriptor for a field with type `java.lang.String` as follows:

```
"Ljava/lang/String;"
```

Descriptors for array types consist of the "`[`" character, followed by the descriptor of the component type of the array. For example, `"[I"` is the descriptor for the `int[]` field type. Section 12.3.3 contains the details of field descriptors and their matching types in the Java programming language.

You can use the `javap` tool (shipped with JDK or Java 2 SDK releases) to generate the field descriptors from class files. Normally `javap` prints out the method and field types in a given class. If you specify the `-s` option (and the `-p` option for exposing private members), `javap` prints JNI descriptors instead:

```
javap -s -p InstanceFieldAccess
```

This gives you output containing the JNI descriptors for the field `s`:

```
...
s Ljava/lang/String;
...
```

Using the `javap` tool helps eliminate mistakes that can occur from deriving JNI descriptor strings by hand.

4.1.3 Accessing Static Fields

Accessing static fields is similar to accessing instance fields. Let us look at a minor variation of the `InstanceFieldAccess` example:

```
class StaticFielcdAccess {
    private static int si;

    private native void accessField();
    public static void main(String args[]) {
        StaticFieldAccess c = new StaticFieldAccess();
        StaticFieldAccess.si = 100;
        c.accessField();
        System.out.println("In Java:");
        System.out.println("  StaticFieldAccess.si = " + si);
    }
    static {
        System.loadLibrary("StaticFieldAccess");
    }
}
```

The StaticFieldAccess class contains a static integer field si. The Static-
FieldAccess.main method creates an object, initializes the static field, and then
calls the native method StaticFieldAccess.accessField. As we will see
shortly, the native method prints out the existing value of the static field and then
sets the field to a new value. To verify that the field has indeed changed, the program prints the static field value again after the native method returns.

Here is the implementation of the StaticFieldAccess.accessField native
method.

```
JNIEXPORT void JNICALL
Java_StaticFieldAccess_accessField(JNIEnv *env, jobject obj)
{
    jfieldID fid;    /* store the field ID */
    jint si;

    /* Get a reference to obj's class */
    jclass cls = (*env)->GetObjectClass(env, obj);

    printf("In C:\n");

    /* Look for the static field si in cls */
    fid = (*env)->GetStaticFieldID(env, cls, "si", "I");
    if (fid == NULL) {
        return; /* field not found */
    }
    /* Access the static field si */
    si = (*env)->GetStaticIntField(env, cls, fid);
    printf("  StaticFieldAccess.si = %d\n", si);
    (*env)->SetStaticIntField(env, cls, fid, 200);
}
```

Running the program with the native library produces the following output:

```
In C:
  StaticFieldAccess.si = 100
In Java:
  StaticFieldAccess.si = 200
```

There are two differences between how you access a static field and how you access an instance field:

1. You call `GetStaticFieldID` for static fields, as opposed to `GetFieldID` for instance fields. `GetStaticFieldID` and `GetFieldID` have the same return type `jfieldID`.

2. Once you have obtained the static field ID, you pass the *class reference*, as opposed to an *object reference*, to the appropriate static field access function.

4.2   Calling Methods

There are several kinds of methods in the Java programming language. *Instance methods* must be invoked on a specific instance of a class, whereas *static methods* may be invoked independent of any instance. We will defer the discussion of *constructors* to the next section.

The JNI supports a complete set of functions that allow you to perform callbacks from native code. The example program below contains a native method that in turn calls an instance method implemented in the Java programming language.

```
class InstanceMethodCall {
    private native void nativeMethod();
    private void callback() {
        System.out.println("In Java");
    }
    public static void main(String args[]) {
        InstanceMethodCall c = new InstanceMethodCall();
        c.nativeMethod();
    }
    static {
        System.loadLibrary("InstanceMethodCall");
    }
}
```

Here is the implementation of the native method:

```
JNIEXPORT void JNICALL
Java_InstanceMethodCall_nativeMethod(JNIEnv *env, jobject obj)
{
    jclass cls = (*env)->GetObjectClass(env, obj);
    jmethodID mid =
        (*env)->GetMethodID(env, cls, "callback", "()V");
    if (mid == NULL) {
        return; /* method not found */
    }
    printf("In C\n");
    (*env)->CallVoidMethod(env, obj, mid);
}
```

Running the above program produces the following output:

```
In C
In Java
```

4.2.1 Calling Instance Methods

The `Java_InstanceMethodCall_nativeMethod` implementation illustrates the two steps required to call an instance method:

- The native method first calls the JNI function `GetMethodID`. `GetMethodID` performs a lookup for the method in the given class. The lookup is based on the name and type descriptor of the method. If the method does not exist, `GetMethodID` returns NULL. At this point, an immediate return from the native method causes a `NoSuchMethodError` to be thrown in the code that called `InstanceMethodCall.nativeMethod`.

- The native method then calls `CallVoidMethod`. `CallVoidMethod` invokes an instance method that has the return type `void`. You pass the object, the method ID, and the actual arguments (though in the above example there are none) to `CallVoidMethod`.

Besides the `CallVoidMethod` function, the JNI also supports method invocation functions with other return types. For example, if the method you called back returned a value of type `int`, then your native method would use `CallIntMethod`. Similarly, you can use `CallObjectMethod` to call methods that return objects, which include `java.lang.String` instances and arrays.

You can use *Call<Type>Method* family of functions to invoke interface methods as well. You must derive the method ID from the interface type. The following

47

code segment, for example, invokes the `Runnable.run` method on a `java.lang.Thread` instance:

```
jobject thd = ...; /* a java.lang.Thread instance */
jmethodID mid;
jclass runnableIntf =
    (*env)->FindClass(env, "java/lang/Runnable");
if (runnableIntf == NULL) {
    ... /* error handling */
}
mid = (*env)->GetMethodID(env, runnableIntf, "run", "()V");
if (mid == NULL) {
    ... /* error handling */
}
(*env)->CallVoidMethod(env, thd, mid);
... /* check for possible exceptions */
```

We have seen in Section 3.3.5 that the `FindClass` function returns a reference to a named class. Here we also use it to obtain a reference to a named interface.

4.2.2 Forming the Method Descriptor

The JNI uses descriptor strings to denote method types in a way similar to how it denotes field types. A method descriptor combines the argument types and the return type of a method. The argument types appear first and are surrounded by one pair of parentheses. Argument types are listed in the order in which they appear in the method declaration. There are no separators between multiple argument types. If a method takes no arguments, this is represented with an empty pair of parentheses. Place the method's return type immediately after the right closing parenthesis for the argument types.

For example, `"(I)V"` denotes a method that takes one argument of type `int` and has return type `void`. `"()D"` denotes a method that takes no arguments and returns a `double`. Do not let C function prototypes such as "int f(void)" mislead you to thinking that `"(V)I"` is a valid method descriptor. Use `"()I"` instead.

Method descriptors may involve class descriptors (§12.3.2). For example, the method:

```
native private String getLine(String);
```

has the following descriptor:

```
"(Ljava/lang/String;)Ljava/lang/String;"
```

Descriptors for array types begin with the "[" character, followed by the descriptor of the array element type. For example, the method descriptor of:

```
public static void main(String[] args);
```

is as follows:

```
"([Ljava/lang/String;)V"
```

Section 12.3.4 gives a complete description of how to form JNI method descriptors. You can use the `javap` tool to print out JNI method descriptors. For example, by running:

```
javap -s -p InstanceMethodCall
```

you obtain the following output:

```
...
private callback ()V
public static main ([Ljava/lang/String;)V
private native nativeMethod ()V
...
```

The `-s` flag informs `javap` to output JNI descriptor strings rather than types as they appear in the Java programming language. The `-p` flag causes `javap` to include information about the private members of the class in its output.

4.2.3 Calling Static Methods

The previous example demonstrates how native code calls an instance method. Similarly, you can perform callbacks to static methods from native code by following these steps:

• Obtain the method ID using `GetStaticMethodID`, as opposed to `GetMethodID`.

• Pass the class, method ID, and arguments to one of the family of static method invocation functions: `CallStaticVoidMethod`, `CallStaticBooleanMethod`, and so on.

There is a key difference between the functions that allow you to call static methods and the functions that allow you to call instance methods. The former takes a class reference as the second argument, whereas the latter takes an object reference as the second argument. For example, you pass the class reference to `CallStaticVoidMethod`, but pass an object reference to `CallVoidMethod`.

49

At the Java programming language level, you can invoke a static method f in class Cls using two alternative syntaxes: either Cls.f or obj.f where obj is an instance of Cls. (The latter is the recommended programming style, however.) In the JNI, you must always specify the class reference when issuing static method calls from native code.

Let us look at an example that makes a callback to a static method from native code. It is a slight variation of the earlier InstanceMethodCall example:

```
class StaticMethodCall {
    private native void nativeMethod();
    private static void callback() {
        System.out.println("In Java");
    }
    public static void main(String args[]) {
        StaticMethodCall c = new StaticMethodCall();
        c.nativeMethod();
    }
    static {
        System.loadLibrary("StaticMethodCall");
    }
}
```

Here is the implementation of the native method:

```
JNIEXPORT void JNICALL
Java_StaticMethodCall_nativeMethod(JNIEnv *env, jobject obj)
{
    jclass cls = (*env)->GetObjectClass(env, obj);
    jmethodID mid =
        (*env)->GetStaticMethodID(env, cls, "callback", "()V");
    if (mid == NULL) {
        return;  /* method not found */
    }
    printf("In C\n");
    (*env)->CallStaticVoidMethod(env, cls, mid);
}
```

Make sure that you pass cls (highlighted in bold), as opposed to obj, to CallStaticVoidMethod. Running the above program produces the following expected output:

```
In C
In Java
```

4.2.4   Calling Instance Methods of a Superclass

You can call instance methods which were defined in a superclass but that have been overridden in the class to which the object belongs. The JNI provides a set of `CallNonvirtual<Type>Method` functions for this purpose. To call a instance method defined in a superclass, you do the following:

- Obtain the method ID from a reference to the superclass using `GetMethodID`, as opposed to `GetStaticMethodID`.

- Pass the object, superclass, method ID, and arguments to one of the family of nonvirtual invocation functions, such as `CallNonvirtualVoidMethod`, `CallNonvirtualBooleanMethod`, and so on.

It is relatively rare that you will need to invoke the instance methods of a superclass. This facility is similar to calling an overridden superclass method, say f, using the following construct in the Java programming language:

```
super.f();
```

`CallNonvirtualVoidMethod` can also be used to invoke constructors, as the next section will illustrate.

4.3   Invoking Constructors

In the JNI, constructors may be invoked following steps similar to those used for calling instance methods. To obtain the method ID of a constructor, pass "`<init>`" as the method name and "V" as the return type in the method descriptor. You can then invoke the constructor by passing the method ID to JNI functions such as `NewObject`. The following code implements the equivalent functionality of the JNI function `NewString`, which constructs a java.lang.String object from the Unicode characters stored in a C buffer:

```
jstring
MyNewString(JNIEnv *env, jchar *chars, jint len)
{
    jclass stringClass;
    jmethodID cid;
    jcharArray elemArr;
    jstring result;

    stringClass = (*env)->FindClass(env, "java/lang/String");
    if (stringClass == NULL) {
        return NULL; /* exception thrown */
    }
```

51

```
/* Get the method ID for the String(char[]) constructor */
cid = (*env)->GetMethodID(env, stringClass,
                              "<init>", "([C)V");
if (cid == NULL) {
    return NULL; /* exception thrown */
}

/* Create a char[] that holds the string characters */
elemArr = (*env)->NewCharArray(env, len);
if (elemArr == NULL) {
    return NULL; /* exception thrown */
}
(*env)->SetCharArrayRegion(env, elemArr, 0, len, chars);

/* Construct a java.lang.String object */
result = (*env)->NewObject(env, stringClass, cid, elemArr);

/* Free local references */
(*env)->DeleteLocalRef(env, elemArr);
(*env)->DeleteLocalRef(env, stringClass);
return result;
}
```

This function is complex enough to deserve careful explanation. First, Find-Class returns a reference to the java.lang.String class. Next, GetMethodID returns the method ID for the string constructor, String(char[] chars). We then call NewCharArray to allocate a character array that holds all the string elements. The JNI function NewObject invokes the constructor specified by the method ID. The NewObject function takes as arguments the reference to the class to be constructed, the method ID of the constructor, and the arguments that need to be passed to the constructor.

The DeleteLocalRef call allows the virtual machine to free the resources used by local references elemArr and stringClass. Section 5.2.1 will provide a detailed description of when and why you should call DeleteLocalRef.

Strings are objects. This example highlights the point further. The example also leads to a question, however. Given that we can implement equivalent functionality using other JNI functions, why does the JNI provide built-in functions such as NewString? The reason is that the built-in string functions are far more efficient than calling the java.lang.String API from native code. String is the most frequently used type of objects, one that deserves special support in the JNI.

It is also possible to invoke constructors using the CallNonvirtualVoid-Method function. In this case, the native code must first create an *uninitialized* object by calling the AllocObject function. The single NewObject call above:

```
result = (*env)->NewObject(env, stringClass, cid, elemArr);
```

may be replaced by an `AllocObject` call followed by a `CallNonvirtualVoid-Method` call:

```
result = (*env)->AllocObject(env, stringClass);
if (result) {
    (*env)->CallNonvirtualVoidMethod(env, result, stringClass,
                                     cid, elemArr);
    /* we need to check for possible exceptions */
    if ((*env)->ExceptionCheck(env)) {
        (*env)->DeleteLocalRef(env, result);
        result = NULL;
    }
}
```

`AllocObject` creates an uninitialized object, and must be used with care so that a constructor is called at most once on each object. The native code should not invoke a constructor on the same object multiple times.

Occasionally you may find it useful to allocate an uninitialized object first and call the constructor sometime later. In most cases, however, you should use `NewObject` and avoid the more error-prone `AllocObject`/`CallNonvirtualVoid-Method` pair.

4.4   Caching Field and Method IDs

Obtaining field and method IDs requires symbolic lookups based on the name and descriptor of the field or method. Symbolic lookups are relatively expensive. In this section, we introduce a technique that can be used to reduce this overhead.

The idea is to compute field and method IDs and cache them for repeated uses later. There are two ways to cache field and method IDs, depending upon whether caching is performed at the point of use of the field or method ID, or in the static initializer of the class that defines the field or method.

4.4.1   Caching at the Point of Use

Field and method IDs may be cached at the point where native code accesses the field values or performs method callbacks. The following implementation of the `Java_InstanceFieldAccess_accessField` function caches the field ID in static variables so that it need not be recomputed upon each invocation of the `InstanceFieldAccess.accessField` method.

```
JNIEXPORT void JNICALL
Java_InstanceFieldAccess_accessField(JNIEnv *env, jobject obj)
{
    static jfieldID fid_s = NULL; /* cached field ID for s */

    jclass cls = (*env)->GetObjectClass(env, obj);
    jstring jstr;
    const char *str;

    if (fid_s == NULL) {
        fid_s = (*env)->GetFieldID(env, cls, "s",
                                    "Ljava/lang/String;");
        if (fid_s == NULL) {
            return; /* exception already thrown */
        }
    }

    printf("In C:\n");

    jstr = (*env)->GetObjectField(env, obj, fid_s);
    str = (*env)->GetStringUTFChars(env, jstr, NULL);
    if (str == NULL) {
        return; /* out of memory */
    }
    printf("  c.s = \"%s\"\n", str);
    (*env)->ReleaseStringUTFChars(env, jstr, str);

    jstr = (*env)->NewStringUTF(env, "123");
    if (jstr == NULL) {
        return; /* out of memory */
    }
    (*env)->SetObjectField(env, obj, fid_s, jstr);
}
```

The highlighted static variable fid_s stores the precomputed field ID for InstanceFieldAccess.s. The static variable is initialized to NULL. When the InstanceFieldAccess.accessField method is called for the first time, it computes the field ID and caches it in the static variable for later use.

You may notice that there is an obvious race condition in the above code. Multiple threads may call the InstanceFieldAccess.accessField method at the same time and compute the same field ID concurrently. One thread may overwrite the static variable fid_s computed by another thread. Luckily, although this race condition leads to duplicated work in multiple threads, it is otherwise harmless. The field IDs computed by multiple threads for the same field in the same class will necessarily be the same.

Following the same idea, we may also cache the method ID for the java.lang.String constructor in the earlier MyNewString example:

```
jstring
MyNewString(JNIEnv *env, jchar *chars, jint len)
{
    jclass stringClass;
    jcharArray elemArr;
    static jmethodID cid = NULL;
    jstring result;

    stringClass = (*env)->FindClass(env, "java/lang/String");
    if (stringClass == NULL) {
        return NULL; /* exception thrown */
    }

    /* Note that cid is a static variable */
    if (cid == NULL) {
        /* Get the method ID for the String constructor */
        cid = (*env)->GetMethodID(env, stringClass,
                            "<init>", "([C)V");
        if (cid == NULL) {
            return NULL; /* exception thrown */
        }
    }

    /* Create a char[] that holds the string characters */
    elemArr = (*env)->NewCharArray(env, len);
    if (elemArr == NULL) {
        return NULL; /* exception thrown */
    }
    (*env)->SetCharArrayRegion(env, elemArr, 0, len, chars);

    /* Construct a java.lang.String object */
    result = (*env)->NewObject(env, stringClass, cid, elemArr);

    /* Free local references */
    (*env)->DeleteLocalRef(env, elemArr);
    (*env)->DeleteLocalRef(env, stringClass);
    return result;
}
```

We compute the method ID for the java.lang.String constructor when MyNewString is called for the first time. The highlighted static variable cid caches the result.

4.4.2   Caching in the Defining Class's Initializer

When we cache a field or method ID at the point of use we must introduce a check to detect whether the IDs have already been cached. Not only does this approach incur a small performance impact on the "fast path" when the IDs have already been cached, but it could lead to duplication of caching and checking as well. For example, if multiple native methods all require access to the same field, then they all need a check to compute and cache the corresponding field ID.

In many situations it is more convenient to initialize the field and method IDs required by a native method before the application can have a chance to invoke the native method. The virtual machine always executes the static initializer of a class before it invokes any of the methods in that class. Thus a suitable place for computing and caching field or method IDs is in the static initializer of the class that defines the fields or methods.

For example, to cache the method ID for `InstanceMethodCall.callback` we introduce a new native method `initIDs`, called from the static initializer of the `InstanceMethodCall` class:

```
class InstanceMethodCall {
    private static native void initIDs();
    private native void nativeMethod();
    private void callback() {
        System.out.println("In Java");
    }
    public static void main(String args[]) {
        InstanceMethodCall c = new InstanceMethodCall();
        c.nativeMethod();
    }
    static {
        System.loadLibrary("InstanceMethodCall");
        initIDs();
    }
}
```

Compared to the original code in Section 4.2, the above program contains two extra lines (highlighted in bold font). The implementation of `initIDs` simply computes and caches the method ID for `InstanceMethodCall.callback`:

```
jmethodID MID_InstanceMethodCall_callback;

JNIEXPORT void JNICALL
Java_InstanceMethodCall_initIDs(JNIEnv *env, jclass cls)
{
    MID_InstanceMethodCall_callback =
        (*env)->GetMethodID(env, cls, "callback", "()V");
}
```

The virtual machine runs the static initializer, and in turn calls the `initIDs` method, before executing any other methods (such as `nativeMethod` or `main`) in the `InstanceMethodCall` class. With the method ID is already cached in a global variable, the native implementation of `InstanceMethodCall.nativeMethod` no longer needs to perform a symbolic lookup:

```
JNIEXPORT void JNICALL
Java_InstanceMethodCall_nativeMethod(JNIEnv *env, jobject obj)
{
    printf("In C\n");
    (*env)->CallVoidMethod(env, obj,
                           MID_InstanceMethodCall_callback);
}
```

4.4.3 Comparison between the Two Approaches to Caching IDs

Caching IDs at the point of use is the reasonable solution if the JNI programmer does not have control over the source of the class that defines the field or method. For example, in the `MyNewString` example, we cannot inject a custom `initIDs` native method into the `java.lang.String` class in order to precompute and cache the method ID for the `java.lang.String` constructor.

Caching at the point of use has a number of disadvantages when compared with caching in the static initializer of the defining class.

- As explained before, caching at the point of use requires a check in the execution fast path and may also require duplicated checks and initialization of the same field or method ID.

- Method and field IDs are only valid until the class is unloaded. If you cache field and method IDs at the point of use you must make sure that the defining class will not be unloaded and reloaded as long as the native code still relies on the value of the cached ID. (The next chapter will show how you can keep a class from being unloaded by creating a reference to that class using the JNI.) On the other hand, if caching is done in the static initializer of the defining class, the cached IDs will automatically be recalculated when the class is unloaded and later reloaded.

Thus, where feasible, it is preferable to cache field and method IDs in the static initializer of their defining classes.

4.5   Performance of JNI Field and Method Operations

After learning how to cache field and method IDs to enhance performance, you might wonder: What are the performance characteristics of accessing fields and calling methods using the JNI? How does the cost of performing a callback from native code (a native/Java callback) compare with the cost of calling a native method (a Java/native call), and with the cost of calling a regular method (a Java/Java call)?

The answer to this question no doubt depends on how efficiently the underlying virtual machine implements the JNI. It is thus impossible to give an exact account of performance characteristics that is guaranteed to apply to a wide variety of virtual machine implementations. Instead, we will analyze the inherent cost of native method calls and JNI field and method operations and provide a general performance guideline for JNI programmers and implementors.

Let us start by comparing the cost of Java/native calls with the cost of Java/Java calls. Java/native calls are potentially slower than Java/Java calls for the following reasons:

- Native methods most likely follow a different calling convention than that used by Java/Java calls inside the Java virtual machine implementation. As a result, the virtual machine must perform additional operations to build arguments and set up the stack frame before jumping to a native method entry point.

- It is common for the virtual machine to inline method calls. Inlining Java/native calls is a lot harder than inlining Java/Java calls.

We estimate that a typical virtual machine may execute a Java/native call roughly two to three times slower than it executes a Java/Java call. Because a Java/Java call takes just a few cycles, the added overhead will be negligible unless the native method performs trivial operations. It is also possible to build virtual machine implementations with Java/native call performance close or equal to that of Java/Java calls. (Such virtual machine implementations, for example, may adopt the JNI calling convention as the internal Java/Java calling convention.)

The performance characteristics of a native/Java callback is technically similar to a Java/native call. In theory, the overhead of native/Java callbacks could also be within two to three times of Java/Java calls. In practice, however, native/Java callbacks are relatively infrequent. Virtual machine implementations do not usually optimize the performance of callbacks. At the time of this writing many production virtual machine implementations are such that the overhead of a native/Java callback can be as much as ten times higher than a Java/Java call.

The overhead of field access using the JNI lies in the cost of calling through the `JNIEnv`. Rather than directly dereferencing objects, the native code has to perform a C function call which in turn dereferences the object. The function call is necessary because it isolates the native code from the internal object representation maintained by the virtual machine implementation. The JNI field access overhead is typically negligible because a function call takes only a few cycles.

CHAPTER 5

Local and Global References

THE JNI exposes instance and array types (such as `jobject`, `jclass`, `jstring`, and `jarray`) as opaque references. Native code never directly inspects the contents of an opaque reference pointer. Instead it uses JNI functions to access the data structure pointed to by an opaque reference. By only dealing with opaque references, you need not worry about internal object layout that is dependent upon a particular Java virtual machine implementation. You do, however, need to learn more about different kinds of references in the JNI:

- The JNI supports three kinds of opaque references: local references, global references, and weak global references.

- Local and global references have different lifetimes. Local references are automatically freed, whereas global and weak global references remain valid until they are freed by the programmer.

- A local or global reference keeps the referenced object from being garbage collected. A weak global reference, on the other hand, allows the referenced object to be garbage collected.

- Not all references can be used in all contexts. It is illegal, for example, to use a local reference after the native method that created the reference returns.

In this chapter, we will discuss these issues in detail. Managing JNI references properly is crucial to writing reliable and space-efficient code.

5.1 Local and Global References

What are local and global references, and how are they different? We will use a series of examples to illustrate local and global references.

5.1.1 Local References

Most JNI functions create local references. For example, the JNI function New-Object creates a new instance and returns a local reference to that instance.

A local reference is valid only within the dynamic context of the native method that creates it, and only within that one invocation of the native method. All local references created during the execution of a native method will be freed once the native method returns.

You must not write native methods that store a local reference in a static variable and expect to use the same reference in subsequent invocations. For example, the following program, which is a modified version of the MyNewString function in Section 4.4.1, uses local references incorrectly.

```
/* This code is illegal */
jstring
MyNewString(JNIEnv *env, jchar *chars, jint len)
{
    static jclass stringClass = NULL;
    jmethodID cid;
    jcharArray elemArr;
    jstring result;

    if (stringClass == NULL) {
        stringClass = (*env)->FindClass(env,
                                      "java/lang/String");
        if (stringClass == NULL) {
            return NULL; /* exception thrown */
        }
    }
    /* It is wrong to use the cached stringClass here,
       because it may be invalid. */
    cid = (*env)->GetMethodID(env, stringClass,
                            "<init>", "([C)V");
    ...
    elemArr = (*env)->NewCharArray(env, len);
    ...
    result = (*env)->NewObject(env, stringClass, cid, elemArr);
    (*env)->DeleteLocalRef(env, elemArr);
    return result;
}
```

We have elided the lines that are not directly relevant to our discussion here. The goal for caching stringClass in a static variable might have been to eliminate the overhead of repeatedly making the following function call:

```
FindClass(env, "java/lang/String");
```

This is not the right approach because FindClass returns a local reference to the java.lang.String class object. To see why this is a problem, suppose that the native method implementation of C.f calls MyNewString:

```
JNIEXPORT jstring JNICALL
Java_C_f(JNIEnv *env, jobject this)
{
    char *c_str = ...;
    ...
    return MyNewString(c_str);
}
```

After the native method C.f returns, the virtual machine frees all local references created during the execution of Java_C_f. These freed local references include the local reference to the class object stored in the stringClass variable. Future MyNewString calls will then attempt to use an invalid local reference, which could lead to memory corruption or system crashes. A code segment such as the following, for example, makes two consecutive calls to C.f and causes MyNewString to encounter the invalid local reference:

```
...
... = C.f(); // The first call is perhaps OK.
... = C.f(); // This would use an invalid local reference.
...
```

There are two ways to invalidate a local reference. As explained before, the virtual machine automatically frees all local references created during the execution of a native method after the native method returns. In addition, programmers may explicitly manage the lifetime of local references using JNI functions such as DeleteLocalRef.

Why do you want to delete local references explicitly if the virtual machine automatically frees them after native methods return? A local reference keeps the referenced object from being garbage collected until the local reference is invalidated. The DeleteLocalRef call in MyNewString, for example, allows the intermediate array object, elemArr, to be garbage collected immediately. Otherwise the virtual machine will only be able to free the elemArr object after the native method that calls MyNewString (such as C.f above) returns.

A local reference may be passed through multiple native functions before it is destroyed. For example, MyNewString returns the string reference created by NewObject. It will then be up to the caller of MyNewString to determine whether to free the local reference returned by MyNewString. In the Java_C_f example, C.f in turn returns the result of MyNewString as the result of the native method call. After the virtual machine receives the local reference from the Java_C_f function, it passes the underlying string object to the caller of C.f and then destroys the local reference that was originally created by the JNI function NewOb-ject.

Local references are also only valid in the thread that creates them. A local reference that is created in one thread cannot be used in another thread. It is a programming error for a native method to store a local reference in a global variable and expect another thread to use the local reference.

5.1.2 Global References

You can use a global reference across multiple invocations of a native method. A global reference can be used across multiple threads and remains valid until it is freed by the programmer. Like a local reference, a global reference ensures that the referenced object will not be garbage collected.

Unlike local references, which are created by most JNI functions, global references are created by just one JNI function, NewGlobalRef. The following version of MyNewString illustrates how to use a global reference. We highlight the differences between the code below and the code that mistakenly cached a local reference in the last section:

```
/* This code is OK */
jstring
MyNewString(JNIEnv *env, jchar *chars, jint len)
{
    static jclass stringClass = NULL;
    ...
    if (stringClass == NULL) {
        jclass localRefCls =
            (*env)->FindClass(env, "java/lang/String");
        if (localRefCls == NULL) {
            return NULL; /* exception thrown */
        }
        /* Create a global reference */
        stringClass = (*env)->NewGlobalRef(env, localRefCls);

        /* The local reference is no longer useful */
        (*env)->DeleteLocalRef(env, localRefCls);

        /* Is the global reference created successfully? */
        if (stringClass == NULL) {
            return NULL; /* out of memory exception thrown */
        }
    }
    ...
}
```

The modified version passes the local reference returned from FindClass to NewGlobalRef, which creates a global reference to the java.lang.String class object. We check whether the NewGlobalRef has successfully created string-Class after deleting localRefCls because the local reference localRefCls needs to be deleted in either case.

5.1.3 Weak Global References

Weak global references are new in Java 2 SDK release 1.2. They are created using NewGlobalWeakRef and freed using DeleteGlobalWeakRef. Like global references, weak global references remain valid across native method calls and across different threads. Unlike global references, weak global references do not keep the underlying object from being garbage collected.

The MyNewString example has shown how to cache a global reference to the java.lang.String class. The MyNewString example could alternatively use a weak global reference to store the cached java.lang.String class. It does not matter whether we use a global reference or a weak global reference because java.lang.String is a system class and will never be garbage collected.

Weak global references become more useful when a reference cached by the native code must not keep the underlying object from being garbage collected. Suppose, for example, a native method mypkg.MyCls.f needs to cache a reference to the class mypkg.MyCls2. Caching the class in a weak global reference allows the mypkg.MyCls2 class to still be unloaded:

```
JNIEXPORT void JNICALL
Java_mypkg_MyCls_f(JNIEnv *env, jobject self)
{
    static jclass myCls2 = NULL;
    if (myCls2 == NULL) {
        jclass myCls2Local =
            (*env)->FindClass(env, "mypkg/MyCls2");
        if (myCls2Local == NULL) {
            return; /* can't find class */
        }
        myCls2 = NewWeakGlobalRef(env, myCls2Local);
        if (myCls2 == NULL) {
            return; /* out of memory */
        }
    }
    ... /* use myCls2 */
}
```

We assume that MyCls and MyCls2 have the same lifetime. (For example, they may be loaded by the same class loader.) Thus we do not consider the case when

MyCls2 is unloaded and later reloaded while MyCls and its native method implementation Java_mypkg_MyCls remain to be in use. If that could happen, we would have to check whether the cached weak reference still points to a live class object or points to a class object that has already been garbage collected. The next section will explain how to perform such checks on weak global references.

5.1.4 Comparing References

Given two local, global, or weak global references, you can check whether they refer to the same object using the IsSameObject function. For example:

```
(*env)->IsSameObject(env, obj1, obj2)
```

returns JNI_TRUE (or 1) if obj1 and obj2 refer to the same object, and returns JNI_FALSE (or 0) otherwise.

A NULL reference in JNI refers to the null object in the Java virtual machine. If obj is a local or a global reference, you may use either

```
(*env)->IsSameObject(env, obj, NULL)
```

or

```
obj == NULL
```

to determine if obj refers to the null object.

The rules for weak global references are somewhat different. NULL weak references refer to the null object. IsSameObject, however, has special uses for weak global references. You can use IsSameObject to determine whether a non-NULL weak global reference still points to a live object. Suppose wobj is a non-NULL weak global reference. The following call:

```
(*env)->IsSameObject(env, wobj, NULL)
```

returns JNI_TRUE if wobj refers to an object that has already been collected, and returns JNI_FALSE if wobj still refers to a live object.

5.2 Freeing References

Each JNI reference consumes a certain amount of memory by itself, in addition to the memory taken by the referred object. As a JNI programmer, you should be aware of the number of references that your program will use at a given time. In particular, you should be aware of the upper bound of the number of local references your program can create at any point during its execution, even though these local references will eventually be freed automatically by the virtual machine. Excessive reference creation, however transient, can lead to memory exhaustion.

5.2.1 Freeing Local References

In most cases, you do not have to worry about freeing local references when implementing a native method. The Java virtual machine frees them for you when the native method returns to the caller. However, there are times when you, the JNI programmer, should explicitly free local references in order to avoid excessive memory usage. Consider the following situations:

- You need to create a large number of local references in a single native method invocation. This may result in an overflow of the internal JNI local reference table. It is a good idea to delete promptly those local references that will not be needed. For example, in the following program segment the native code iterates through a potentially large array of strings. After each iteration, the native code should explicitly free the local reference to the string element as follows:

```
for (i = 0; i < len; i++) {
    jstring jstr = (*env)->GetObjectArrayElement(env, arr, i);
    ... /* process jstr */
    (*env)->DeleteLocalRef(env, jstr);
}
```

- You want to write a utility function that is called from unknown contexts. The MyNewString example shown in Section 4.3 illustrates the use of DeleteLocalRef to delete promptly local references in a utility function. Otherwise there will be two local references that remains allocated after each call to the MyNewString function.

- Your native method does not return at all. For example, a native method may enter an infinite event dispatch loop. It is crucial to release local references created inside the loop so that they do not accumulate indefinitely, resulting in a memory leak.

- Your native method accesses a large object, thereby creating a local reference to the object. The native method then performs additional computation before returning to the caller. The local reference to the large object will prevent the object from being garbage collected until the native method returns, even if the object is no longer used in the remainder of the native method. For example, in the following program segment, because there is an explicit call to DeleteLocalRef beforehand, the garbage collector may be able to free the object referred to by `lref` when the execution is inside the function `lengthy-Computation`:

```
/* A native method implementation */
JNIEXPORT void JNICALL
Java_pkg_Cls_func(JNIEnv *env, jobject this)
{
    lref = ...                /* a large Java object */
    ...                       /* last use of lref */
    (*env)->DeleteLocalRef(env, lref);

    lengthyComputation();     /* may take some time */
    return;                   /* all local refs are freed */
}
```

5.2.2   Managing Local References in Java 2 SDK Release 1.2

Java 2 SDK release 1.2 provides an additional set of functions for managing the lifetime of local references. These functions are `EnsureLocalCapacity`, `NewLocalRef`, `PushLocalFrame`, and `PopLocalFrame`.

The JNI specification dictates that the virtual machine automatically ensures that each native method can create at least 16 local references. Experience shows that this provides enough capacity for the majority of native methods that do not contain complex interactions with objects in the Java virtual machine. If, however, there is a need to create additional local references, a native method may issue an `EnsureLocalCapacity` call to make sure that space for a sufficient number of local references is available. For example, a slight variation of a previous example above reserves enough capacity for all local references created during the loop execution if sufficient memory is available:

```
/* The number of local references to be created is equal to
   the length of the array. */
if ((*env)->EnsureLocalCapacity(env, len)) < 0) {
    ... /* out of memory */
}
for (i = 0; i < len; i++) {
    jstring jstr = (*env)->GetObjectArrayElement(env, arr, i);
    ... /* process jstr */
    /* DeleteLocalRef is no longer necessary */
}
```

Of course, the above version is likely to consume more memory that the previous version which promptly deletes local references.

Alternatively, the Push/PopLocalFrame functions allow programmers to create nested scopes of local references. For example, we may also rewrite the same example as follows:

```
#define N_REFS ... /* the maximum number of local references
                       used in each iteration */
for (i = 0; i < len; i++) {
    if ((*env)->PushLocalFrame(env, N_REFS) < 0) {
        ... /* out of memory */
    }
    jstr = (*env)->GetObjectArrayElement(env, arr, i);
    ... /* process jstr */
    (*env)->PopLocalFrame(env, NULL);
}
```

PushLocalFrame creates a new scope for specific number of local references. PopLocalFrame destroys the topmost scope, freeing all local references in that scope.

The advantage of using the Push/PopLocalFrame functions is that they make it possible to manage the lifetime of local references without having to worry about every single local reference that might be created during execution. In the above example, if the computation that processes jstr creates additional local references, these local references will be freed after PopLocalFrame returns.

The NewLocalRef function is useful when you write utility functions that are expected to return a local reference. We will demonstrate the use of the NewLocalRef function in Section 5.3.

The native code may create local references beyond the default capacity of 16 or the capacity reserved in a PushLocalFrame or EnsureLocalCapacity call. The virtual machine implementation will try to allocate the memory needed for the local reference. There is no guarantee, however, that memory will be available. The virtual machine exits if it fails to allocate the memory. You should reserve enough memory for local references and free local references promptly to avoid such unexpected virtual machine exits.

Java 2 SDK release 1.2 supports a command-line option -verbose:jni. When this option is enabled, the virtual machine implementation reports excessive local reference creation beyond the reserved capacity.

5.2.3 Freeing Global References

You should call DeleteGlobalRef when your native code no longer needs access to a global reference. If you fail to call this function the Java virtual machine will not garbage collect the corresponding object, even when the object is no longer used anywhere else in the system.

You should call `DeleteWeakGlobalRef` when your native code no longer needs access to a weak global reference. If you fail to call this function the Java virtual machine will still be able to garbage collect the underlying object, but will not be able to reclaim the memory consumed by the weak global reference itself.

5.3 Rules for Managing References

We are now ready to go through the rules for managing JNI references in native code, based on what we have covered in previous sections. The objective is to eliminate unnecessary memory usage and object retention.

There are, in general, two kinds of native code: functions that directly implement native methods and utility functions that are used in arbitrary contexts.

When writing functions that directly implement native methods, you need to be careful about excessive local reference creation in loops and unnecessary local reference creation caused by native methods that do not return. It is acceptable to leave up to 16 local references in use for the virtual machine to delete after the native method returns. Native method calls must not cause global or weak global references to accumulate because global and weak global references are not freed automatically after native methods return.

When writing native utility functions you must be careful not to leak any local references on any execution path throughout the function. Because a utility function may be called repeatedly from an unanticipated context, any unnecessary reference creation may cause memory overflow.

- When a utility function that returns a primitive type is called, it must not have the side effect of accumulating additional local, global, or weak global references.

- When a utility function that returns a reference type is called, it must not accumulate extra local, global, or weak global references, other than the reference it returns as result.

It is acceptable for a utility function to create some global or weak global references for the purpose of caching because only the very first call creates these references.

If a utility function returns a reference, you should make the kind of returned reference part of the function specification. It should not return a local reference some of the time and a global reference at other times. The caller needs to know the type of the reference returned by a utility function in order to manage its own JNI references correctly. For example, the following code calls a utility function `GetInfoString` repeatedly. We need to know the type of reference returned by

GetInfoString to be able to free the returned JNI reference properly after each iteration.

```
while (JNI_TRUE) {
    jstring infoString = GetInfoString(info);
    ... /* process infoString */

    ??? /* we need to call DeleteLocalRef, DeleteGlobalRef,
           or DeleteWeakGlobalRef depending on the type of
           reference returned by GetInfoString. */
}
```

In Java 2 SDK release 1.2, the NewLocalRef function sometimes is useful to ensure that a utility function always returns a local reference. To illustrate, let us make another (somewhat contrived) change to the MyNewString function. The following version caches a frequently requested string (say, "CommonString") in a global reference:

```
jstring
MyNewString(JNIEnv *env, jchar *chars, jint len)
{
    static jstring result;

    /* wstrncmp compares two Unicode strings */
    if (wstrncmp("CommonString", chars, len) == 0) {
        /* refers to the global ref caching "CommonString" */
        static jstring cachedString = NULL;
        if (cachedString == NULL) {
            /* create cachedString for the first time */
            jstring cachedStringLocal = ... ;
            /* cache the result in a global reference */
            cachedString =
                (*env)->NewGlobalRef(env, cachedStringLocal);
        }
        return (*env)->NewLocalRef(env, cachedString);
    }

    ... /* create the string as a local reference and store in
           result as a local reference */
    return result;
}
```

The normal path returns a string as a local reference. As explained before, we must store the cached string in a global reference so that it can be accessed in multiple native method invocations and from multiple threads. The highlighted line creates a new local reference that refers to the same object as the cached global reference. As part of the contract with its callers, MyNewString always returns a local reference.

The Push/PopLocalFrame functions are especially convenient for managing the lifetime of local references. If you called PushLocalFrame on entry to a native function, calling PopLocalFrame before the native function returns ensures that all local references created during native function execution will be freed. The Push/PopLocalFrame functions are efficient. You are strongly encouraged to use them.

If you call PushLocalFrame on function entry, remember to call Pop-LocalFrame in all function exit paths. For example, the following function has one call to PushLocalFrame but needs multiple calls to PopLocalFrame:

```
jobject f(JNIEnv *env, ...)
{
    jobject result;
    if ((*env)->PushLocalFrame(env, 10) < 0) {
        /* frame not pushed, no PopLocalFrame needed */
        return NULL;
    }
    ...
    result = ...;
    if (...) {
        /* remember to pop local frame before return */
        result = (*env)->PopLocalFrame(env, result);
        return result;
    }
    ...
    result = (*env)->PopLocalFrame(env, result);
    /* normal return */
    return result;
}
```

Failing to place PopLocalFrame calls properly would lead to undefined behavior, such as virtual machine crashes.

The above example also illustrates why it is sometimes useful to specify the second argument to PopLocalFrame. The result local reference is initially created in the new frame constructed by PushLocalFrame. PopLocalFrame converts its second argument, result, to a new local reference in the previous frame before popping the topmost frame.

CHAPTER 6

Exceptions

WE have encountered numerous situations in which native code checks for possible errors after making JNI function calls. This chapter examines how native code can detect and recover from these error conditions.

We will focus on errors that occur as the result of issuing JNI function calls, not arbitrary errors that happen in native code. If a native method makes an operating systems call, it simply follows the documented way of checking for possible failures in the system call. If, on the other hand, the native method issues a callback to a Java API method, then it must follow the steps described in this chapter to properly check for and recover from possible exceptions that have occurred in the method execution.

6.1 Overview

We introduce JNI exception handling functions through a series of examples.

6.1.1 Caching and Throwing Exceptions in Native Code

The program below shows how to declare a native method that throws an exception. The CatchThrow class declares the doit native method and specifies that it throws an IllegalArgumentException:

```
class CatchThrow {
    private native void doit()
        throws IllegalArgumentException;
    private void callback() throws NullPointerException {
        throw new NullPointerException("CatchThrow.callback");
    }
```

```
public static void main(String args[]) {
    CatchThrow c = new CatchThrow();
    try {
        c.doit();
    } catch (Exception e) {
        System.out.println("In Java:\n\t" + e);
    }
}
static {
    System.loadLibrary("CatchThrow");
}
```

The CatchThrow.main method calls the native method doit, implemented as follows:

```
JNIEXPORT void JNICALL
Java_CatchThrow_doit(JNIEnv *env, jobject obj)
{
    jthrowable exc;
    jclass cls = (*env)->GetObjectClass(env, obj);
    jmethodID mid =
        (*env)->GetMethodID(env, cls, "callback", "()V");
    if (mid == NULL) {
        return;
    }
    (*env)->CallVoidMethod(env, obj, mid);
    exc = (*env)->ExceptionOccurred(env);
    if (exc) {
        /* We don't do much with the exception, except that
           we print a debug message for it, clear it, and
           throw a new exception. */
        jclass newExcCls;
        (*env)->ExceptionDescribe(env);
        (*env)->ExceptionClear(env);
        newExcCls = (*env)->FindClass(env,
                    "java/lang/IllegalArgumentException");
        if (newExcCls == NULL) {
            /* Unable to find the exception class, give up. */
            return;
        }
        (*env)->ThrowNew(env, newExcCls, "thrown from C code");
    }
}
```

Running the program with the native library produces the following output:

```
java.lang.NullPointerException:
        at CatchThrow.callback(CatchThrow.java)
        at CatchThrow.doit(Native Method)
        at CatchThrow.main(CatchThrow.java)
In Java:
        java.lang.IllegalArgumentException: thrown from C code
```

The callback method throws a NullPointerException. When the CallVoid-Method returns control to the native method, the native code will detect this exception by calling the JNI function ExceptionOccurred. In our example, when an exception is detected, the native code outputs a descriptive message about the exception by calling ExceptionDescribe, clears the exception using Exception-Clear, and throws an IllegalArgumentException instead.

A pending exception raised through the JNI (by calling ThrowNew, for example) does not immediately disrupt the native method execution. This is different from how exceptions behave in the Java programming language. When an exception is thrown in the Java programming language, the virtual machine automatically transfers the control flow to the nearest enclosing try/catch statement that matches the exception type. The virtual machine then clears the pending exception and executes the exception handler. In contrast, JNI programmers must explicitly implement the control flow after an exception has occurred.

6.1.2 A Utility Function

Throwing an exception involves first finding the exception class and then issuing a call to the ThrowNew function. To simplify the task, we can write a utility function that throws a named exception:

```
void
JNU_ThrowByName(JNIEnv *env, const char *name, const char *msg)
{
    jclass cls = (*env)->FindClass(env, name);
    /* if cls is NULL, an exception has already been thrown */
    if (cls != NULL) {
        (*env)->ThrowNew(env, cls, msg);
    }
    /* free the local ref */
    (*env)->DeleteLocalRef(env, cls);
}
```

In this book, the JNU prefix stands for **JNI** Utilities. JNU_ThrowByName first finds the exception class using the FindClass function. If FindClass fails (returns NULL), the virtual machine must have thrown an exception (such as NoClassDefFoundError). In this case JNU_ThrowByName does not attempt to throw another exception. If FindClass succeeds, we throw the named exception by calling ThrowNew. When JNU_ThrowByName returns, it guarantees that there is a pending exception, although the pending exception was not necessarily what is specified by the name argument. We make sure to delete the local reference to the exception class created in this function. Passing NULL to DeleteLocalRef is a no-op, which is an appropriate action if FindClass fails and returns NULL.

6.2 Proper Exception Handling

JNI programmers must foresee possible exception conditions and write code that checks for and handles these cases. Proper exception handling is sometimes tedious but is necessary in order to produce robust applications.

6.2.1 Checking for Exceptions

There are two ways to check whether an error has occurred.

1. Most JNI functions use a distinct return value (such as NULL) to indicate that an error has occurred. The error return value also implies that there is a pending exception in the current thread. (Encoding error conditions in the return value is common practice in C.)

   The following example illustrates using the NULL value returned by Get-FieldID in checking for errors. The example consists of two parts: a class Window that defines a number of instance fields (handle, length, and width) and a native method that caches the field IDs of these fields. Even though these fields exist in the Window class, we still need to check for possible errors returned from GetFieldID because the virtual machine may not be able to allocate the memory needed to represent a field ID.

```
/* a class in the Java programming language */
public class Window {
    long handle;
    int length;
    int width;
    static native void initIDs();
    static {
        initIDs();
    }
}
```

```
/* C code that implements Window.initIDs */
jfieldID FID_Window_handle;
jfieldID FID_Window_length;
jfieldID FID_Window_width;

JNIEXPORT void JNICALL
Java_Window_initIDs(JNIEnv *env, jclass classWindow)
{
    FID_Window_handle =
        (*env)->GetFieldID(env, classWindow, "handle", "J");
    if (FID_Window_handle == NULL) {   /* important check. */
        return; /* error occurred. */
    }
    FID_Window_length =
        (*env)->GetFieldID(env, classWindow, "length", "I");
    if (FID_Window_length == NULL) {   /* important check. */
        return; /* error occurred. */
    }
    FID_Window_width =
        (*env)->GetFieldID(env, classWindow, "width", "I");
    /* no checks necessary; we are about to return anyway */
}
```

2. When using a JNI function whose return value cannot flag that an error has occurred, native code must rely on the raised exception to do error checks. The JNI function that performs checks for a pending exception in the current thread is ExceptionOccurred. (ExceptionCheck was also added in Java 2 SDK release 1.2.) For example, the JNI function CallIntMethod cannot encode an error condition in the return value. Typical choices of error condition return values, such as NULL and -1, do not work because they could be legal values returned by the method that was called. Consider a Fraction class whose floor method returns the integral part of the value of the fraction, and some native code that calls this method.

```
public class Fraction {
    // details such as constructors omitted
    int over, under;
    public int floor() {
        return Math.floor((double)over/under);
    }
}
```

```
/* Native code that calls Fraction.floor. Assume method ID
   MID_Fraction_floor has been initialized elsewhere. */
void f(JNIEnv *env, jobject fraction)
{
    jint floor = (*env)->CallIntMethod(env, fraction,
                                       MID_Fraction_floor);
    /* important: check if an exception was raised */
    if ((*env)->ExceptionCheck(env)) {
        return;
    }
    ... /* use floor */
}
```

When the JNI function returns a distinct error code, the native code may still check for exceptions explicitly by calling, for example, ExceptionCheck. However, it is more efficient to check for the distinct error return value instead. *If a JNI function returns its error value, a subsequent ExceptionCheck call in the current thread is guaranteed to return JNI_TRUE.*

6.2.2   Handling Exceptions

Native code may handle a pending exception in two ways:

- The native method implementation can choose to return immediately, causing the exception to be handled in the caller.

- The native code can clear the exception by calling ExceptionClear and then execute its own exception handling code.

It is extremely important to check, handle, and clear a pending exception before calling any subsequent JNI functions. Calling most JNI functions with a pending exception—with an exception that you have not explicitly cleared—may lead to unexpected results. You can call only a small number of JNI functions safely when there is a pending exception in the current thread. Section 11.8.2 specifies the complete list of these JNI functions. Generally speaking, when there is a pending exception you can call the JNI functions that are designed to handle exceptions and the JNI functions that release various virtual machine resources exposed through the JNI.

It is often necessary to be able to free resources when exceptions occur. In the following example, the native method first obtains the contents of a string by issuing a GetStringChars call. It calls ReleaseStringChars if a subsequent operation fails:

```
JNIEXPORT void JNICALL
Java_pkg_Cls_f(JNIEnv *env, jclass cls, jstring jstr)
{
    const jchar *cstr = (*env)->GetStringChars(env, jstr);
    if (c_str == NULL) {
        return;
    }
    ...
    if (...) { /* exception occurred */
        (*env)->ReleaseStringChars(env, jstr, cstr);
        return;
    }
    ...
    /* normal return */
    (*env)->ReleaseStringChars(env, jstr, cstr);
}
```

The first call to `ReleaseStringChars` is issued when there is a pending exception. The native method implementation releases the string resource and returns immediately afterwards without first clearing the exception.

6.2.3 Exceptions in Utility Functions

Programmers writing utility functions should pay special attention to ensure that exceptions are propagated to the caller native method. In particular, we emphasize the following two issues:

- Preferably, utility functions should provide a special return value to indicate that an exception has occurred. This simplifies the caller's task of checking for pending exceptions.

- In addition, utility functions should follow the rules (§5.3) for managing local references in exception handling code.

To illustrate, let us introduce a utility function that performs a callback based on the name and descriptor of an instance method:

```
jvalue
JNU_CallMethodByName(JNIEnv *env,
                     jboolean *hasException,
                     jobject obj,
                     const char *name,
                     const char *descriptor, ...)
{
    va_list args;
    jclass clazz;
    jmethodID mid;
```

```
jvalue result;
if ((*env)->EnsureLocalCapacity(env, 2) == JNI_OK) {
    clazz = (*env)->GetObjectClass(env, obj);
    mid = (*env)->GetMethodID(env, clazz, name,
                                descriptor);
    if (mid) {
        const char *p = descriptor;
        /* skip over argument types to find out the
            return type */
        while (*p != ')') p++;
        /* skip ')' */
        p++;
        va_start(args, descriptor);
        switch (*p) {
        case 'V':
            (*env)->CallVoidMethodV(env, obj, mid, args);
            break;
        case '[':
        case 'L':
            result.l = (*env)->CallObjectMethodV(
                                env, obj, mid, args);
            break;
        case 'Z':
            result.z = (*env)->CallBooleanMethodV(
                                env, obj, mid, args);
            break;
        case 'B':
            result.b = (*env)->CallByteMethodV(
                                env, obj, mid, args);
            break;
        case 'C':
            result.c = (*env)->CallCharMethodV(
                                env, obj, mid, args);
            break;
        case 'S':
            result.s = (*env)->CallShortMethodV(
                                env, obj, mid, args);
            break;
        case 'I':
            result.i = (*env)->CallIntMethodV(
                                env, obj, mid, args);
            break;
        case 'J':
            result.j = (*env)->CallLongMethodV(
                                env, obj, mid, args);
            break;
        case 'F':
            result.f = (*env)->CallFloatMethodV(
```

```
                                                env, obj, mid, args);
                break;
            case 'D':
                result.d = (*env)->CallDoubleMethodV(
                                            env, obj, mid, args);
                break;
            default:
                (*env)->FatalError(env, "illegal descriptor");
            }
            va_end(args);
        }
        (*env)->DeleteLocalRef(env, clazz);
    }
    if (hasException) {
        *hasException = (*env)->ExceptionCheck(env);
    }
    return result;
}
```

JNU_CallMethodByName takes, among other arguments, a pointer to a jboolean. The jboolean will be set to JNI_FALSE if everything succeeds and to
JNI_TRUE if an exception occurs at any point during the execution of this function.
This gives the caller of JNU_CallMethodByName an obvious way to check for possible exceptions.

JNU_CallMethodByName first makes sure that it can create two local references: one for the class reference and the other for the result returned from the
method call. Next, it obtains the class reference from the object and looks up the
method ID. Depending on the return type, the switch statement dispatches to the
corresponding JNI method call function. After the callback returns, if hasExcep-
tion is not NULL, we call ExceptionCheck to check for pending exceptions.

The ExceptionCheck function is new in Java 2 SDK release 1.2. It is similar
to the ExceptionOccurred function. The difference is that ExceptionCheck does
not return a reference to the exception object, but returns JNI_TRUE when there is
a pending exception and returns JNI_FALSE when there is no pending exception.
ExceptionCheck simplifies local reference management when the native code
only needs to know whether an exception has occurred but needs not obtain a reference to the exception object. The previous code would have to be rewritten as
follows in JDK release 1.1:

```
    if (hasException) {
        jthrowable exc = (*env)->ExceptionOccurred(env);
        *hasException = exc != NULL;
        (*env)->DeleteLocalRef(env, exc);
    }
```

The additional `DeleteLocalRef` call is necessary in order to delete the local reference to the exception object.

Using the `JNU_CallMethodByName` function we can rewrite the implementation of `InstanceMethodCall.nativeMethod` in Section 4.2 as follows:

```
JNIEXPORT void JNICALL
Java_InstanceMethodCall_nativeMethod(JNIEnv *env, jobject obj)
{
    printf("In C\n");
    JNU_CallMethodByName(env, NULL, obj, "callback", "()V");
}
```

We need not check for exceptions after the `JNU_CallMethodByName` call because the native method returns immediately afterwards.

CHAPTER 7

The Invocation Interface

THIS chapter illustrates how you can embed a Java virtual machine in your native application. A Java virtual machine implementation is typically shipped as a native library. Native applications can link against this library and use the invocation interface to load the Java virtual machine. Indeed, the standard launcher command (java) in JDK or Java 2 SDK releases is no more than a simple C program linked with the Java virtual machine. The launcher parses the command line arguments, loads the virtual machine, and runs Java applications through the invocation interface.

7.1 Creating the Java Virtual Machine

To illustrate the invocation interface, let's look at a C program that loads a Java virtual machine and calls the Prog.main method defined as follows:

```
public class Prog {
    public static void main(String[] args) {
        System.out.println("Hello World " + args[0]);
    }
}
```

The following C program, invoke.c, loads a Java virtual machine and invokes Prog.main.

```
#include <jni.h>

#define PATH_SEPARATOR ';' /* define it to be ':' on Solaris */
#define USER_CLASSPATH "." /* where Prog.class is */

main() {
    JNIEnv *env;
    JavaVM *jvm;
    jint res;
    jclass cls;
    jmethodID mid;
    jstring jstr;
    jclass stringClass;
    jobjectArray args;

#ifdef JNI_VERSION_1_2
    JavaVMInitArgs vm_args;
    JavaVMOption options[1];
    options[0].optionString =
        "-Djava.class.path=" USER_CLASSPATH;
    vm_args.version = 0x00010002;
    vm_args.options = options;
    vm_args.nOptions = 1;
    vm_args.ignoreUnrecognized = JNI_TRUE;
    /* Create the Java VM */
    res = JNI_CreateJavaVM(&jvm, (void**)&env, &vm_args);
#else
    JDK1_1InitArgs vm_args;
    char classpath[1024];
    vm_args.version = 0x00010001;
    JNI_GetDefaultJavaVMInitArgs(&vm_args);
    /* Append USER_CLASSPATH to the default system class path */
    sprintf(classpath, "%s%c%s",
            vm_args.classpath, PATH_SEPARATOR, USER_CLASSPATH);
    vm_args.classpath = classpath;
    /* Create the Java VM */
    res = JNI_CreateJavaVM(&jvm, &env, &vm_args);
#endif /* JNI_VERSION_1_2 */

    if (res < 0) {
        fprintf(stderr, "Can't create Java VM\n");
        exit(1);
    }
    cls = (*env)->FindClass(env, "Prog");
    if (cls == NULL) {
        goto destroy;
    }
```

```
        mid = (*env)->GetStaticMethodID(env, cls, "main",
                                        "([Ljava/lang/String;)V");
        if (mid == NULL) {
            goto destroy;
        }
        jstr = (*env)->NewStringUTF(env, " from C!");
        if (jstr == NULL) {
            goto destroy;
        }
        stringClass = (*env)->FindClass(env, "java/lang/String");
        args = (*env)->NewObjectArray(env, 1, stringClass, jstr);
        if (args == NULL) {
            goto destroy;
        }
        (*env)->CallStaticVoidMethod(env, cls, mid, args);

    destroy:
        if ((*env)->ExceptionOccurred(env)) {
            (*env)->ExceptionDescribe(env);
        }
        (*jvm)->DestroyJavaVM(jvm);
    }
```

The code conditionally compiles an initialization structure JDK1_1InitArgs that is specific to the virtual machine implementation in JDK release 1.1. Java 2 SDK release 1.2 still supports JDK1_1InitArgs, although it introduces a general-purpose virtual machine initialization structure called JavaVMInitArgs. The constant JNI_VERSION_1_2 is defined in Java 2 SDK release 1.2, but not in JDK release 1.1.

When it targets the 1.1 release, the C code begins with a call to JNI_GetDefaultJavaVMInitArgs to obtain the default virtual machine settings. JNI_GetDefaultJavaVMInitArgs returns such values as the heap size, stack size, default class path, and so on, in the vm_args parameter. We then append the directory in which Prog.class resides to vm_args.classpath.

When it targets the 1.2 release, the C code creates a JavaVMInitArgs structure. The virtual machine initialization arguments are stored in a JavaVMOption array. You can set both common options (e.g., -Djava.class.path=.) and implementation-specific options (e.g., -Xmx64m) that directly correspond to java command line options. Setting ignoreUnrecognized field to JNI_TRUE instructs the virtual machine to ignore unrecognized implementation-specific options.

After setting up the virtual machine initialization structure, the C program calls JNI_CreateJavaVM to load and initialize the Java virtual machine. The JNI_CreateJavaVM function fills in two return values:

- An interface pointer, `jvm`, to the newly created Java virtual machine.

- The `JNIEnv` interface pointer `env` for the current thread. Recall that native code accesses JNI functions through the `env` interface pointer.

When the `JNI_CreateJavaVM` function returns successfully, the current native thread has bootstrapped itself into the Java virtual machine. At this point it is running just like a native method. Thus it can, among other things, issue JNI calls to invoke the `Prog.main` method.

Eventually the program calls the `DestroyJavaVM` function to unload the Java virtual machine. (Unfortunately, you cannot unload the Java virtual machine implementation in JDK release 1.1 or Java 2 SDK release 1.2. `DestroyJavaVM` always returns an error code in these releases.)

Running the above program produces:

```
Hello World from C!
```

7.2   Linking Native Applications with the Java Virtual Machine

The invocation interface requires you to link programs such as `invoke.c` with a Java virtual machine implementation. How you link with the Java virtual machine depends on whether the native application is intended to be deployed with only a particular virtual machine implementation or it is designed to work with a variety of virtual machine implementations from different vendors.

7.2.1   Linking with a Known Java Virtual Machine

You may decide that your native application will be deployed only with a particular virtual machine implementation. In this case you can link the native application with the native library that implements the virtual machine. For example, with the JDK 1.1 release for Solaris, you can use the following command to compile and link `invoke.c`:

```
cc -I<jni.h dir> -L<libjava.so dir> -lthread -ljava invoke.c
```

The `-lthread` option indicates that we use the Java virtual machine implementation with native thread support (§8.1.5). The `-ljava` option specifies that `libjava.so` is the Solaris shared library that implements the Java virtual machine.

On Win32 with the Microsoft Visual C++ compiler, the command line to compile and link the same program with JDK 1.1 release is:

```
cl -I<jni.h dir> -MD invoke.c -link <javai.lib dir>\javai.lib
```

Of course, you need to supply the correct include and library directories that correspond to the JDK installation on your machine. The -MD option ensures that your native application is linked with the Win32 multithreaded C library, the same C library used by the Java virtual machine implementation in JDK 1.1 and Java 2 SDK 1.2 releases. The cl command consults the javai.lib file, shipped with JDK release 1.1 on Win32, for linkage information about invocation interface functions such as JNI_CreateJavaVM implemented in the virtual machine. The actual JDK 1.1 virtual machine implementation used at run time is contained in a separate dynamic link library file called javai.dll. In contrast, the same Solaris shared library (.so file) is used both at link time and at run time.

With Java 2 SDK release 1.2, virtual machine library names have changed to libjvm.so on Solaris and to jvm.lib and jvm.dll on Win32. In general, different vendors may name their virtual machine implementations differently.

Once compilation and linking are complete you can run the resulting executable from the command line. You may get an error that the system cannot find either a shared library or a dynamic link library. On Solaris, if the error message indicates that the system cannot find the shared library libjava.so (or libjvm.so in Java 2 SDK release 1.2), then you need to add the directory containing the virtual machine library to your LD_LIBRARY_PATH variable. On a Win32 system, the error message may indicate that it cannot find the dynamic link library javai.dll (or jvm.dll in Java 2 SDK release 1.2). If this is the case, add the directory containing the DLL to your PATH environment variable.

7.2.2 Linking with Unknown Java Virtual Machines

You cannot link the native application with one specific library that implements a virtual machine if the application is intended to work with virtual machine implementations from different vendors. Because the JNI does not specify the name of the native library that implements a Java virtual machine, you should be prepared to work with Java virtual machine implementations that are shipped under different names. For example, on Win32 the virtual machine is shipped as javai.dll in JDK release 1.1 and as jvm.dll in Java 2 SDK release 1.2.

The solution is to use run-time dynamic linking to load the particular virtual machine library needed by the application. The name of the virtual machine library can then be easily configured in an application-specific way. For example, the following Win32 code finds the function entry point for JNI_CreateJavaVM given the path of a virtual machine library:

```
/* Win32 version */
void *JNU_FindCreateJavaVM(char *vmlibpath)
{
    HINSTANCE hVM = LoadLibrary(vmlibpath);
    if (hVM == NULL) {
        return NULL;
    }
    return GetProcAddress(hVM, "JNI_CreateJavaVM");
}
```

LoadLibrary and GetProcAddress are the API functions for dynamic linking on Win32. Although LoadLibrary can accept either the name (such as "jvm") or the path (such as "C:\\jdk1.2\\jre\\bin\\classic\\jvm.dll") of the native library that implements the Java virtual machine, it is preferable that you pass the absolute path of the native library to JNU_FindCreateJavaVM. Relying on LoadLibrary to search for jvm.dll makes your application susceptible to configuration changes, such as additions to the PATH environment variable.

The Solaris version is similar:

```
/* Solaris version */
void *JNU_FindCreateJavaVM(char *vmlibpath)
{
    void *libVM = dlopen(vmlibpath, RTLD_LAZY);
    if (libVM == NULL) {
        return NULL;
    }
    return dlsym(libVM, "JNI_CreateJavaVM");
}
```

The dlopen and dlsym functions support dynamically linking shared libraries on Solaris.

7.3   Attaching Native Threads

Suppose that you have a multithreaded application such as a web server written in C. As HTTP requests come in, the server creates a number of native threads to handle the HTTP requests concurrently. We would like to embed a Java virtual machine in this server so that multiple threads can perform operations in the Java virtual machine at the same time, as illustrated in Figure 7.1.

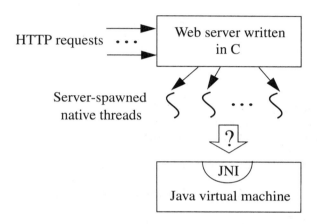

Figure 7.1   Embedding the Java virtual machine in a web server

Server-spawned native methods may have a shorter life span than the Java virtual machine. Therefore, we need a way to attach a native thread to a Java virtual machine that is already running, perform JNI calls in the attached native thread, and then detach the native thread from the virtual machine without disrupting other attached threads.

The following example, `attach.c`, illustrates how to attach native threads to a virtual machine using the invocation interface. This program is written using the Win32 thread API. Similar versions can be written for Solaris and other operating systems.

```
            /* Note: This program only works on Win32 */
            #include <windows.h>
            #include <jni.h>
            JavaVM *jvm; /* The virtual machine instance */

            #define PATH_SEPARATOR ';'
            #define USER_CLASSPATH "." /* where Prog.class is */

            void thread_fun(void *arg)
            {
                jint res;
                jclass cls;
                jmethodID mid;
                jstring jstr;
                jclass stringClass;
                jobjectArray args;
                JNIEnv *env;
                char buf[100];
                int threadNum = (int)arg;
                /* Pass NULL as the third argument */
            #ifdef JNI_VERSION_1_2
                res = (*jvm)->AttachCurrentThread(jvm, (void**)&env, NULL);
            #else
                res = (*jvm)->AttachCurrentThread(jvm, &env, NULL);
            #endif
                if (res < 0) {
                    fprintf(stderr, "Attach failed\n");
                    return;
                }
                cls = (*env)->FindClass(env, "Prog");
                if (cls == NULL) {
                    goto detach;
                }
                mid = (*env)->GetStaticMethodID(env, cls, "main",
                                              "([Ljava/lang/String;)V");
                if (mid == NULL) {
                    goto detach;
                }
                sprintf(buf, " from Thread %d", threadNum);
                jstr = (*env)->NewStringUTF(env, buf);
                if (jstr == NULL) {
                    goto detach;
                }
                stringClass = (*env)->FindClass(env, "java/lang/String");
                args = (*env)->NewObjectArray(env, 1, stringClass, jstr);
                if (args == NULL) {
                    goto detach;
                }
```

```
        (*env)->CallStaticVoidMethod(env, cls, mid, args);

    detach:
        if ((*env)->ExceptionOccurred(env)) {
            (*env)->ExceptionDescribe(env);
        }
        (*jvm)->DetachCurrentThread(jvm);
}

main() {
    JNIEnv *env;
    int i;
    jint res;

#ifdef JNI_VERSION_1_2
    JavaVMInitArgs vm_args;
    JavaVMOption options[1];
    options[0].optionString =
        "-Djava.class.path=" USER_CLASSPATH;
    vm_args.version = 0x00010002;
    vm_args.options = options;
    vm_args.nOptions = 1;
    vm_args.ignoreUnrecognized = TRUE;
    /* Create the Java VM */
    res = JNI_CreateJavaVM(&jvm, (void**)&env, &vm_args);
#else
    JDK1_1InitArgs vm_args;
    char classpath[1024];
    vm_args.version = 0x00010001;
    JNI_GetDefaultJavaVMInitArgs(&vm_args);
    /* Append USER_CLASSPATH to the default system class path */
    sprintf(classpath, "%s%c%s",
            vm_args.classpath, PATH_SEPARATOR, USER_CLASSPATH);
    vm_args.classpath = classpath;
    /* Create the Java VM */
    res = JNI_CreateJavaVM(&jvm, &env, &vm_args);
#endif /* JNI_VERSION_1_2 */

    if (res < 0) {
        fprintf(stderr, "Can't create Java VM\n");
        exit(1);
    }
    for (i = 0; i < 5; i++)
        /* We pass the thread number to every thread */
        _beginthread(thread_fun, 0, (void *)i);
    Sleep(1000); /* wait for threads to start */
    (*jvm)->DestroyJavaVM(jvm);
}
```

The `attach.c` program is a variation of `invoke.c`. Rather than calling `Prog.main` in the main thread, the native code starts five threads. Once it has spawned the threads it waits for them to start and then calls `DestroyJavaVM`. Each spawned thread attaches itself to the Java virtual machine, invokes the `Prog.main` method, and finally detaches itself from the virtual machine before it terminates. `DestroyJavaVM` returns after all five threads terminate. We ignore the return value of `DestroyJavaVM` for now because this function is not fully implemented in JDK release 1.1 and Java 2 SDK release 1.2.

`JNI_AttachCurrentThread` takes `NULL` as its third argument. Java 2 SDK release 1.2 introduces the `JNI_ThreadAttachArgs` structure. It allows you to specify additional arguments, such as the thread group to which you would like to attach. The details of the `JNI_ThreadAttachArgs` structure is described as part of the specification for `JNI_AttachCurrentThread` in Section 13.2.

When the program executes the function `DetachCurrentThread` it frees all local references belonging to the current thread.

Running the program produces the following output:

```
Hello World from thread 1
Hello World from thread 0
Hello World from thread 4
Hello World from thread 2
Hello World from thread 3
```

The exact order of output will likely vary depending on random factors in thread scheduling.

CHAPTER **8**

Additional JNI Features

WE have discussed the JNI features used for writing native methods and embedding a Java virtual machine implementation in a native application. This chapter introduces the remaining JNI features.

8.1 JNI and Threads

The Java virtual machine supports multiple threads of control concurrently executing in the same address space. This concurrency introduces a degree of complexity that you do not have in a single-threaded environment. Multiple threads may access the same objects, the same file descriptors—in short, the same shared resources—at the same time.

To get the most out of this section, you should be familiar with the concepts of multithreaded programming. You should know how to write Java applications that utilize multiple threads and how to synchronize access of shared resources. A good reference on multithreaded programming in the Java programming language is *Concurrent Programming in Java™, Design Principles and Patterns*, by Doug Lea (Addison-Wesley, 1997).

8.1.1 Constraints

There are certain constraints that you must keep in mind when writing native methods that are to run in a multithreaded environment. By understanding and programming within these constraints, your native methods will execute safely no matter how many threads simultaneously execute a given native method. For example:

- A JNIEnv pointer is only valid in the thread associated with it. You must not pass this pointer from one thread to another, or cache and use it in multiple threads. The Java virtual machine passes a native method the same JNIEnv pointer in consecutive invocations from the same thread, but passes different JNIEnv pointers when invoking that native method from different threads.

93

Avoid the common mistake of caching the JNIEnv pointer of one thread and using the pointer in another thread.

- Local references are valid only in the thread that created them. You must not pass local references from one thread to another. You should always convert local references to global references whenever there is a possibility that multiple threads may use the same reference.

8.1.2 Monitor Entry and Exit

Monitors are the primitive synchronization mechanism on the Java platform. Each object can be dynamically associated with a monitor. The JNI allows you to synchronize using these monitors, thus implementing the functionality equivalent to a synchronized block in the Java programming language:

```
synchronized (obj) {
    ...                     // synchronized block
}
```

The Java virtual machine guarantees that a thread acquires the monitor associated with the object obj before it executes any statements in the block. This ensures that there can be at most one thread that holds the monitor and executes inside the synchronized block at any given time. A thread blocks when it waits for another thread to exit a monitor.

Native code can use JNI functions to perform equivalent synchronization on JNI references. You can use the MonitorEnter function to enter the monitor and the MonitorExit function to exit the monitor:

```
if ((*env)->MonitorEnter(env, obj) != JNI_OK) {
    ... /* error handling */
}
...     /* synchronized block */
if ((*env)->MonitorExit(env, obj) != JNI_OK) {
    ... /* error handling */
};
```

Executing the code above, a thread must first enter the monitor associated with obj before executing any code inside the synchronized block. The Monitor-Enter operation takes a jobject as an argument and blocks if another thread has already entered the monitor associated with the jobject. Calling MonitorExit when the current thread does not own the monitor results in an error and causes an IllegalMonitorStateException to be raised. The above code contains a matched pair of MonitorEnter and MonitorExit calls, yet we still need to check for possible errors. Monitor operations may fail if, for example, the underlying thread implementation cannot allocate the resources necessary to perform the monitor operation.

`MonitorEnter` and `MonitorExit` work on `jclass`, `jstring`, and `jarray` types, which are special kinds of `jobject` references.

Remember to match a `MonitorEnter` call with the appropriate number of `MonitorExit` calls, especially in code that handles errors and exceptions:

```
if ((*env)->MonitorEnter(env, obj) != JNI_OK) ...;
...
if ((*env)->ExceptionOccurred(env)) {
    ... /* exception handling */
    /* remember to call MonitorExit here */
    if ((*env)->MonitorExit(env, obj) != JNI_OK) ...;
}
... /* Normal execution path.
if ((*env)->MonitorExit(env, obj) != JNI_OK) ...;
```

Failure to call `MonitorExit` will most likely lead to deadlocks. By comparing the above C code segment with the code segment at the beginning of this section, you can appreciate how much easier it is to program with the Java programming language than with the JNI. Thus, it is preferable to express synchronization constructs in the Java programming language. If, for example, a static native method needs to enter the monitor associated with its defining class, you should define a static synchronized native method as opposed to performing JNI-level monitor synchronization in native code.

8.1.3 Monitor Wait and Notify

The Java API contains several other methods that are useful for thread synchronization. They are `Object.wait`, `Object.notify`, and `Object.notifyAll`. No JNI functions are supplied that correspond directly to these methods because monitor wait and notify operations are not as performance critical as monitor enter and exit operations. Native code may instead use the JNI method call mechanism to invoke the corresponding methods in the Java API:

```
/* precomputed method IDs */
static jmethodID MID_Object_wait;
static jmethodID MID_Object_notify;
static jmethodID MID_Object_notifyAll;

void
JNU_MonitorWait(JNIEnv *env, jobject object, jlong timeout)
{
    (*env)->CallVoidMethod(env, object, MID_Object_wait,
                                 timeout);
}

void
JNU_MonitorNotify(JNIEnv *env, jobject object)
{
    (*env)->CallVoidMethod(env, object, MID_Object_notify);
}

void
JNU_MonitorNotifyAll(JNIEnv *env, jobject object)
{
    (*env)->CallVoidMethod(env, object, MID_Object_notifyAll);
}
```

We assume that the method IDs for Object.wait, Object.notify, and Object.notifyAll have been calculated elsewhere and are cached in the global variables. Like in the Java programming language, you can call the above monitor-related functions only when holding the monitor associated with the jobject argument.

8.1.4 Obtaining a JNIEnv Pointer in Arbitrary Contexts

We explained earlier that a JNIEnv pointer is only valid in its associated thread. This is generally not a problem for native methods because they receive the JNIEnv pointer from the virtual machine as the first argument. Occasionally, however, it may be necessary for a piece of native code not called directly from the virtual machine to obtain the JNIEnv interface pointer that belongs to the current thread. For example, the piece of native code may belong to a "callback" function called by the operating system, in which case the JNIEnv pointer will probably not be available as an argument.

You can obtain the JNIEnv pointer for the current thread by calling the AttachCurrentThread function of the invocation interface:

```
JavaVM *jvm; /* already set */

f()
{
    JNIEnv *env;
    (*jvm)->AttachCurrentThread(jvm, (void **)&env, NULL);
    ... /* use env */
}
```

When the current thread is already attached to the virtual machine, `Attach-CurrentThread` returns the `JNIEnv` interface pointer that belongs to the current thread.

There are many ways to obtain the `JavaVM` pointer: by recording it when the virtual machine is created, by querying for the created virtual machines using `JNI_GetCreatedJavaVMs`, by calling the JNI function `GetJavaVM` inside a regular native method, or by defining a `JNI_OnLoad` handler. Unlike the `JNIEnv` pointer, the `JavaVM` pointer remains valid across multiple threads so it can be cached in a global variable.

Java 2 SDK release 1.2 provides a new invocation interface function `GetEnv` so that you can check whether the current thread is attached to the virtual machine, and, if so, to return the `JNIEnv` pointer that belongs to the current thread. `GetEnv` and `AttachCurrentThread` are functionally equivalent if the current thread is already attached to the virtual machine.

8.1.5 Matching the Thread Models

Suppose that native code to be run in multiple threads accesses a global resource. Should the native code use JNI functions `MonitorEnter` and `MonitorExit`, or use the native thread synchronization primitives in the host environment (such as `mutex_lock` on Solaris)? Similarly, if the native code needs to create a new thread, should it create a `java.lang.Thread` object and perform a callback of `Thread.start` through the JNI, or should it use the native thread creation primitive in the host environment (such as `thr_create` on Solaris)?

The answer is that all of these approaches work if the Java virtual machine implementation supports a *thread model* that matches that used by the native code. The thread model dictates how the system implements essential thread operations such as scheduling, context switching, synchronization, and blocking in system calls. In a *native thread* model the operating system manages all the essential thread operations. In a *user thread* model, on the other hand, the application code implements the thread operations. For example, the "Green thread" model shipped with JDK and Java 2 SDK releases on Solaris uses the ANSI C functions `setjmp` and `longjmp` to implement context switches.

Many modern operating systems (such as Solaris and Win32) support a native thread model. Unfortunately, some operating systems still lack native thread support. Instead, there may be one or many user thread packages on these operating systems.

If you write application strictly in the Java programming language, you need not worry about the underlying thread model of the virtual machine implementation. The Java platform can be ported to any host environment that supports the required set of thread primitives. Most native and user thread packages provide the necessary thread primitives for implementing a Java virtual machine.

JNI programmers, on the other hand, must pay attention to thread models. The application using native code may not function properly if the Java virtual implementation and the native code have a different notion of threading and synchronization. For example, a native method could be blocked in a synchronization operation in its own thread model, but the Java virtual machine, running in a different thread model, may not be aware that the thread executing the native method is blocked. The application deadlocks because no other threads will be scheduled.

The thread models match if the native code uses the same thread model as the Java virtual machine implementation. If the Java virtual machine implementation uses native thread support, the native code can freely invoke thread-related primitives in the host environment. If the Java virtual machine implementation is based on a user thread package, the native code should either link with the same user thread package or rely on no thread operations at all. The latter may be harder to achieve than you think: most C library calls (such as I/O and memory allocation functions) perform thread synchronization underneath. Unless the native code performs pure computation and makes no library calls, it is likely to use thread primitives indirectly.

Most virtual machine implementations support only a particular thread model for JNI native code. Implementations that support native threads are the most flexible, hence native threads, when available, are typically preferred on a given host environment. Virtual machine implementations that rely on a particular user thread package may be severely limited as to the type of native code with which they can operate.

Some virtual machine implementations may support a number of different thread models. A more flexible type of virtual machine implementation may even allow you to provide a custom thread model implementation for virtual machine's internal use, thus ensuring that the virtual machine implementation can work with your native code. Before embarking on a project likely to require native code, you should consult the documentation that comes with your virtual machine implementation for thread model limitations.

8.2 Writing Internationalized Code

Special care must be taken to write code that works well in multiple locales. The JNI gives programmers complete access to the internationalization features of the Java platform. We will use string conversion as an example because file names and messages may contain non-ASCII characters in many locales.

The Java virtual machine represents strings in the Unicode format. Although some native platforms (such as Windows NT) also provide Unicode support, most represent strings in locale-specific encodings.

Do not use GetStringUTFChars and GetStringUTFRegion functions to convert between jstrings and locale-specific strings unless UTF-8 happens to be the native encoding on the platform. UTF-8 strings are useful when representing names and descriptors (such as the arguments to GetMethodID) that are to be passed to JNI functions, but are not appropriate for representing locale-specific strings such as file names.

8.2.1 Creating jstrings from Native Strings

Use the String(byte[] bytes) constructor to convert a native string into a jstring. The following utility function creates a jstring from a locale-specific native C string:

```
jstring JNU_NewStringNative(JNIEnv *env, const char *str)
{
    jstring result;
    jbyteArray bytes = 0;
    int len;
    if ((*env)->EnsureLocalCapacity(env, 2) < 0) {
        return NULL; /* out of memory error */
    }
    len = strlen(str);
    bytes = (*env)->NewByteArray(env, len);
    if (bytes != NULL) {
        (*env)->SetByteArrayRegion(env, bytes, 0, len,
                                   (jbyte *)str);
        result = (*env)->NewObject(env, Class_java_lang_String,
                                   MID_String_init, bytes);
        (*env)->DeleteLocalRef(env, bytes);
        return result;
    } /* else fall through */
    return NULL;
}
```

The function creates a byte array, copies the native C string into the byte array, and finally invokes the String(byte[] bytes) constructor to create the resulting jstring object. Class_java_lang_String is a global reference to the java.lang.String class, and MID_String_init is the method ID of the string constructor. Because this is a utility function, we make sure to delete the local reference to the byte array created temporarily to store the characters.

Delete the call to EnsureLocalCapacity if you need to use this function with JDK release 1.1.

8.2.2 Translating jstrings to Native Strings

Use the String.getBytes method to convert a jstring to the appropriate native encoding. The following utility function translates a jstring to a locale-specific native C string:

```
char *JNU_GetStringNativeChars(JNIEnv *env, jstring jstr)
{
    jbyteArray bytes = 0;
    jthrowable exc;
    char *result = 0;
    if ((*env)->EnsureLocalCapacity(env, 2) < 0) {
        return 0; /* out of memory error */
    }
    bytes = (*env)->CallObjectMethod(env, jstr,
                                    MID_String_getBytes);
    exc = (*env)->ExceptionOccurred(env);
    if (!exc) {
        jint len = (*env)->GetArrayLength(env, bytes);
        result = (char *)malloc(len + 1);
        if (result == 0) {
            JNU_ThrowByName(env, "java/lang/OutOfMemoryError",
                            0);
            (*env)->DeleteLocalRef(env, bytes);
            return 0;
        }
        (*env)->GetByteArrayRegion(env, bytes, 0, len,
                                    (jbyte *)result);
        result[len] = 0; /* NULL-terminate */
    } else {
        (*env)->DeleteLocalRef(env, exc);
    }
    (*env)->DeleteLocalRef(env, bytes);
    return result;
}
```

The function passes the `java.lang.String` reference to the `String.get-Bytes` method and then copies the elements of the byte array to a newly allocated C array. `MID_String_getBytes` is the precomputed method ID of the `String.getBytes` method. Because this is a utility function, we make sure to delete the local references to the byte array and the exception object. Keep in mind that deleting a JNI reference to the exception object does not clear the pending exception.

Once again, delete the call to `EnsureLocalCapacity` if you need to use this function with JDK release 1.1.

8.3 Registering Native Methods

Before an application executes a native method it goes through a two-step process to load the native library containing the native method implementation and then link to the native method implementation:

1. `System.loadLibrary` locates and loads the named native library. For example, `System.loadLibrary("foo")` may cause `foo.dll` to be loaded on Win32.

2. The virtual machine locates the native method implementation in one of the loaded native libraries. For example, a `Foo.g` native method call requires locating and linking the native function `Java_Foo_g`, which may reside in `foo.dll`.

This section will introduce another way to accomplish the second step. Instead of relying on the virtual machine to search for the native method in the already loaded native libraries, the JNI programmer can manually link native methods by registering a function pointer with a class reference, method name, and method descriptor:

```
JNINativeMethod nm;
nm.name = "g";
/* method descriptor assigned to signature field */
nm.signature = "()V";
nm.fnPtr = g_impl;
(*env)->RegisterNatives(env, cls, &nm, 1);
```

The above code registers the native function `g_impl` as the implementation of the `Foo.g` native method:

```
void JNICALL g_impl(JNIEnv *env, jobject self);
```

The native function `g_impl` does not need to follow the JNI naming convention because only function pointers are involved, nor does it need to be exported from the library (thus there is no need to declare the function using JNIEXPORT). The native function g_impl must still, however, follow the JNICALL calling convention.

The RegisterNatives function is useful for a number of purposes:

- It is sometimes more convenient and more efficient to register a large number of native method implementations eagerly, as opposed to letting the virtual machine link these entries lazily.

- You may call RegisterNatives multiple times on a method, allowing the native method implementation to be updated at runtime.

- RegisterNatives is particularly useful when a native application embeds a virtual machine implementation and needs to link with a native method implementation defined in the native application. The virtual machine would not be able to find this native method implementation automatically because it only searches in native libraries, not the application itself.

8.4 Load and Unload Handlers

Load and unload handlers allow the native library to export two functions: one to be called when System.loadLibrary loads the native library, the other to be called when the virtual machine unloads the native library. This feature was added in Java 2 SDK release 1.2.

8.4.1 The JNI_OnLoad Handler

When System.loadLibrary loads a native library, the virtual machine searches for the following exported entry in the native library:

```
JNIEXPORT jint JNICALL JNI_OnLoad(JavaVM *jvm, void *reserved);
```

You can invoke any JNI functions in an implementation of JNI_Onload. A typical use of the JNI_OnLoad handler is caching the JavaVM pointer, class references, or method and field IDs, as shown in the following example:

```
JavaVM *cached_jvm;
jclass Class_C;
jmethodID MID_C_g;
```

```
JNIEXPORT jint JNICALL
JNI_OnLoad(JavaVM *jvm, void *reserved)
{
    JNIEnv *env;
    jclass cls;
    cached_jvm = jvm;   /* cache the JavaVM pointer */

    if ((*jvm)->GetEnv(jvm, (void **)&env, JNI_VERSION_1_2)) {
        return JNI_ERR; /* JNI version not supported */
    }
    cls = (*env)->FindClass(env, "C");
    if (cls == NULL) {
        return JNI_ERR;
    }
    /* Use weak global ref to allow C class to be unloaded */
    Class_C = (*env)->NewWeakGlobalRef(env, cls);
    if (Class_C == NULL) {
        return JNI_ERR;
    }
    /* Compute and cache the method ID */
    MID_C_g = (*env)->GetMethodID(env, cls, "g", "()V");
    if (MID_C_g == NULL) {
        return JNI_ERR;
    }
    return JNI_VERSION_1_2;
}
```

The JNI_OnLoad function first caches the JavaVM pointer in the global variable cached_jvm. It then obtains the JNIEnv pointer by calling GetEnv. It finally loads the C class, caches the class reference, and computes the method ID for C.g. The JNI_OnLoad function returns JNI_ERR (§12.4) on error and otherwise returns the JNIEnv version JNI_VERSION_1_2 needed by the native library.

We will explain in the next section why we cache the C class in a weak global reference instead of a global reference.

Given a cached JavaVM interface pointer it is trivial to implement a utility function that allows the native code to obtain the JNIEnv interface pointer for the current thread (§8.1.4) :

```
JNIEnv *JNU_GetEnv()
{
    JNIEnv *env;
    (*cached_jvm)->GetEnv(cached_jvm,
                          (void **)&env,
                          JNI_VERSION_1_2);
    return env;
}
```

8.4.2   The JNI_OnUnload Handler

Intuitively, the virtual machine calls the JNI_OnUnload handler when it unloads a JNI native library. This is not precise enough, however. When does the virtual machine determine that it can unload a native library? Which thread runs the JNI_OnUnload handler?

The rules of unloading native libraries are as follows:

- The virtual machine associates each native library with the class loader L of the class C that issues the System.loadLibrary call.

- The virtual machine calls the JNI_OnUnload handler and unloads the native library after it determines that the class loader L is no longer a live object. Because a class loader refers to all the classes it defines, this implies that C can be unloaded as well.

- The JNI_OnUnload handler runs in a finalizer, and is either invoked synchroniously by java.lang.System.runFinalization or invoked asynchronously by the virtual machine.

Here is the definition of a JNI_OnUnload handler that cleans up the resources allocated by the JNI_OnLoad handler in the last section:

```
JNIEXPORT void JNICALL
JNI_OnUnload(JavaVM *jvm, void *reserved)
{
    JNIEnv *env;
    if ((*jvm)->GetEnv(jvm, (void **)&env, JNI_VERSION_1_2)) {
        return;
    }
    (*env)->DeleteWeakGlobalRef(env, Class_C);
    return;
}
```

The JNI_OnUnload function deletes the weak global reference to the C class created in the JNI_OnLoad handler. We need not delete the method ID MID_C_g because the virtual machine automatically reclaims the resources needed to represent C's method IDs when unloading its defining class C.

We are now ready to explain why we cache the C class in a weak global reference instead of a global reference. A global reference would keep C alive, which in turn would keep C's class loader alive. Given that the native library is associated with C's class loader L, the native library would not be unloaded and JNI_OnUnload would not be called.

The JNI_OnUnload handler runs in a finalizer. In contrast, the JNI_OnLoad handler runs in the thread that initiates the System.loadLibrary call. Because JNI_OnUnload runs in an unknown thread context, to avoid possible deadlocks, you should avoid complex synchronization and locking operations in JNI_OnUnload. The JNI_OnUnload handler typically carries out simple tasks such as releasing the resources allocated by the native library.

The JNI_OnUnload handler runs when the class loader that loaded the library and all classes defined by that class loader are no longer alive. The JNI_OnUnload handler must not use these classes in any way. In the above JNI_OnUnload definition, you must not perform any operations that assume Class_C still refers to a valid class. The DeleteWeakGlobalRef call in the example frees the memory for the weak global reference itself, but does not manipulate the referred class C in any way.

In summary, you should be careful when writing JNI_OnUnload handlers. Avoid complex locking operations that may introduce deadlocks. Keep in mind that classes have been unloaded when the JNI_OnUnload handler is invoked.

8.5 Reflection Support

Reflection generally refers to manipulating language-level constructs at runtime. For example, reflection allows you to discover at run time the name of arbitrary class objects and the set of fields and methods defined in the class. Reflection support is provided at the Java programming language level through the java.lang.reflect package as well as some methods in the java.lang.Object and java.lang.Class classes. Although you can always call the corresponding Java API to carry out reflective operations, the JNI provides the following functions to make the frequent reflective operations from native code more efficient and convenient:

- GetSuperclass returns the superclass of a given class reference.

- IsAssignableFrom checks whether instances of one class can be used when instances of another class are expected.

- GetObjectClass returns the class of a given jobject reference.

- IsInstanceOf checks whether a jobject reference is an instance of a given class.

- FromReflectedField and ToReflectedField allow the native code to convert between field IDs and java.lang.reflect.Field objects. They are new additions in Java 2 SDK release 1.2.

- FromReflectedMethod and ToReflectedMethod allow the native code to convert between method IDs, java.lang.reflect.Method objects and java.lang.reflect.Constructor objects. They are new additions in Java 2 SDK release 1.2.

105

8.6 JNI Programming in C++

The JNI presents a slightly simpler interface for C++ programmers. The jni.h file contains a set of definitions so that C++ programmers can write, for example:

```
jclass cls = env->FindClass("java/lang/String");
```

instead of in C:

```
jclass cls = (*env)->FindClass(env, "java/lang/String");
```

The extra level of indirection on env and the env argument to FindClass are hidden from the programmer. The C++ compiler inlines the C++ member function calls to their equivalent C counterparts; the resulting code is exactly the same. There is no inherent performance difference between using the JNI in C or C++.

In addition, the jni.h file also defines a set of dummy C++ classes to enforce the subtyping relationships among different jobject subtypes:

```
// JNI reference types defined in C++
class _jobject {};
class _jclass : public _jobject {};
class _jstring : public _jobject {};
...
typedef _jobject* jobject;
typedef _jclass*  jclass;
typedef _jstring* jstring;
...
```

The C++ compiler is able to detect at compile time if you pass in, for example, a jobject to GetMethodID:

```
// ERROR: pass jobject as a jclass:
jobject obj = env->NewObject(...);
jmethodID mid =  env->GetMethodID(obj, "foo", "()V");
```

Because GetMethodID expects a jclass reference, the C++ compiler will give an error message. In the C type definitions for JNI, jclass is the same as jobject:

```
typedef jobject jclass;
```

Therefore, a C compiler is not able to detect that you have mistakenly passed a jobject instead of jclass.

The added type hierarchy in C++ sometimes necessitates additional casting. In C, you can fetch a string from an array of strings and assign the result to a jstring:

```
jstring jstr = (*env)->GetObjectArrayElement(env, arr, i);
```

In C++, however, you need to insert an explicit conversion:

```
jstring jstr = (jstring)env->GetObjectArrayElement(arr, i);
```

CHAPTER **9**

Leveraging Existing Native Libraries

ONE of the applications of the JNI is to write native methods that leverage code in existing native libraries. A typical approach, covered in this chapter, is to produce a class library that *wraps* a set of native functions.

This chapter first discusses the most straightforward way to write wrapper classes — *one-to-one mapping*. We then introduce a technique, *shared stubs*, that simplifies the task of writing wrapper classes.

One-to-one mapping and shared stubs are both techniques for wrapping native functions. At the end of this chapter, we will also discuss how to wrap native data structures using *peer classes*.

The approaches described in this chapter directly expose a native library using native methods, and thus have the disadvantage of making an application calling such native methods dependent on that native library. Such an application may run only on an operating system that supplies the native library. A preferred approach is to declare operating system-independent native methods. Only the native functions implementing those native methods use the native libraries directly, limiting the need for porting to those native functions. The application, including the native method declarations, does not need to be ported.

9.1 One-to-One Mapping

Let us begin with a simple example. Suppose that we want to write a wrapper class that exposes the `atol` function in the standard C library:

```
long atol(const char *str);
```

The `atol` function parses a string and returns the decimal value represented by the string. There is perhaps little reason to define such a native method in practice because the `Integer.parseInt` method, part of the Java API, supplies the equivalent functionality. Evaluating `atol("100")`, for example, results in the integer value `100`. We define a wrapper class as follows:

```
public class C {
    public static native int atol(String str);
    ...
}
```

For the sake of illustrating JNI programming in C++, we will implement native methods in this chapter using C++ (§8.6). The C++ implementation of the `C.atol` native method is as follows:

```
JNIEXPORT jint JNICALL
Java_C_atol(JNIEnv *env, jclass cls, jstring str)
{
    const char *cstr = env->GetStringUTFChars(str, 0);
    if (cstr == NULL) {
        return 0; /* out of memory */
    }
    int result = atol(cstr);
    env->ReleaseStringUTFChars(str, cstr);
    return result;
}
```

The implementation is quite straightforward. We use `GetStringUTFChars` to convert the Unicode string because decimal numbers are ASCII characters.

Let us now examine a more complex example that involves passing structure pointers to a C function. Suppose that we want to write a wrapper class that exposes the `CreateFile` function from the Win32 API:

```
typedef void * HANDLE;
typedef long DWORD;
typedef struct {...} SECURITY_ATTRIBUTES;

HANDLE CreateFile(
    const char *fileName,        // file name
    DWORD desiredAccess,         // access (read-write) mode
    DWORD shareMode,             // share mode
    SECURITY_ATTRIBUTES *attrs,  // security attributes
    DWORD creationDistribution,  // how to create
    DWORD flagsAndAttributes,    // file attributes
    HANDLE templateFile          // file with attr. to copy
);
```

The `CreateFile` function supports a number of Win32-specific features not available in the platform-independent Java File API. For example, the `Create-File` function may be used to specify special access modes and file attributes, to open Win32 named pipes, and to handle serial port communications.

We will not discuss further details of the `CreateFile` function in this book. The focus will be on how `CreateFile` may be mapped to a native method defined in a wrapper class called `Win32`:

```
public class Win32 {
    public static native int CreateFile(
        String fileName,          // file name
        int desiredAccess,        // access (read-write) mode
        int shareMode,            // share mode
        int[] secAttrs,           // security attributes
        int creationDistribution, // how to create
        int flagsAndAttributes,   // file attributes
        int templateFile);        // file with attr. to copy
    ...
}
```

The mapping from the `char` pointer type to `String` is obvious. We map the native Win32 type `long` (DWORD) to `int` in the Java programming language. The Win32 type `HANDLE`, an opaque 32-bit pointer type, is also mapped to `int`.

Because of potential differences in how fields are laid out in memory, we do not map C structures to classes in the Java programming language. Instead, we use an array to store the contents of the C structure `SECURITY_ATTRIBUTES`. The caller may also pass `null` as `secAttrs` to specify the default Win32 security attributes. We will not discuss the contents of the `SECURITY_ATTRIBUTES` structure or how to encode that in an `int` array.

A C++ implementation of the above native method is as follows:

```
JNIEXPORT jint JNICALL Java_Win32_CreateFile(
        JNIEnv *env,
        jclass cls,
        jstring  fileName,          // file name
        jint desiredAccess,         // access (read-write) mode
        jint shareMode,             // share mode
        jintArray secAttrs,         // security attributes
        jint creationDistribution,  // how to create
        jint flagsAndAttributes,    // file attributes
        jint templateFile)          // file with attr. to copy
{
    jint result = 0;
    jint *cSecAttrs = NULL;
    if (secAttrs) {
        cSecAttrs = env->GetIntArrayElements(secAttrs, 0);
        if (cSecAttrs == NULL) {
            return 0; /* out of memory */
        }
    }
```

```
char *cFileName = JNU_GetStringNativeChars(env, fileName);
if (cFileName) {
    /* call the real Win32 function */
    result = (jint)CreateFile(cFileName,
                    desiredAccess,
                    shareMode,
                    (SECURITY_ATTRIBUTES *)cSecAttrs,
                    creationDistribution,
                    flagsAndAttributes,
                    (HANDLE)templateFile);
    free(cFileName);
}
/* else fall through, out of memory exception thrown */
if (secAttrs) {
    env->ReleaseIntArrayElements(secAttrs, cSecAttrs, 0);
}
return result;
}
```

First, we convert the security attributes stored in the int array into a jint array. If the secAttrs argument is a NULL reference, we pass NULL as the security attribute to the Win32 CreateFile function. Next, we call the utility function JNU_GetStringNativeChars (§8.2.2) to obtain the file name represented as a locale-specific C string. Once we have converted the security attributes and file name, we pass the results of the conversions and the remaining arguments to the Win32 CreateFile function.

We take care to check for exceptions and release virtual machine resources (such as cSecAttrs).

The C.atol and Win32.CreateFile examples demonstrate a common approach to writing wrapper classes and native methods. Each native function (for example, CreateFile) maps to a single native *stub* function (for example, Java_Win32_CreateFile), which in turn maps to a single native method definition (for example, Win32.CreateFile). In one-to-one mapping, the stub function serves two purposes:

1. The stub adapts the native function's argument passing convention to what is expected by the Java virtual machine. The virtual machine expects the native method implementation to follow a given naming convention and to accept two additional arguments (the JNIEnv pointer and the "this" pointer).

2. The stub converts between Java programming language types and native types. For example, the Java_Win32_CreateFile function translates the jstring file name to a locale-specific C string.

112

9.2 Shared Stubs

The one-to-one mapping approach requires you to write one stub function for each native function you want to wrap. This becomes tedious when you are faced with the task of writing wrapper classes for a large number of native functions. In this section we introduce the concept of shared stubs and demonstrate how shared stubs may be used to simplify the task of writing wrapper classes.

A shared stub is a native method that dispatches to other native functions. The shared stub is responsible for converting the argument types from what is provided by the caller to what is accepted by the native functions.

We will soon introduce a shared stub class CFunction, but first let us show how it can simplify the implementation of the C.atol method:

```
public class C {
    private static CFunction c_atol =
        new CFunction("msvcrt.dll", // native library name
                      "atol",        // C function name
                      "C");          // calling convention
    public static int atol(String str) {
        return c_atol.callInt(new Object[] {str});
    }
    ...
}
```

C.atol is no longer a native method (and thus no longer needs a stub function). Instead, C.atol is defined using the CFunction class. The CFunction class internally implements a shared stub. The static variable C.c_atol stores a CFunction object that corresponds to the C function atol in the msvcrt.dll library (the multithreaded C library on Win32). The CFunction constructor call also specifies that atol follows the C calling convention (§11.4). Once the c_atol field is initialized, calls to the C.atol method need only to redispatch through c_atol.callInt, the *shared stub*.

The CFunction class belongs to a class hierarchy that we will build up and use shortly:

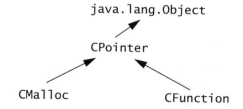

Instances of the CFunction class denote a pointer to a C function. CFunction is a subclass of CPointer, which denotes arbitrary C pointers:

```
public class CFunction extends CPointer {
    public CFunction(String lib,      // native library name
                     String fname,    // C function name
                     String conv) {   // calling convention
        ...
    }
    public native int callInt(Object[] args);
    ...
}
```

The callInt method takes as its argument an array of java.lang.Object. It inspects the types of the elements in the array, converts them (from jstring to char *, for example), and passes them as arguments to the underlying C function. The callInt method then returns the result of the underlying C function as an int. The CFunction class can define methods such as callFloat or callDouble to handle C functions with other return types.

The CPointer class is defined as follows:

```
public abstract class CPointer {
    public native void copyIn(
            int bOff,      // offset from a C pointer
            int[] buf,     // source data
            int off,       // offset into source
            int len);      // number of elements to be copied
    public native void copyOut(...);
    ...
}
```

CPointer is an abstract class that supports arbitrary access to C pointers. The copyIn method, for example, copies a number of elements from an int array to the location pointed to by the C pointer. This method should be used with care because it can easily be used to corrupt arbitrary memory locations in the address space. Native methods such as CPointer.copyIn are as unsafe as direct pointer manipulation in C.

CMalloc is a subclass of CPointer that points to a block of memory allocated in the C heap using malloc:

```
public class CMalloc extends CPointer {
    public CMalloc(int size) throws OutOfMemoryError { ... }
    public native void free();
    ...
}
```

The `CMalloc` constructor allocates a memory block of the given size in the C heap. The `CMalloc.free` method releases the memory block.

Equipped with the `CFunction` and `CMalloc` classes, we can reimplement `Win32.CreateFile` as follows:

```
public class Win32 {
    private static CFunction c_CreateFile =
        new CFunction ("kernel32.dll",      // native library name
                       "CreateFileA",       // native function
                       "JNI");              // calling convention

    public static int CreateFile(
        String fileName,            // file name
        int desiredAccess,          // access (read-write) mode
        int shareMode,              // share mode
        int[] secAttrs,             // security attributes
        int creationDistribution,   // how to create
        int flagsAndAttributes,     // file attributes
        int templateFile)           // file with attr. to copy
    {
        CMalloc cSecAttrs = null;
        if (secAttrs != null) {
            cSecAttrs = new CMalloc(secAttrs.length * 4);
            cSecAttrs.copyIn(0, secAttrs, 0, secAttrs.length);
        }
        try {
            return c_CreateFile.callInt(new Object[] {
                        fileName,
                        new Integer(desiredAccess),
                        new Integer(shareMode),
                        cSecAttrs,
                        new Integer(creationDistribution),
                        new Integer(flagsAndAttributes),
                        new Integer(templateFile)});
        } finally {
            if (secAttrs != null) {
                cSecAttrs.free();
            }
        }
    }
    ...
}
```

We cache the `CFunction` object in a static variable. The Win32 API `Create-File` is exported from `kernel32.dll` as `CreateFileA`. Another exported entry, `CreateFileW`, takes a Unicode string as the file name argument. This function follows the JNI calling convention, which is the standard Win32 calling convention (stdcall).

The Win32.CreateFile implementation first allocates a memory block in the C heap that is big enough to hold the security attributes temporarily. It then packages all arguments in an array and invokes the underlying C function CreateFileA through the shared dispatcher. Finally the Win32.CreateFile method frees the C memory block used to hold the security attributes. We call cSecAttrs.free in a finally clause to make sure the temporarily C memory is freed even if the c_CreateFile.callInt call raises an exception.

9.3   One-to-One Mapping versus Shared Stubs

One-to-one mapping and shared stubs are two ways of building wrapper classes for native libraries. Each has its own advantages.

The main advantage of shared stubs is that the programmer need not write a large number of stub functions in native code. Once a shared stub implementation such as CFunction is available, the programmer may be able to build wrapper classes without writing a single line of native code.

Shared stubs must be used with care, however. With shared stubs, programmers are essentially writing C code in the Java programming language. This defeats the type safety of the Java programming language. Mistakes in using shared stubs can lead to corrupted memory and application crashes.

The advantage of one-to-one mapping is that it is typically more efficient in converting the data types that are transferred between the Java virtual machine and native code. Shared stubs, on the other hand, can handle at most a predetermined set of argument types and cannot achieve optimal performance even for these argument types. The caller of CFunction.callInt always has to create an Integer object for each int argument. This adds both space and time overhead to the shared stubs scheme.

In practice, you need to balance performance, portability, and short-term productivity. Shared stubs may be suitable for leveraging inherently nonportable native code that can tolerate a slight performance degradation, whereas one-to-one mapping should be used in cases where top performance is necessary or where portability matters.

9.4   Implementation of Shared Stubs

We have so far treated CFunction, CPointer, and CMalloc classes as black boxes. This section describes how they may be implemented using the basic JNI features.

9.4.1 The CPointer Class

We look at the CPointer class first because it is the superclass of both CFunction and CMalloc. The abstract class CPointer contains a 64-bit field, peer, that stores the underlying C pointer:

```
public abstract class CPointer {
    protected long peer;
    public native void copyIn(int bOff, int[] buf,
                                int off,int len);
    public native void copyOut(...);
    ...
}
```

The C++ implementation of native methods such as copyIn is straightforward:

```
JNIEXPORT void JNICALL
Java_CPointer_copyIn__I_3III(JNIEnv *env, jobject self,
    jint boff, jintArray arr, jint off, jint len)
{
    long peer = env->GetLongField(self, FID_CPointer_peer);
    env->GetIntArrayRegion(arr, off, len, (jint *)peer + boff);
}
```

FID_CPointer_peer is the precomputed field ID for CPointer.peer. The native method implementation uses the long name encoding scheme (§11.3) to resolve conflicts with implementations of overloaded copyIn native methods for other array types in the CPointer class.

9.4.2 The CMalloc Class

The CMalloc class adds two native methods used to allocate and free C memory blocks:

```
public class CMalloc extends CPointer {
    private static native long malloc(int size);
    public CMalloc(int size) throws OutOfMemoryError {
        peer = malloc(size);
        if (peer == 0) {
            throw new OutOfMemoryError();
        }
    }
    public native void free();
    ...
}
```

The CMalloc constructor calls a native method CMalloc.malloc, and throws an OutOfMemoryError if CMalloc.malloc fails to return a newly allocated memory block in the C heap. We can implement the CMalloc.malloc and CMalloc.free methods as follows:

```
JNIEXPORT jlong JNICALL
Java_CMalloc_malloc(JNIEnv *env, jclass cls, jint size)
{
    return (jlong)malloc(size);
}

JNIEXPORT void JNICALL
Java_CMalloc_free(JNIEnv *env, jobject self)
{
    long peer = env->GetLongField(self, FID_CPointer_peer);
    free((void *)peer);
}
```

9.4.3   The CFunction Class

The CFunction class implementation requires the use of dynamic linking support in the operating system as well as CPU-specific assembly code. The implementation presented below is targeted specifically toward the Win32/Intel x86 environment. Once you understand the principles behind implementing the CFunction class, you can follow the same steps to implement it on other platforms.

The CFunction class is defined as follows:

```
public class CFunction extends CPointer {
    private static final int CONV_C = 0;
    private static final int CONV_JNI = 1;
    private int conv;
    private native long find(String lib, String fname);

    public CFunction(String lib,      // native library name
                     String fname,    // C function name
                     String conv) {   // calling convention
        if (conv.equals("C")) {
            conv = CONV_C;
        } else if (conv.equals("JNI")) {
            conv = CONV_JNI;
        } else {
            throw new IllegalArgumentException(
                    "bad calling convention");
        }
        peer = find(lib, fname);
    }
```

```
        public native int callInt(Object[] args);
        ...
}
```

The CFunction class declares a private field conv used to store the calling convention of the C function. The CFunction.find native method is implemented as follows:

```
JNIEXPORT jlong JNICALL
Java_CFunction_find(JNIEnv *env, jobject self, jstring lib,
                    jstring fun)
{
    void *handle;
    void *func;
    char *libname;
    char *funname;

    if ((libname = JNU_GetStringNativeChars(env, lib))) {
        if ((funname = JNU_GetStringNativeChars(env, fun))) {
            if ((handle = LoadLibrary(libname))) {
                if (!(func = GetProcAddress(handle, funname))) {
                    JNU_ThrowByName(env,
                        "java/lang/UnsatisfiedLinkError",
                        funname);
                }
            } else {
                JNU_ThrowByName(env,
                    "java/lang/UnsatisfiedLinkError",
                    libname);
            }
            free(funname);
        }
        free(libname);
    }
    return (jlong)func;
}
```

CFunction.find converts the library name and function name to locale-specific C strings, and then calls the Win32 API functions LoadLibrary and GetProcAddress to locate the C function in the named native library.

The callInt method, implemented as follows, carries out the main task of redispatching to the underlying C function:

```c
JNIEXPORT jint JNICALL
Java_CFunction_callInt(JNIEnv *env, jobject self,
                       jobjectArray arr)
{
#define MAX_NARGS 32
    jint ires;
    int nargs, nwords;
    jboolean is_string[MAX_NARGS];
    word_t args[MAX_NARGS];

    nargs = env->GetArrayLength(arr);
    if (nargs > MAX_NARGS) {
        JNU_ThrowByName(env,
                    "java/lang/IllegalArgumentException",
                    "too many arguments");
        return 0;
    }

    // convert arguments
    for (nwords = 0; nwords < nargs; nwords++) {
        is_string[nwords] = JNI_FALSE;
        jobject arg = env->GetObjectArrayElement(arr, nwords);

        if (arg == NULL) {
            args[nwords].p = NULL;
        } else if (env->IsInstanceOf(arg, Class_Integer)) {
            args[nwords].i =
                env->GetIntField(arg, FID_Integer_value);
        } else if (env->IsInstanceOf(arg, Class_Float)) {
            args[nwords].f =
                env->GetFloatField(arg, FID_Float_value);
        } else if (env->IsInstanceOf(arg, Class_CPointer)) {
            args[nwords].p = (void *)
                env->GetLongField(arg, FID_CPointer_peer);
        } else if (env->IsInstanceOf(arg, Class_String)) {
            char * cstr =
                JNU_GetStringNativeChars(env, (jstring)arg);
            if ((args[nwords].p = cstr) == NULL) {
                goto cleanup; // error thrown
            }
            is_string[nwords] = JNI_TRUE;
        } else {
            JNU_ThrowByName(env,
                "java/lang/IllegalArgumentException",
                "unrecognized argument type");
            goto cleanup;
        }
        env->DeleteLocalRef(arg);
    }
```

```
    void *func =
        (void *)env->GetLongField(self, FID_CPointer_peer);
    int conv = env->GetIntField(self, FID_CFunction_conv);

    // now transfer control to func.
    ires = asm_dispatch(func, nwords, args, conv);

cleanup:
    // free all the native strings we have created
    for (int i = 0; i < nwords; i++) {
        if (is_string[i]) {
            free(args[i].p);
        }
    }
    return ires;
}
```

We assume that we have set up a number of global variables for caching the appropriate class references and field IDs. For example, global variable FID_CPointer_peer caches the field ID for CPointer.peer and global variable Class_String is a global reference to the java.lang.String class object. The word_t type represents a machine word and is defined as follows:

```
typedef union {
    jint i;
    jfloat f;
    void *p;
} word_t;
```

The Java_CFunction_callInt function iterates through the argument array, and checks the type of each element:

- If the element is a null reference, it is passed as a NULL pointer to the C function.

- If the element is an instance of the java.lang.Integer class, the integer value is fetched and passed to the C function.

- If the element is an instance of the java.lang.Float class, the floating-point value is fetched and passed to the C function.

- If the element is an instance of the CPointer class, the peer pointer is fetched and passed to the C function.

- If the argument is an instance of java.lang.String, it is converted to a locale-specific C string and passed to the C function.

- Otherwise, an IllegalArgumentException is thrown.

We carefully check for possible errors during argument conversion and free all the temporary storage allocated for C strings before returning from the `Java_CFunction_callInt` function.

The code that transfers the arguments from the temporary buffer `args` to the C function needs to manipulate the C stack directly. It is written in inlined assembly:

```
int asm_dispatch(void *func,     // pointer to the C function
                 int nwords,     // number of words in args array
                 word_t *args,   // start of the argument data
                 int conv)       // calling convention 0: C
                                 //                    1: JNI
{
    __asm {
        mov esi, args
        mov edx, nwords
        // word address -> byte address
        shl edx, 2
        sub edx, 4
        jc  args_done

        // push the last argument first
    args_loop:
        mov eax, DWORD PTR [esi+edx]
        push eax
        sub edx, 4
        jge SHORT args_loop
    args_done:
        call func

        // check for calling convention
        mov edx, conv
        or edx, edx
        jnz jni_call

        // pop the arguments
        mov edx, nwords
        shl edx, 2
        add esp, edx
    jni_call:
        // done, return value in eax
    }
}
```

The assembly routine copies the arguments onto the C stack, then redispatches to the C function `func`. After `func` returns, the `asm_dispatch` routine checks `func`'s calling convention. If `func` follows the C calling convention, `asm_dispatch` pops the arguments passed to `func`. If `func` follows the JNI calling convention, `asm_dispatch` does not pop the arguments; `func` pops the arguments before it returns.

9.5 Peer Classes

One-to-one mapping and shared stubs both address the problem of wrapping native functions. We also encountered the problem of wrapping native data structures in the course of constructing the shared stubs implementation. Recall the definition of the `CPointer` class:

```
public abstract class CPointer {
    protected long peer;
    public native void copyIn(int bOff, int[] buf,
                                  int off, int len);
    public native void copyOut(...);
    ...
}
```

It contains a 64-bit `peer` field that refers to the native data structure (in this case, a piece of memory in the C address space). Subclasses of `CPointer` assign specific meanings to the `peer` field. The `CMalloc` class, for example, uses the `peer` field to point to a chunk of memory in the C heap:

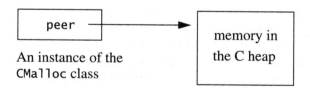

An instance of the
`CMalloc` class

memory in
the C heap

Classes that directly correspond to native data structures, such as `CPointer` and `CMalloc`, are called *peer classes*. You can construct peer classes for a variety of native data structures, including, for example:

- file descriptors
- socket descriptors
- windows or other graphics user interface components

9.5.1   Peer Classes in the Java Platform

The current JDK and Java 2 SDK releases (1.1 and 1.2) use peer classes internally to implement the `java.io`, `java.net`, and `java.awt` packages. An instance of the `java.io.FileDescriptor` class, for example, contains a private field `fd` that represents a native file descriptor:

```
// Implementation of the java.io.FileDescriptor class
public final class FileDescriptor {
    private int fd;
    ...
}
```

Suppose that you want to perform a file operation that is not supported by the Java platform API. You might be tempted to use the JNI to find out the underlying native file descriptor of a `java.io.FileDescriptor` instance. The JNI allows you to access a private field, as long as you know its name and type. You might think that you could then perform the native file operation directly on that file descriptor. This approach, however, has a couple of problems:

- First, you are relying on one `java.io.FileDescriptor` implementation that stores the native file descriptor in a private field called `fd`. There is no guarantee, however, that future implementations from Sun or third-party implementations of the `java.io.FileDescriptor` class will still use the same private field name `fd` for the native file descriptor. Native code that assumes the name of the peer field may fail to work with a different implementation of the Java platform.

- Second, the operation you perform directly on the native file descriptor may disrupt the internal consistency of the peer class. For example, `java.io.FileDescriptor` instances maintain an internal state indicating whether the underlying native file descriptor has been closed. If you use native code to bypass the peer class and close the underlying file descriptor, the state maintained in the `java.io.FileDescriptor` instance will no longer be consistent with the true state of the native file descriptor. Peer class implementations typically assume that they have exclusive access to the underlying native data structure.

The only way to overcome these problems is to define your own peer classes that wrap native data structures. In the above case, you can define your own file descriptor peer class that supports the required set of operations. This approach does not let you use your own peer classes to implement Java API classes. You cannot, for example, pass your own file descriptor instance to a method that expects a `java.io.FileDescriptor` instance. You can, however, easily define your own peer class that implements a standard interface in the Java API. This is a strong argument for designing APIs based on interfaces instead of classes.

9.5.2 Freeing Native Data Structures

Peer classes are defined in the Java programming language; thus instances of peer classes will be garbage collected automatically. You need to make sure, however, that the underlying native data structures will be freed as well.

Recall that the `CMalloc` class contains a `free` method for explicitly freeing the `malloc`'ed C memory:

```
public class CMalloc extends CPointer {
    public native void free();
    ...
}
```

You must remember to call `free` on instances of the `CMalloc` class; otherwise a `CMalloc` instance may be garbage collected, but its corresponding `malloc`'ed C memory will never be reclaimed.

Some programmers like to put a finalizer in peer classes such as `CMalloc`:

```
public class CMalloc extends CPointer {
    public native synchronized void free();
    protected void finalize() {
        free();
    }
    ...
}
```

The virtual machine calls the `finalize` method before it garbage collects an instance of `CMalloc`. Even if you forget to call `free`, the `finalize` method frees the `malloc`'ed C memory for you.

You need to make a small change to the `CMalloc.free` native method implementation to account for the possibility that it may be called multiple times. You also need to make `CMalloc.free` a synchronized method to avoid thread race conditions:

```
JNIEXPORT void JNICALL
Java_CMalloc_free(JNIEnv *env, jobject self)
{
    long peer = env->GetLongField(self, FID_CPointer_peer);
    if (peer == 0) {
        return; /* not an error, freed previously */
    }
    free((void *)peer);
    peer = 0;
    env->SetLongField(self, FID_CPointer_peer, peer);
}
```

We set the peer field using two statements:

```
peer = 0;
env->SetLongField(self, FID_CPointer_peer, peer);
```

instead of one statement:

```
env->SetLongField(self, FID_CPointer_peer, 0);
```

because C++ compilers will regard the literal 0 as a 32-bit integer, as opposed to a 64-bit integer. Some C++ compilers allow you to specify 64-bit integer literals, but using 64-bit literals will not be as portable.

Defining a finalize method is a proper safeguard, but *you should never rely on finalizers as the sole means of freeing native data structures.* The reason is that the native data structures may consume much more resources than their peer instances. The Java virtual machine may not garbage collect and finalize instances of peer classes fast enough to free up their native counterparts.

Defining a finalizer has performance consequences as well. It is typically slower to create and reclaim instances of classes with finalizers than to create and reclaim those without finalizers.

If you can always ensure that you manually free the native data structure for peer classes, you need not define a finalizer. You should make sure, however, to free native data structures in all paths of execution; otherwise you may have created a resource leak. *Pay special attention to possible exceptions thrown during the process of using a peer instance.* Always free native data structures in a finally clause:

```
CMalloc cptr = new CMalloc(10);
try {
    ... // use cptr
} finally {
    cptr.free();
}
```

The `finally` clause ensures that `cptr` is freed even if an exception occurs inside the `try` block.

9.5.3 Backpointers to Peer Instances

We have shown that peer classes typically contain a private field that refers to the underlying native data structure. In some cases it is desirable to also include a reference from the native data structure to instances of the peer class. This happens, for example, when the native code needs to initiate callbacks to instance methods in the peer class.

Suppose that we are building a hypothetical user interface component called `KeyInput`. `KeyInput`'s native C++ component, `key_input`, receives an event as a `key_pressed` C++ function call from the operating system when the user presses a key. The `key_input` C++ component reports the operating system event to the `KeyInput` instance by calling the `keyPressed` method on the `KeyInput` instance. The arrows in the figure below indicate how a key press event is originated by a user key press and propagated from the `key_input` C++ component to the `KeyInput` peer instance:

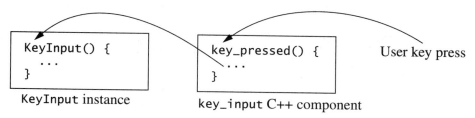

The `KeyInput` peer class is defined as follows:

```
class KeyInput {
    private long peer;
    private native long create();
    private native void destroy(long peer);
    public KeyInput() {
        peer = create();
    }
    public destroy() {
        destroy(peer);
    }
    private void keyPressed(int key) {
        ... /* process the key event */
    }
}
```

The `create` native method implementation allocates an instance of the C++ structure `key_input`. C++ structures are similar to C++ classes, with the only difference being that all members are by default public as opposed to private. We use a C++ structure instead of a C++ class in this example mainly to avoid confusion with classes in the Java programming language.

```
// C++ structure, native counterpart of KeyInput
struct key_input {
    jobject back_ptr;        // back pointer to peer instance
    int key_pressed(int key); // called by the operating system
};

JNIEXPORT jlong JNICALL
Java_KeyInput_create(JNIEnv *env, jobject self)
{
    key_input *cpp_obj = new key_input();
    cpp_obj->back_ptr = env->NewGlobalRef(self);
    return (jlong)cpp_obj;
}

JNIEXPORT void JNICALL
Java_KeyInput_destroy(JNIEnv *env, jobject self, jlong peer)
{
    key_input *cpp_obj = (key_input*)peer;
    env->DeleteGlobalRef(cpp_obj->back_ptr);
    delete cpp_obj;
    return;
}
```

The `create` native method allocates the C++ structure and initializes its `back_ptr` field to a global reference to the `KeyInput` peer instance. The `destroy` native method deletes the global reference to the peer instance and the C++ structure referred to by the peer instance. The `KeyInput` constructor calls the `create` native method to set up the links between a peer instance and its native counterpart:

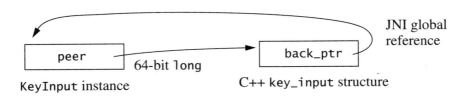

When the user presses a key, the operating system calls the C++ member function `key_input::key_pressed`. This member function responds to events by issuing a callback to the `keyPressed` method on the `KeyInput` peer instance.

```
// returns 0 on success, -1 on failure
int key_input::key_pressed(int key)
{
    jboolean has_exception;
    JNIEnv *env = JNU_GetEnv();
    JNU_CallMethodByName(env,
                            &has_exception,
                            java_peer,
                            "keyPressed",
                            "()V",
                            key);
    if (has_exception) {
        env->ExceptionClear();
        return -1;
    } else {
        return 0;
    }
}
```

The `key_press` member function clears any exceptions after the callback and returns error conditions to the operating system using the -1 return code. Refer to Sections 6.2.3 and 8.4.1 for the definitions of `JNU_CallMethodByName` and `JNU_GetEnv` utility functions respectively.

Let us discuss one final issue before concluding this section. Suppose that you add a `finalize` method in the `KeyInput` class to avoid potential memory leaks:

```
class KeyInput {
    ...
    public synchronized destroy() {
        if (peer != 0) {
            destroy(peer);
            peer = 0;
        }
    }
    protect void finalize() {
        destroy();
    }
}
```

The `destroy` method checks whether the `peer` field is zero, and sets the `peer` field to zero after calling the overloaded `destroy` native method. It is defined as a synchronized method to avoid race conditions.

129

The above code will not work as you might expect, however. The virtual machine will never garbage collect any KeyInput instances unless you call destroy explicitly. The KeyInput constructor creates a JNI global reference to the KeyInput instance. The global reference prevents the KeyInput instance from being garbage collected. You can overcome this problem by using a weak global reference instead of a global reference:

```
JNIEXPORT jlong JNICALL
Java_KeyInput_create(JNIEnv *env, jobject self)
{
    key_input *cpp_obj = new key_input();
    cpp_obj->back_ptr = env->NewWeakGlobalRef(self);
    return (jlong)cpp_obj;
}

JNIEXPORT void JNICALL
Java_KeyInput_destroy(JNIEnv *env, jobject self, jlong peer)
{
    key_input *cpp_obj = (key_input*)peer;
    env->DeleteWeakGlobalRef(cpp_obj->back_ptr);
    delete cpp_obj;
    return;
}
```

CHAPTER **10**

Traps and Pitfalls

To highlight the important techniques covered in previous chapters, this chapter covers a number of mistakes commonly made by JNI programmers. Each mistake described here has occurred in real-world projects.

10.1 Error Checking

The most common mistake when writing native methods is forgetting to check whether an error condition has occurred. Unlike the Java programming language, native languages do not offer standard exception mechanisms. The JNI does not rely on any particular native exception mechanism (such as C++ exceptions). As a result, programmers *are required* to perform explicit checks after every JNI function call that could possibly raise an exception. Not all JNI functions raise exceptions, but most can. Exception checks are tedious, but are necessary to ensure that the application using native methods is robust.

The tediousness of error checking greatly emphasizes the need to limit native code to those well-defined subsets of an application where it is necessary to use the JNI (§10.5).

10.2 Passing Invalid Arguments to JNI Functions

The JNI functions do not attempt to detect or recover from invalid arguments. If you pass NULL or (jobject)0xFFFFFFFF to a JNI function that expects a reference, the resulting behavior is undefined. In practice this could either lead to incorrect results or virtual machine crashes. Java 2 SDK release 1.2 provides you with a command-line option -Xcheck:jni. This option instructs the virtual machine to detect and report many, though not all, cases of native code passing illegal arguments to JNI functions. Checking the validity of arguments incurs a significant amount of overhead and thus is not enabled by default.

Not checking the validity of arguments is a common practice in C and C++ libraries. Code that uses the library is responsible for making sure that all the arguments passed to library functions are valid. If, however, you are used to the Java programming language, you may have to adjust to this particular aspect of the lack of safety in JNI programming.

10.3 Confusing `jclass` with `jobject`

The differences between instance references (a value of the `jobject` type) and class references (a value of the `jclass` type) can be confusing when first using the JNI.

Instance references correspond to arrays and instances of `java.lang.Object` or one of its subclasses. Class references correspond to `java.lang.Class` instances, which represent class types.

An operation such as `GetFieldID`, which takes a `jclass`, is a class operation because it gets the field descriptor from a class. In contrast, `GetIntField`, which takes a `jobject`, is an instance operation because it gets the value of a field from an instance. The association of `jobject` with instance operations and the association of `jclass` with class operations are consistent across all JNI functions, so it is easy to remember that class operations are distinct from instance operations.

10.4 Truncating `jboolean` Arguments

A `jboolean` is an 8-bit unsigned C type that can store values from 0 to 255. The value 0 corresponds to the constant `JNI_FALSE`, and the values from 1 to 255 correspond to `JNI_TRUE`. But 32-bit or 16-bit values greater than 255 whose lower 8 bits are 0 pose a problem.

Suppose you have defined a function `print` that takes an argument `condition` whose type is `jboolean`:

```
void print(jboolean condition)
{
    /* C compilers generate code that truncates condition
       to its lower 8 bits. */
    if (condition) {
        printf("true\n");
    } else {
        printf("false\n");
    }
}
```

There is nothing wrong with the previous definition. However, the following innocent-looking call to `print` will produce a somewhat unexpected result:

```
int n = 256; /* the value 0x100, whose lower 8 bits are all 0 */
print(n);
```

We passed a non-zero value (256) to `print` expecting that it would represent true. But because all bits other than the lower 8 are truncated, the argument evaluates to 0. The program prints "`false`," contrary to expectations.

A good rule of thumb when coercing integral types, such as `int`, to `jboolean` is always to evaluate conditions on the integral type, thereby avoiding inadvertent errors during coercion. You can rewrite the call to `print` as follows:

```
n = 256;
print (n ? JNI_TRUE : JNI_FALSE);
```

10.5 Boundaries between Java Application and Native Code

A common question when designing a Java application supported by native code is "What, and how much, should be in native code?" The boundaries between the native code and the rest of the application written in the Java programming language are application-specific, but there are some generally applicable principles:

- Keep the boundaries *simple.* Complex control flow that goes back and forth between the Java virtual machine and native code can be hard to debug and maintain. Such control flow also gets in the way of optimizations performed by high-performance virtual machine implementations. For example, it is much easier for a virtual machine implementation to inline methods defined in the Java programming language than to inline native methods defined in C and C++.

- Keep the code on the native code side *minimal.* There are compelling reasons to do so. Native code is neither portable nor type-safe. Error checking in native code is tedious (§10.1). It is good software engineering to keep such parts to a minimum.

- Keep native code *isolated.* In practice, this could mean that all native methods are in the same package or in the same class, isolated from the rest of the application. The package or the class containing native methods essentially becomes the "porting layer" for the application.

The JNI provides access to virtual machine functionality such as class loading, object creation, field access, method calls, thread synchronization, and so

133

forth. It is sometimes tempting to express complex interactions with Java virtual machine functionality in native code, when in fact it is simpler to accomplish the same task in the Java programming language. The following example shows why "Java programming in native code" is bad practice. Consider a simple statement that creates a new thread written in the Java programming language:

```
new JobThread().start();
```

The same statement can also be written in native code:

```
/* Assume these variables are precomputed and cached:
 *      Class_JobThread:  the class "JobThread"
 *      MID_Thread_init:  method ID of constructor
 *      MID_Thread_start: method ID of Thread.start()
 */
aThreadObject =
    (*env)->NewObject(env, Class_JobThread, MID_Thread_init);
if (aThreadObject == NULL) {
    ... /* out of memory */
}
(*env)->CallVoidMethod(env, aThreadObject, MID_Thread_start);
if ((*env)->ExceptionOccurred(env)) {
    ... /* thread did not start */
}
```

The native code is much more complex than its equivalent written in the Java programming language despite the fact that we have omitted the lines of code needed for error checks.

Rather than writing a complex segment of native code manipulating the Java virtual machine, it is often preferable to define an auxiliary method in the Java programming language and have the native code issue a callback to the auxiliary method.

10.6 Confusing IDs with References

The JNI exposes objects as references. Classes, strings, and arrays are special types of references. The JNI exposes methods and fields as IDs. An ID is not a reference. Do not call a class reference a "class ID" or a method ID a "method reference."

References are virtual machine resources that can be managed explicitly by native code. The JNI function `DeleteLocalRef`, for example, allows native code to delete a local reference. In contrast, field and method IDs are managed by the virtual machine and remain valid until their defining class is unloaded. Native code cannot explicitly delete a field or method ID before the the virtual machine unloads the defining class.

Native code may create multiple references that refer to the same object. A global and a local reference, for example, may refer to the same object. In contrast, a unique field or method ID is derived for the same *definition* of a field or a method. If class A defines method f and class B inherits f from A, the two Get-MethodID calls in the following code always return the same result:

```
jmethodID MID_A_f = (*env)->GetMethodID(env, A, "f", "()V");
jmethodID MID_B_f = (*env)->GetMethodID(env, B, "f", "()V");
```

10.7 Caching Field and Method IDs

Native code obtains field or method IDs from the virtual machine by specifying the name and type descriptor of the field or method as strings (§4.1, §4.2). Field and method lookups using name and type strings are slow. It often pays off to cache the IDs. Failure to cache field and method IDs is a common performance problem in native code.

In some cases caching IDs is more than a performance gain. A cached ID may be necessary to ensure that the correct field or method is accessed by native code. The following example illustrates how the failure to cache a field ID can lead to a subtle bug:

```
class C {
    private int i;
    native void f();
}
```

Suppose that the native method f needs to obtain the value of the field i in an instance of C. A straightforward implementation that does not cache an ID accomplishes this in three steps: 1) get the class of the object; 2) look up the field ID for i from the class reference; and 3) access the field value based on the object reference and field ID:

```
// No field IDs cached.
JNIEXPORT void JNICALL
Java_C_f(JNIEnv *env, jobject this) {
    jclass cls = (*env)->GetObjectClass(env, this);
    ... /* error checking */
    jfieldID fid = (*env)->GetFieldID(env, cls, "i", "I");
    ... /* error checking */
    ival = (*env)->GetIntField(env, this, fid);
    ... /* ival now has the value of this.i */
}
```

The code works fine until we define another class D as a subclass of C, and declare a private field also named "i" in D:

```
// Trouble in the absence of ID caching
class D extends C {
    private int i;
    D() {
        f(); // inherited from C
    }
}
```

When D's constructor calls C.f, the native method receives an instance of D as the this argument, cls refers to the D class, and fid represents D.i. At the end of the native method, ival contains the value of D.i, instead of C.i. This might not be what you expected when implementing native method C.f.

The solution is to compute and cache the field ID at the time when you are certain that you have a class reference to C, not D. Subsequent accesses from this cached ID will always refer to the right field C.i. Here is the corrected version:

```
// Version that caches IDs in static initializers
class C {
    private int i;
    native void f();
    private static native void initIDs();
    static {
        initIDs(); // Call an initializing native method
    }
}
```

The modified native code is:

```
static jfieldID FID_C_i;

JNIEXPORT void JNICALL
Java_C_initIDs(JNIEnv *env, jclass cls) {
    /* Get IDs to all fields/methods of C that
       native methods will need. */
    FID_C_i = (*env)->GetFieldID(env, cls, "i", "I");
}

JNIEXPORT void JNICALL
Java_C_f(JNIEnv *env, jobject this) {
    ival = (*env)->GetIntField(env, this, FID_C_i);
    ... /* ival is always C.i, not D.i */
}
```

The field ID is computed and cached in C's static initializer. This guarantees that the field ID for C.i will be cached, and thus the native method implementation Java_C_f will read the value of C.i independent of the actual class of the this object.

Caching may be needed for some method calls as well. If we change the above example slightly so that classes C and D each have their own definition of a *private* method g, f needs to cache the method ID of C.g to avoid accidentally calling D.g. Caching is not needed for making correct virtual method calls. Virtual methods by definition dynamically bind to the instance on which the method is invoked. Thus you can safely use the JNU_CallMethodByName utility function (§6.2.3) to call virtual methods. The previous example tells us, however, why we do not define a similar JNU_GetFieldByName utility function.

10.8   Terminating Unicode Strings

Unicode strings obtained from GetStringChars or GetStringCritical are not NULL-terminated. Call GetStringLength to find out the number of 16-bit Unicode characters in a string. Some operating systems, such as Windows NT, expect two trailing zero byte values to terminate Unicode strings. You cannot pass the result of GetStringChars to Windows NT APIs that expect a Unicode string. You must make another copy of the string and insert the two trailing zero byte values.

10.9   Violating Access Control Rules

The JNI does not enforce class, field, and method access control restrictions that can be expressed at the Java programming language level through the use of modifiers such as `private` and `final`. It is possible to write native code to access or modify fields of an object even though doing so at the Java programming language level would lead to an `IllegalAccessException`. JNI's permissiveness was a conscious design decision, given that native code can access and modify any memory location in the heap anyway.

Native code that bypasses source-language-level access checks may have undesirable effects on program execution. For example, an inconsistency may be created if a native method modifies a `final` field after a just-in-time (JIT) compiler has inlined accesses to the field. Similarly, native methods should not modify immutable objects such as fields in instances of `java.lang.String` or `java.lang.Integer`. Doing so may lead to breakage of invariants in the Java platform implementation.

10.10   Disregarding Internationalization

Strings in the Java virtual machine consist of Unicode characters, whereas native strings are typically in a locale-specific encoding. Use utility functions such as `JNU_NewStringNative` (§8.2.1) and `JNU_GetStringNativeChars` (§8.2.2) to translate between Unicode `jstring`s and locale-specific native strings of the underlying host environment. Pay special attention to message strings and file names, which typically are internationalized. If a native method gets a file name as a `jstring`, the file name must be translated to a native string before being passed to a C library routine.

The following native method, `MyFile.open`, opens a file and returns the file descriptor as its result:

```
JNIEXPORT jint JNICALL
Java_MyFile_open(JNIEnv *env, jobject self, jstring name,
                jint mode)
{
    jint result;
    char *cname = JNU_GetStringNativeChars(env, name);
    if (cname == NULL) {
        return 0;
    }
    result = open(cname, mode);
    free(cname);
    return result;
}
```

We translate the jstring argument using the JNU_GetStringNativeChars function because the open system call expects the file name to be in the locale-specific encoding.

10.11 Retaining Virtual Machine Resources

A common mistake in native methods is forgetting to free virtual machine resources. Programmers need to be particularly careful in code paths that are only executed when there is an error. The following code segment, a slight modification of an example in Section 6.2.2, misses a ReleaseStringChars call:

```
JNIEXPORT void JNICALL
Java_pkg_Cls_f(JNIEnv *env, jclass cls, jstring jstr)
{
    const jchar *cstr =
        (*env)->GetStringChars(env, jstr, NULL);
    if (cstr == NULL) {
        return;
    }
    ...
    if (...) { /* exception occurred */
        /* misses a ReleaseStringChars call */
        return;
    }
    ...
    /* normal return */
    (*env)->ReleaseStringChars(env, jstr, cstr);
}
```

Forgetting to call the ReleaseStringChars function may cause either the jstring object to be pinned indefinitely, leading to memory fragmentation, or the C copy to be retained indefinitely, a memory leak.

There must be a corresponding ReleaseStringChars call whether or not GetStringChars has made a copy of the string. The following code fails to release virtual machine resources properly:

```
/* The isCopy argument is misused here! */
JNIEXPORT void JNICALL
Java_pkg_Cls_f(JNIEnv *env, jclass cls, jstring jstr)
{
    jboolean isCopy;
    const jchar *cstr = (*env)->GetStringChars(env, jstr,
                                               &isCopy);
    if (cstr == NULL) {
        return;
    }
    ... /* use cstr */
    /* This is wrong. Always need to call ReleaseStringChars. */
    if (isCopy) {
        (*env)->ReleaseStringChars(env, jstr, cstr);
    }
}
```

The call to ReleaseStringChars is still needed even when isCopy is JNI_FALSE so that the virtual machine will unpin the jstring elements.

10.12   Excessive Local Reference Creation

Excessive local reference creation causes programs to retain memory unnecessarily. An unnecessary local reference wastes memory both for the referenced object and for the reference itself.

Pay special attention to long-running native methods, local references created in loops, and utility functions. Take advantage of the new Push/PopLocalFrame functions in Java 2 SDK release 1.2 to manage local references more effectively. Refer to Section 5.2.1 and Section 5.2.2 for a more detailed discussion of this problem.

You can specify the -verbose:jni option in Java 2 SDK 1.2 to ask the virtual machine to detect and report excessive local reference creation. Suppose that you run a class Foo with this option:

```
% java -verbose:jni Foo
```

and the output contains the following:

```
***ALERT: JNI local ref creation exceeded capacity
         (creating: 17, limit: 16).
      at Baz.g (Native method)
      at Bar.f (Compiled method)
      at Foo.main (Compiled method)
```

It is likely that the native method implementation for `Baz.g` fails to manage local references properly.

10.13 Using Invalid Local References

Local references are valid only inside a single invocation of a native method. Local references created in a native method invocation are freed automatically after the native function that implements the method returns. Native code should not store a local reference in a global variable and expect to use it in later invocations of the native method.

Local references are valid only within the thread in which they are created. You should not pass a local reference from one thread to another. Create a global reference when it is necessary to pass a reference across threads.

10.14 Using the `JNIEnv` across Threads

The `JNIEnv` pointer, passed as the first argument to every native method, can only be used in the thread with which it is associated. It is wrong to cache the `JNIEnv` interface pointer obtained from one thread, and use that pointer in another thread. Section 8.1.4 explains how you can obtain the `JNIEnv` interface pointer for the current thread.

10.15 Mismatched Thread Models

The JNI works only if the host native code and the Java virtual machine implementation share the same thread model (§8.1.5). For example, programmers cannot attach native platform threads to an embedded Java virtual machine implemented using a user thread package.

On Solaris, Sun ships a virtual machine implementation that is based on a user thread package known as *Green threads*. If your native code relies on Solaris native thread support, it will not work with a Green-thread-based Java virtual machine implementation. You need a virtual machine implementation that is designed to work with Solaris native threads. Native threads support in Solaris JDK release 1.1 requires a separate download. The native threads support is bundled with Solaris Java 2 SDK release 1.2.

Sun's virtual machine implementation on Win32 supports native threads by default, and can be easily embedded into native Win32 applications.

Part Three: Specification

CHAPTER 11

Overview of the JNI Design

THIS chapter gives an overview of the JNI design. Where necessary, we also provide the underlying technical motivation. The design overview serves as the specification for key JNI concepts such as the JNIEnv interface pointer, local and global references, and field and method IDs. The technical motivation aims at helping the reader to understand various design trade-offs. On a few occasions, we will discuss how certain features may be implemented. The purpose of such discussion is not to present a practical implementation strategy, but instead to clarify the subtle semantic issues.

The concept of a programming interface that bridges different languages is not new. For example, C programs can typically call functions written in languages such as FORTRAN and assembly. Similarly, implementations of programming languages such as LISP and Smalltalk support a variety of foreign function interfaces.

The JNI addresses an issue similar to that addressed by the interoperability mechanisms supported by other languages. There is, however, a significant difference between the JNI and the interoperability mechanisms used in many other languages. The JNI is not designed for a particular implementation of the Java virtual machine. Rather, it is a native interface that can be supported by every implementation of the Java virtual machine. We will further elaborate on this as we describe the JNI design goals.

11.1 Design Goals

The most important goal of the JNI design is ensuring that it offers *binary compatibility* among different Java virtual machine implementations on a given host environment. The same native library binary will run on different virtual machine implementations on a given host environment without the need for recompilation.

To achieve this goal, the JNI design cannot make any assumptions about the internal details of the Java virtual machine implementation. Because Java virtual machine implementation technologies are evolving rapidly, we must be careful to avoid introducing any constraints that may interfere with advanced implementation techniques in the future.

The second goal of JNI design is *efficiency*. To support time-critical code, the JNI imposes as little overhead as possible. We will see, however, that our first goal, the need for implementation-independence, sometimes requires us to adopt a slightly less efficient design than we might have otherwise. We strike a compromise between efficiency and implementation-independence.

Lastly, the JNI must be functionally *complete*. It must expose enough Java virtual machine functionality to enable native methods and applications to accomplish useful tasks.

It is not the goal of JNI to be the only native programming interface supported by a given Java virtual machine implementation. A standard interface benefits programmers who would like to load their native code libraries into different Java virtual machine implementations. In some cases, however, a lower-level implementation-specific interface may achieve higher performance. In other cases, the programmer might use a higher-level interface to build software components.

11.2   Loading Native Libraries

Before an application can invoke a native method, the virtual machine must locate and load a native library that contains an implementation of the native method.

11.2.1   Class Loaders

Native libraries are located by *class loaders*. Class loaders have many uses in the Java virtual machine including, for example, loading class files, defining classes and interfaces, providing namespace separation among software components, resolving symbolic references among different classes and interfaces, and finally, locating native libraries. We assume that you have a basic understanding of class loaders, so we will not go into the details of how they load and link classes in the Java virtual machine. You can find out more details on class loaders in the paper *Dynamic Class Loading in the Java Virtual Machine*, by Sheng Liang and Gilad Bracha, published in the proceedings of the ACM Conference on Object Oriented Programming Systems, Languages, and Applications (OOPSLA), 1998.

Class loaders provide the namespace separation needed to run multiple components (such as the applets downloaded from different web sites) inside an instance of the same virtual machine. A class loader maintains a separate namespace by mapping class or interface names to actual class or interface types represented as objects in the Java virtual machine. Each class or interface type is associated with its *defining loader*, the loader that initially reads the class file and defines the class or interface object. Two class or interface types are the same only when they have the same name and the same defining loader. For example, in Figure 11.1, class loaders L1 and L2 each define a class named C. These two classes named C are not the same. Indeed, they contain two different f methods that have distinct return types.

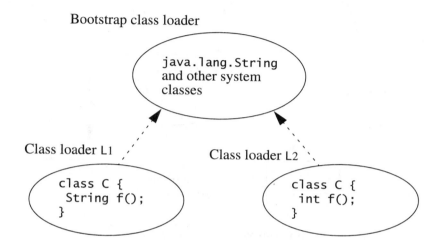

Figure 11.1   Two classes of the same name loaded by different class loaders

    The dotted lines in the above figure represent the *delegation* relationships among class loaders. A class loader may ask another class loader to load a class or an interface on its behalf. For example, both L1 and L2 delegate to the bootstrap class loader for loading the system class java.lang.String. Delegation allows system classes to be shared among all class loaders. This is necessary because type safety would be violated if, for example, application and system code had different notions of what the type java.lang.String was.

11.2.2   Class Loaders and Native Libraries

Now suppose the method f in both classes C are native methods. The virtual machine locates the native implementation for both C.f methods using the name "C_f". To ensure that each C class links with the correct native function, each class loader must maintain its own set of native libraries, as shown in Figure 11.2.

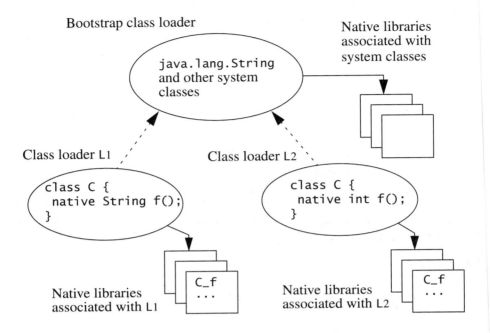

Figure 11.2   Associating native libraries with class loaders

Because each class loader maintains a set of native libraries, the programmer may use a single library to store all the native methods needed by any number of classes as long as those classes have the same defining loader.

Native libraries will automatically be unloaded by the virtual machine when their corresponding class loaders are garbage collected (§11.2.5).

11.2.3   Locating Native Libraries

Native libraries are loaded by the System.loadLibrary method. In the following example, the static initializer of class Cls loads a platform-specific native library in which the native method f is defined:

```
package pkg;
class Cls {
    native double f(int i, String s);
    static {
        System.loadLibrary("mypkg");
    }
}
```

The argument to System.loadLibrary is a library name chosen by the programmer. Software developers are responsible for choosing native library names that minimize the chance of name clashes. The virtual machine follows a standard, but host environment specific, convention to convert the library name to a native library name. For example, the Solaris operating system converts the name mypkg to libmypkg.so, while the Win32 operating system converts the same mypkg name to mypkg.dll.

When the Java virtual machine starts up, it constructs a list of directories that will be used to locate native libraries for application classes. The contents of the list are dependent upon the host environment and the virtual machine implementation. For example, under the Win32 JDK or Java 2 SDK releases, the list of directories consists of the Windows system directories, the current working directory, and the entries in the PATH environment variable. Under the Solaris JDK or Java 2 SDK releases, the list of directories consists of the entries in the LD_LIBRARY_PATH environment variable.

System.loadLibrary throws an UnsatisfiedLinkError if it fails to load the named native library. System.loadLibrary completes silently if an earlier call to System.loadLibrary has already loaded the same native library. If the underlying operating system does not support dynamic linking, all native methods must be prelinked with the virtual machine. In this case, the virtual machine completes the System.loadLibrary calls without actually loading the library.

The virtual machine internally maintains a list of loaded native libraries for each class loader. It follows three steps to determine which class loader should be associated with a newly loaded native library:

1. determine the *immediate* caller of System.loadLibrary

2. identify the class that defines the caller

3. obtain the defining loader of the caller class

In the following example, the native library foo will be associated with C's defining loader:

```
class C {
    static {
        System.loadLibrary("foo");
    }
}
```

Java 2 SDK release 1.2 introduces a new ClassLoader.findLibrary method that allows the programmer to specify a custom library loading policy that is specific to a given class loader. The ClassLoader.findLibrary method takes a platform-independent library name (such as mypkg) as an argument, and:

- either returns `null` to instruct the virtual machine to follow the default library search path,

- or returns a host-environment-dependent absolute path of the library file (such as `"c:\\mylibs\\mypkg.dll"`).

`ClassLoader.findLibrary` is typically used with another method added in the Java 2 SDK release 1.2, `System.mapLibraryName`. `System.mapLibrary-Name` maps platform-independent library names (such as `mypkg`) to platform-dependent library file names (such as `mypkg.dll`).

You can override the default library search path in Java 2 SDK release 1.2 by setting the property `java.library.path`. For example, the following command line starts up a program Foo which needs to load a native library in the `c:\mylibs` directory:

```
java -Djava.library.path=c:\mylibs Foo
```

11.2.4 A Type Safety Restriction

The virtual machine does not allow a given JNI native library to be loaded by more than one class loader. Attempting to load the same native library by multiple class loaders causes an `UnsatisfiedLinkError` to be thrown. The purpose of this restriction is to make sure that namespace separation based on class loaders is preserved in native libraries. Without this restriction, it becomes much easier to mistakenly intermix classes and interfaces from different class loaders through native methods. Consider a native method `Foo.f` that caches its own defining class `Foo` in a global reference:

```
JNIEXPORT void JNICALL
Java_Foo_f(JNIEnv *env, jobject self)
{
    static jclass cachedFooClass; /* cached class Foo */
    if (cachedFooClass == NULL) {
        jclass fooClass = (*env)->FindClass(env, "Foo");
        if (fooClass == NULL) {
            return; /* error */
        }
        cachedFooClass = (*env)->NewGlobalRef(env, fooClass);
        if (cachedFooClass == NULL) {
            return; /* error */
        }
    }
    assert((*env)->IsInstanceOf(env, self, cachedFooClass));
    ... /* use cachedFooClass */
}
```

150

We expect the assertion to succeed because Foo.f is an instance method and self refers to an instance of Foo. The assertion could fail, however, if two different Foo classes are loaded by class loaders L1 and L2 and both Foo classes are linked with the previous implementation of Foo.f. The cachedFooClass global reference will be created for the Foo class whose f method is invoked first. A later invocation of the f method of the other Foo class will cause the assertion to fail.

JDK release 1.1 did not properly enforce native library separation among class loaders. This means that it would be possible for two classes in different class loaders to link with the same native method. As shown by the previous example, the approach in JDK release 1.1 leads to the following two problems:

- A class may mistakenly link with native libraries that were loaded by a class with the same name in a different class loader.

- Native methods can easily mix classes from different class loaders. This breaks the namespace separation offered by class loaders, and leads to type safety problems.

11.2.5 Unloading Native Libraries

The virtual machine unloads a native library after it garbage collects the class loader associated with the native library. Because classes refer to their defining loaders, this implies that the virtual machine has also unloaded the class whose static initializer called System.loadLibrary and loaded the native library (§11.2.2).

11.3 Linking Native Methods

The virtual machine attempts to link each native method before invoking it for the first time. The earliest time that a native method f can be linked is the first invocation of a method g, where there is a reference from the method body of g to f. Virtual machine implementations should not try to link a native method too early. Doing so could lead to unexpected linkage errors because the native library that implements the native method may not have been loaded.

Linking a native method involves the following steps:

- Determining the class loader of the class that defines the native method.

- Searching the set of native libraries associated with this class loader to locate the native function that implements the native method.

- Setting up the internal data structures so that all future calls to the native method will jump directly to the native function.

The virtual machine deduces the name of the native function from the name of the native method by concatenating the following components:

- the prefix "Java_"
- an encoded fully qualified class name
- an underscore ("_") separator
- an encoded method name
- for overloaded native methods, two underscores ("__") followed by the encoded argument descriptor

The virtual machine iterates through all native libraries associated with the defining loader to search for a native function with an appropriate name. For each native library, the virtual machine looks first for the short name, that is, the name without the argument descriptor. It then looks for the long name, which is the name with the argument descriptor. Programmers need to use the long name only when a native method is overloaded with another native method. However, this is not a problem if the native method is overloaded with a non-native method. The latter does not reside in a native library.

In the following example, the native method g does not have to be linked using the long name because the other method g is not a native method.

```
class Cls1 {
    int g(int i) { ... } // regular method
    native int g(double d);
}
```

The JNI adopts a simple name-encoding scheme to ensure that all Unicode characters translate into valid C function names. The underscore ("_") character separates the components of fully qualified class names. Because a name or type descriptor never begins with a number, we can use _0, ..., _9 for escape sequences, as illustrated below:

Escape Sequence	Denotes
_0XXXX	a Unicode character XXXX
_1	the character "_"
_2	the character ";" in descriptors
_3	the character "[" in descriptors

If native functions matching an encoded native method name are present in multiple native libraries, the function in the native library that is loaded first is linked with the native method. If no function matches the native method name, an UnsatisfiedLinkError is thrown.

The programmer can also call the JNI function RegisterNatives to register the native methods associated with a class. The RegisterNatives function is particularly useful with statically linked functions.

11.4   Calling Conventions

The calling convention determines how a native function receives arguments and returns results. There is no standard calling convention among various native languages, or among different implementations of the same language. For example, it is common for different C++ compilers to generate code that follows different calling conventions.

It would be difficult, if not impossible, to require the Java virtual machine to interoperate with a wide variety of native calling conventions. The JNI requires the native methods to be written in a specified standard calling convention on a given host environment. For example, the JNI follows the C calling convention on UNIX and the stdcall convention on Win32.

When programmers need to call functions that follow a different calling convention, they must write stub routines that adapt the JNI calling conventions to those of the appropriate native language.

11.5   The JNIEnv Interface Pointer

Native code accesses virtual machine functionality by calling various functions exported through the JNIEnv *interface pointer.*

11.5.1   Organization of the JNIEnv Interface Pointer

A JNIEnv interface pointer is a pointer to thread-local data, which in turn contains a pointer to a function table. Every interface function is at a predefined offset in the table. The JNIEnv interface is organized like a C++ virtual function table and is also like a Microsoft COM interface. Figure 11.3 illustrates a set of JNIEnv interface pointers.

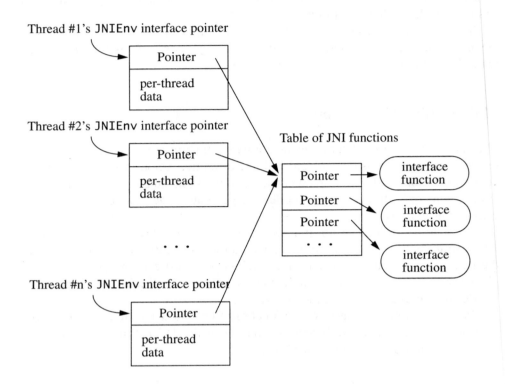

Figure 11.3   Thread Local JNIEnv Interface Pointers

Functions that implement a native method receive the JNIEnv interface pointer as their first argument. The virtual machine is guaranteed to pass the same interface pointer to native method implementation functions called from the same thread. However, a native method can be called from different threads, and therefore may be passed different JNIEnv interface pointers. Although the interface pointer is thread-local, the doubly indirected JNI function table is shared among multiple threads.

The reason the JNIEnv interface pointer refers to a thread-local structure is that some platforms do not have efficient support for thread-local storage access. By passing around a thread-local pointer, the JNI implementation inside the virtual machine can avoid many thread-local storage access operations that it would otherwise have to perform.

Because the JNIEnv interface pointer is thread-local, native code must not use the JNIEnv interface pointer belonging to one thread in another thread. Native code may use the JNIEnv pointer as a thread ID that remains unique for the lifetime of the thread.

11.5.2 Benefits of an Interface Pointer

There are several advantages of using an interface pointer, as opposed to hard-wired function entries:

- Most importantly, because the JNI function table is passed as an argument to each native method, native libraries do not have to link with a particular implementation of the Java virtual machine. This is crucial because different vendors may name their virtual machine implementations differently. Having each native library be self-contained is a prerequisite for the same native library binary to work with virtual machine implementations from different vendors on a given host environment.

- Second, by not using hard-wired function entries, a virtual machine implementation may choose to provide multiple versions of JNI function tables. For example, the virtual machine implementation may support two JNI function tables: one performs thorough illegal argument checks, and is suitable for debugging; the other performs the minimal amount of checking required by the JNI specification, and is therefore more efficient. Java 2 SDK release 1.2 supports a -Xcheck:jni option that optionally turns on additional checks for JNI functions.

- Finally, multiple JNI function tables make it possible to support multiple versions of JNIEnv-like interfaces in the future. Although we do not yet foresee the need to do so, a future version of the Java platform can support a new JNI function table, in addition to the one pointed to by the JNIEnv interface in the 1.1 and 1.2 releases. Java 2 SDK release 1.2 introduces a JNI_Onload function, which can be defined by a native library to indicate the version of the JNI function table needed by the native library. Future implementations of Java virtual machines can simultaneously support multiple versions of JNI function tables, and pass the correct version to individual native libraries depending upon their needs.

11.6 Passing Data

Primitive data types, such as integers, characters, and so on, are copied between the Java virtual machine and native code. Objects, on the other hand, are passed by reference. Each reference contains a direct pointer to the underlying object. The pointer to the object is never directly used by native code. From the native code's point of view, references are opaque.

Passing references, instead of direct pointers to objects, enables the virtual machine to manage objects in more flexible ways. Figure 11.4 illustrates one such flexibility. While native code is holding a reference, the virtual machine may perform a garbage collection that results in the object being copied from one area of memory to another. The virtual machine can automatically update the content of the reference so that although the object has moved, the reference is still valid.

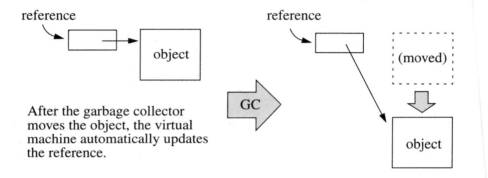

Figure 11.4   Relocating an Object while Native Code Holds a Reference

11.6.1   Global and Local References

The JNI creates two kinds of object references for native code: local and global references. Local references are valid for the duration of a native method invocation and are automatically freed after the native method returns. Global references remain valid until they are explicitly freed.

Objects are passed to native methods as local references. Most JNI functions return local references. The JNI allows the programmer to create global references from local references. JNI functions that take objects as arguments accept both global and local references. A native method may return either a local or a global reference to the virtual machine as its result.

Local references are only valid in the thread in which they are created. Native code must not pass local references from one thread to another.

A NULL reference in the JNI refers to the null object in the Java virtual machine. A local or global reference whose value is not NULL does not refer to a null object.

11.6.2 Implementing Local References

To implement local references, the Java virtual machine creates a registry for each transition of control from the virtual machine to a native method. A registry maps nonmovable local references to object pointers. Objects in the registery cannot be garbage collected. All objects passed to the native method, including those that are returned as the results of JNI function calls, are automatically added to the registry. The registry is deleted after the native method returns, allowing its entries to be garbage collected. Figure 11.5 illustrates how the local references registry is created and deleted. The Java virtual machine frame that corresponds to the native method contains a pointer to the local reference registry. A method D.f calls native method C.g. C.g is implemented by the C function Java_C_g. The virtual machine creates a local reference registry before entering Java_C_g and deletes the local reference registry after Java_C_g returns.

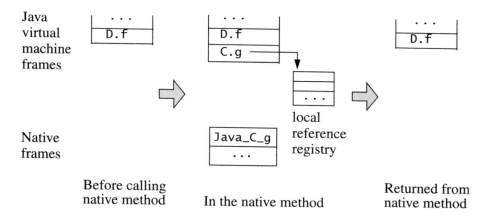

Figure 11.5   Creating and Deleting a Local Reference Registry

There are different ways to implement a registry, such as using a stack, a table, a linked list, or a hash table. Although reference counting may be used to avoid duplicated entries in the registry, a JNI implementation is not obliged to detect and collapse duplicate entries.

Local references cannot be implemented faithfully by conservatively scanning the native stack. Native code may store local references into global or C heap data structures.

11.6.3 Weak Global References

Java 2 SDK release 1.2 introduces a new kind of global reference: weak global references. Unlike normal global references, a weak global reference allows the referenced object to be garbage collected. After the underlying object is garbage collected, a weak global reference is cleared. Native code can test whether a weak global reference is cleared by using `IsSameObject` to compare the reference against NULL.

11.7 Accessing Objects

The JNI provides a rich set of accessor functions for references to objects. This means that the same native method implementation works no matter how the virtual machine represents objects internally. This is a crucial design decision enabling the JNI to be supported by any virtual machine implementation.

The overhead of using accessor functions through opaque references is higher than that of direct access to C data structures. We believe that, in most cases, native methods perform nontrivial tasks that overshadow the cost of the extra function call.

11.7.1 Accessing Primitive Arrays

The function call overhead is not acceptable, however, for repeated access to values of primitive data types in large objects, such as integer arrays and strings. Consider native methods that are used to perform vector and matrix calculations. It would be grossly inefficient to iterate through an integer array and retrieve every element with a function call.

One solution introduces a notion of "pinning" so that the native method can ask the virtual machine not to move the contents of an array. The native method then receives a direct pointer to the elements. This approach, however, has two implications:

- The garbage collector must support pinning. In many implementations, pinning is undesirable because it complicates garbage collection algorithms and leads to memory fragmentation.

- The virtual machine must lay out primitive arrays contiguously in memory. Although this is the natural implementation for most primitive arrays, boolean arrays can be implemented as packed or unpacked. A packed boolean array uses one bit for each element, whereas an unpacked one typically uses one byte for each element. Therefore, native code that relies on the exact layout of boolean arrays will not be portable.

The JNI adopts a compromise that addresses both of the above problems.

First, the JNI provides a set of functions (for example, `GetIntArrayRegion` and `SetIntArrayRegion`) to copy primitive array elements between a segment of a primitive array and a native memory buffer. Use these functions if the native method needs to access only a small number of elements in a large array or if the native method needs to make a copy of the array anyway.

Second, programmers can use another set of functions (for example, `GetIntArrayElements`) to try to obtain a pinned version of array elements. Depending upon the virtual machine implementation, however, these functions may cause storage allocation and copying. Whether these functions in fact copy the array depends upon the virtual machine implementation as follows:

- If the garbage collector supports pinning, and the layout of the array is the same as that of a native array of the same type, then no copying is needed.

- Otherwise, the array is copied to a nonmovable memory block (for example, in the C heap) and the necessary format conversion is performed. A pointer to the copy is returned.

Native code calls a third set of functions (for example, `ReleaseIntArrayElements`) to inform the virtual machine that the native code no longer needs to access the array elements. When that happens, the virtual machine either unpins the array or reconciles the original array with its nonmovable copy and frees the copy.

This approach provides flexibility. A garbage collector algorithm can make separate decisions about copying or pinning for each array. Under a particular implementation scheme the garbage collector might copy small arrays, but pin large arrays.

Finally, Java 2 SDK release 1.2 introduces two new functions: `GetPrimitiveArrayCritical` and `ReleasePrimitiveArrayCritical`. These functions can be used in ways similar to, for example, `GetIntArrayElements` and `ReleaseIntArrayElements`. There are, however, significant restrictions on the native code after it obtains a pointer to array elements using `GetPrimitiveArrayCritical` and before it releases the pointer using `ReleasePrimitiveArrayCritical`. Inside a "critical region" the native code should not run for an indefinite period of time, must not invoke arbitrary JNI functions, and must not perform operations that might cause the current thread to block and wait for another thread in the virtual machine. Given these restrictions, the virtual machine can temporarily disable garbage collection while giving the native code direct access to array elements. Because no pinning support is needed, `GetPrimitive-`

ArrayCritical is more likely to return a direct pointer to the primitive array elements than, for example, GetIntArrayElements.

A JNI implementation must ensure that native methods running in multiple threads can simultaneously access the same array. For example, the JNI may keep an internal counter for each pinned array so that one thread does not unpin an array that is also pinned by another thread. Note that the JNI does not need to lock primitive arrays for exclusive access by a native method. Simultaneously updating an array from different threads is allowed, although this leads to nondeterministic results.

11.7.2 Fields and Methods

The JNI allows native code to access fields and to call methods defined in the Java programming language. The JNI identifies methods and fields by their symbolic names and type descriptors. A two-step process factors out the cost of locating the field or method from its name and descriptor. For example, to read an integer instance field i in class cls, native code first obtains a field ID, as follows:

```
jfieldID fid = env->GetFieldID(env, cls, "i", "I");
```

The native code can then use the field ID repeatedly, without the cost of field lookup, as follows:

```
jint value = env->GetIntField(env, obj, fid);
```

A field or method ID remains valid until the virtual machine unloads the class or interface that defines the corresponding field or method. After the class or interface is unloaded, the method or field ID becomes invalid.

Programmers can derive a field or method ID from the classes or interfaces where the corresponding field or method can be resolved. The field or method can be defined in the class or interface itself or inherited from superclasses or superinterfaces. *The Java™ Virtual Machine Specification* contains the precise rules of resolving fields and methods. *The JNI implementation must derive the same field or method ID for a given name and descriptor from two classes or interfaces if the same field or method definition is resolved from these two classes or interfaces.* For example, if B defines field fld, and C inherits fld from B, then the programmer is guaranteed to obtain the same field ID for field name "fld" from both classes B and C.

The JNI does not impose any restrictions on how field and method IDs are implemented internally.

Note that you need both the field name and field descriptor to obtain a field ID from a given class or interface. This might seem unnecessary because fields cannot be overloaded in the Java programming language. It is legal, however, to have overloaded fields in a class file, and to run such class files on Java virtual machines. Therefore, the JNI is able to handle legal class files that are not generated by a compiler for the Java programming language.

Programmers can use the JNI to call methods or access fields only if they already know the names and types of the methods or fields. In comparison, the Java Core Reflection API allows programmers to determine the set of fields and methods in a given class or interface. It is sometimes useful to be able to reflect on class or interface types in native code as well. Java 2 SDK release 1.2 provides new JNI functions that are designed to work with the existing Java Core Reflection API. The new functions include one pair that converts between JNI field IDs and instances of the `java.lang.reflect.Field` class, and another pair that converts between JNI method IDs and instances of the `java.lang.reflect.Method` class.

11.8 Errors and Exceptions

Errors made in JNI programming are different from exceptions that occur in the Java virtual machine implementation. Programmer errors are caused by misuses of JNI functions. The programmer, for example, may mistakenly pass an object reference instead of a class reference to `GetFieldID`. Java virtual machine exceptions are raised, for example, by out-of-memory situations that occur when native code tries to allocate an object through the JNI.

11.8.1 No Checking for Programming Errors

The JNI functions do not check for programming errors. Passing illegal arguments to JNI functions results in undefined behavior. The reason for this design decision is as follows:

- Forcing JNI functions to check for all possible error conditions degrades the performance in all (typically correct) native methods.

- In many cases there is not enough runtime type information to perform such checking.

Most C library functions do not guard against programming errors. The `printf` function, for example, usually triggers a runtime error instead of returning an error code when it receives an invalid address. Forcing C library functions to check for all possible error conditions would likely result in such checks being duplicated, once in the user code and then again in the library.

Although the JNI specification does not require the virtual machine to check for programming errors, virtual machine implementations are encouraged to provide checks for common mistakes. For example, a virtual machine may perform more checking in a debug version of the JNI function table (§11.5.2).

11.8.2   Java Virtual Machine Exceptions

The JNI does not rely on exception handling mechanisms in native programming languages. Native code may cause the Java virtual machine to throw an exception by calling Throw or ThrowNew. A pending exception is recorded in the current thread. Unlike exceptions thrown in the Java programming language, exceptions thrown in native code do not immediately disrupt the current execution.

There is no standard exception handling mechanism in native languages. Thus, JNI programmers are expected to check for and handle exceptions after each operation that can potentially throw an exception. JNI programmers may deal with an exception in two ways:

- The native method may choose to return immediately, causing the exception to be thrown in the code that initiated the native method call.

- The native code may clear the exception by calling ExceptionClear and then execute its own exception-handling code.

It is extremely important to check, handle, and clear a pending exception before calling any subsequent JNI functions. Calling most JNI functions with a pending exception leads to undefined results. The following is the complete list of JNI functions that can be called safely when there is a pending exception:

```
ExceptionOccurred
ExceptionDescribe
ExceptionClear
ExceptionCheck

ReleaseStringChars
ReleaseStringUTFchars
ReleaseStringCritical
Release<Type>ArrayElements
ReleasePrimitiveArrayCritical
DeleteLocalRef
DeleteGlobalRef
DeleteWeakGlobalRef
MonitorExit
```

The first four functions are directly related to exception handling. The remaining ones are common in that they release various virtual machine resources exposed through the JNI. It is often necessary to be able to free resources when exceptions occur.

11.8.3 Asynchronous Exceptions

One thread may raise an asynchronous exception in another thread by calling `Thread.stop`. An asynchronous exception does not affect the execution of native code in the current thread until:

- the native code calls one of the JNI functions that could raise synchronous exceptions, or
- the native code uses `ExceptionOccurred` to check for synchronous and asynchronous exceptions explicitly.

Only those JNI functions that could potentially raise synchronous exceptions check for asynchronous exceptions.

Native methods may insert `ExceptionOccurred` checks in necessary places (such as in tight loops without other exception checks) to ensure that the current thread responds to asynchronous exceptions in a reasonable amount of time.

The Java thread API that generates asynchronous exceptions, `Thread.stop`, has been deprecated in Java 2 SDK release 1.2. Programmers are strongly discouraged from using `Thread.stop` because it generally leads to unreliable programs. This is particularly a problem for JNI code. For example, many JNI libraries written today do not carefully follow the rules of checking for asynchronous exceptions described in this section.

CHAPTER 12

JNI Types

THIS chapter specifies the standard data types defined by the JNI. C and C++ code should include the header file jni.h before referring to these types.

12.1 Primitive and Reference Types

The JNI defines a set of C/C++ types that correspond to the primitive and reference types in the Java programming language.

12.1.1 Primitive Types

The following table describes the primitive types in the Java programming language and the corresponding types in the JNI. Like their counterparts in the Java programming language, all primitive types in the JNI have well-defined sizes.

Java Language Type	Native Type	Description
boolean	jboolean	unsigned 8 bits
byte	jbyte	signed 8 bits
char	jchar	unsigned 16 bits
short	jshort	signed 16 bits
int	jint	signed 32 bits
long	jlong	signed 64 bits
float	jfloat	32 bits
double	jdouble	64 bits

The jsize integer type is used to describe cardinal indices and sizes:

```
typedef jint jsize;
```

12.1.2   Reference Types

The JNI includes a number of reference types that correspond to different kinds of reference types in the Java programming language. JNI reference types are organized in the hierarchy shown below.

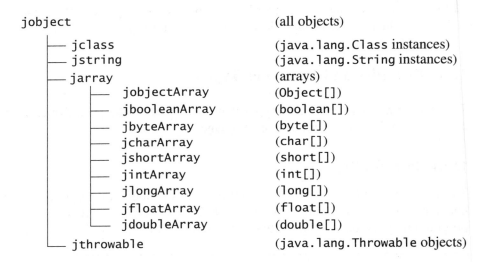

```
jobject                                   (all objects)
      ├── jclass                          (java.lang.Class instances)
      ├── jstring                         (java.lang.String instances)
      ├── jarray                          (arrays)
      │         ├── jobjectArray          (Object[])
      │         ├── jbooleanArray         (boolean[])
      │         ├── jbyteArray            (byte[])
      │         ├── jcharArray            (char[])
      │         ├── jshortArray           (short[])
      │         ├── jintArray             (int[])
      │         ├── jlongArray            (long[])
      │         ├── jfloatArray           (float[])
      │         └── jdoubleArray          (double[])
      └── jthrowable                      (java.lang.Throwable objects)
```

When used in the C programming language, all other JNI reference types are defined to be the same as jobject. For example:

```
typedef jobject jclass;
```

When used in the C++ programming language, the JNI introduces a set of dummy classes to express the subtyping relationship among various reference types:

```
class _jobject {};
class _jclass : public _jobject {};
class _jthrowable : public _jobject {};
```

```
class _jstring : public _jobject {};
class _jarray : public _jobject {};
class _jbooleanArray : public _jarray {};
class _jbyteArray : public _jarray {};
class _jcharArray : public _jarray {};
class _jshortArray : public _jarray {};
class _jintArray : public _jarray {};
class _jlongArray : public _jarray {};
class _jfloatArray : public _jarray {};
class _jdoubleArray : public _jarray {};
class _jobjectArray : public _jarray {};

typedef _jobject *jobject;
typedef _jclass *jclass;
typedef _jthrowable *jthrowable;
typedef _jstring *jstring;
typedef _jarray *jarray;
typedef _jbooleanArray *jbooleanArray;
typedef _jbyteArray *jbyteArray;
typedef _jcharArray *jcharArray;
typedef _jshortArray *jshortArray;
typedef _jintArray *jintArray;
typedef _jlongArray *jlongArray;
typedef _jfloatArray *jfloatArray;
typedef _jdoubleArray *jdoubleArray;
typedef _jobjectArray *jobjectArray;
```

12.1.3 The jvalue Type

The jvalue type is a union of the reference types and primitive types. It is defined as follows:

```
typedef union jvalue {
    jboolean z;
    jbyte    b;
    jchar    c;
    jshort   s;
    jint     i;
    jlong    j;
    jfloat   f;
    jdouble  d;
    jobject  l;
} jvalue;
```

12.2   Field and Method IDs

Method and field IDs are regular C pointer types:

```
struct _jfieldID;                 /* opaque structure */
typedef struct _jfieldID *jfieldID;   /* field ID */
struct _jmethodID;                /* opaque structure */
typedef struct _jmethodID *jmethodID; /* method ID */
```

12.3   String Formats

The JNI uses C strings to represent class names, field and method names, and field and method descriptors. These strings are in the UTF-8 format.

12.3.1   UTF-8 Strings

UTF-8 strings are encoded so that character sequences that contain only non-null ASCII characters can be represented using only one byte per character, but characters of up to 16 bits can be represented. All characters in the range '\u0001' to '\u007F' are represented by a single byte, as follows:

0	bits 6-0

The seven bits of data in the byte give the value of the character that is represented. The null character ('\u000') and characters in the range '\u0080' to '\u07FF' are represented by a pair of bytes, x and y, as follows:

x: | 1 | 1 | 0 | bits 10-6 | y: | 1 | 0 | bits 5-0 |

The bytes represent the character with the value $((x \,\&\, 0x1f) << 6) + (y \,\&\, 0x3f)$.

    Characters in the range '\u0800' to '\uFFFF' are represented by three bytes, x, y, and z:

x: | 1 | 1 | 1 | 0 | bits 15-12 | y: | 1 | 0 | bits 11-6 | z: | 1 | 0 | bits 5-0 |

The character with the value $((x \,\&\, 0xf) << 12) + (y \,\&\, 0x3f) << 6) + (z \,\&\, 0x3f)$ is represented by the three bytes.

There are two differences between this format and the standard UTF-8 format. First, the null byte (byte)0 is encoded using the two-byte format rather than the one-byte format. This means that JNI UTF-8 strings never have embedded nulls. Second, only the one-byte, two-byte, and three-byte formats are used. The JNI does not recognize the longer UTF-8 formats.

12.3.2 Class Descriptors

A class descriptor represents the name of a class or an interface. It can be derived from a fully qualified class or interface name as defined in *The Java™ Language Specification* by substituting the "." character with the "/" character. For example, the class descriptor for java.lang.String is:

    "java/lang/String"

Array classes are formed using the "[" character followed by the field descriptor (§12.3.3) of the element type. The class descriptor for "int[]" is:

    "[I"

and the class descriptor for "double[][][]" is:

    "[[[D"

12.3.3 Field Descriptors

The field descriptors for eight primitive types are as follows:

Field Descriptor	Java Language Type
Z	boolean
B	byte
C	char
S	short
I	int
J	long
F	float
D	double

Field descriptors of reference types begin with the "L" character, followed by the class descriptor, and terminated by the ";" character. Field descriptors of array types are formed following the same rule as class descriptors of array classes. The following are some examples of field descriptors for reference types and their Java programming language counterparts.

Field Descriptor	Java Language Type
"Ljava/lang/String;"	String
"[I"	int[]
"[Ljava/lang/Object;"	Object[]

12.3.4 Method Descriptors

Method descriptors are formed by placing the field descriptors of all argument types in a pair of parentheses, and following that by the field descriptor of the return type. There are no spaces or other separator characters between the argument types. "V" is used to denote the void method return type. Constructors use "V" as their return type, and use "<init>" as their name.

Here are some examples of JNI method descriptors and their corresponding method and constructor types.

Method Descriptor	Java Language Type
"()Ljava/lang/String;"	String f();
"(ILjava/lang/Class;)J"	long f(int i, Class c);
"([B)V"	String(byte[] bytes);

12.4 Constants

JNIEXPORT and JNICALL are macros used to specify the calling and linkage convention of both JNI functions and native method implementations. The programmer must place the JNIEXPORT macro before the function return type and the JNICALL macro between the function name and the return type. For example:

```
JNIEXPORT jint JNICALL
Java_pkg_Cls_f(JNIEnv *env, jobject this);
```

is the prototype for a C function that implements pkg.Cls.f, whereas:

```
jint (JNICALL *f_ptr)(JNIEnv *env, jobject this);
```

is the function pointer variable that can be assigned the Java_pkg_Cls_f function.
JNI_FALSE and JNI_TRUE are constants defined for the jboolean type:

```
#define JNI_FALSE  0
#define JNI_TRUE   1
```

JNI_OK represents the successful return value of JNI functions, and JNI_ERR is sometimes used to represent error conditions.

```
#define JNI_OK     0
#define JNI_ERR    (-1)
```

Not all error conditions are represented by JNI_ERR because the JNI specification does not currently include a standard set of error codes. JNI functions return JNI_OK on success, and a negative number on failure.

The following two constants are used in functions that release the native copy of primitive arrays. An example of such functions is ReleaseIntArrayElements. JNI_COMMIT forces the native array to be copied back to the original array in the Java virtual machine. JNI_ABORT frees the memory allocated for the native array without copying back the new contents.

```
#define JNI_COMMIT 1
#define JNI_ABORT  2
```

Java 2 SDK release 1.2 introduces two constants representing the JNI version numbers.

```
#define JNI_VERSION_1_1 0x00010001 /* JNI version 1.1 */
#define JNI_VERSION_1_2 0x00010002 /* JNI version 1.2 */
```

A native application may determine whether it is being compiled against the 1.1 or 1.2 version of the jni.h file by performing the following conditional compilation:

```
#ifdef JNI_VERSION_1_2
/* compiling against Java 2 SDK 1.2's jni.h */
#else
/* compiling against JDK 1.1's jni.h */
#endif
```

The following constants represent the special error codes returned by the GetEnv function, which is part of the JavaVM Interface:

```
#define JNI_EDETACHED (-2)    /* thread detached from the VM */
#define JNI_EVERSION  (-3)    /* JNI version error */
```

CHAPTER 13

JNI Functions

THIS chapter specifies the JNI functions. We will use the term "must" to describe the restrictions placed on JNI programmers. For example, when a certain JNI function *must* receive a non-NULL object, it is the programmer's responsibility not to pass NULL to that function. As a result, a JNI implementation does not need to check for possibly receiving NULL pointers in that function. If the programmer passes NULL to that function, the resulting behavior is undefined.

We will begin with a summary of JNI functions. The main body of the chapter contains the detailed specifications of all JNI functions.

13.1 Summary of the JNI Functions

The JNI functions fall into one of four categories depending on where they are defined and what they are used for. First of all, a virtual machine implementation exports a set of native functions. These functions are part of the invocation interface. They can be used to accomplish tasks such as creating a *virtual machine instance* in a native application. Second, the JavaVM interface represents a virtual machine instance. The JavaVM interface provides functions that allow, for example, native threads to attach to a virtual machine instance. Third, a native library that implements native methods may export special handler functions that are called when a virtual machine implementation loads and unloads the native library. Finally, the JNIEnv interface supports JNI features such as creating objects, accessing fields, and calling methods.

13.1.1 Directly-Exported Invocation Interface Functions

A virtual machine implementation directly exports the following three functions as part of the invocation interface:

```
JNI_GetDefaultJavaVMInitArgs
JNI_CreateJavaVM
JNI_GetCreatedJavaVMs
```

The `JNI_GetDefaultJavaVMInitArgs` function provides the values of default initialization arguments used to create a virtual machine instance. The information is specific to the virtual machine implementation in JDK release 1.1. This function is no longer useful in Java 2 SDK release 1.2 but is still supported for backward compatibility.

The `JNI_CreateJavaVM` function creates a virtual machine instance according to a given set of initialization arguments. You specify initialization arguments in JDK release 1.1 by setting the fields of a C structure. Java 2 SDK release 1.2 supports a more flexible way to specify the initialization arguments but still supports the same JDK 1.1 style initialization structure for backward compatibility.

The `JNI_GetCreatedJavaVMs` function returns all virtual machine instances that have been created in the current process. A particular JNI implementation need not be able to create more than one virtual machine instance in the same process. Neither JDK release 1.1 nor Java 2 SDK release 1.2 supports the creation of more than one virtual machine instance in the same process.

A native application that embeds a virtual machine instance can invoke any of these functions. The native application may either link against the virtual machine library that exports these functions, or use native dynamic linking mechanisms to load the virtual machine library and locate any of the exported functions at run time.

13.1.2 The JavaVM Interface

The `JavaVM` interface is a pointer to a pointer to a function table. The first three entries in the function table are reserved for future compatibility with the Microsoft COM interface and are set to `NULL`. The remaining four entries are part of the invocation interface:

```
DestroyJavaVM
AttachCurrentThread
DetachCurrentThread
GetEnv
```

Unlike the `JNIEnv` interface pointer, which is specific to a single thread, a `JavaVM` interface pointer represents an entire virtual machine instance and is valid for all threads in the virtual machine instance.

The `DestroyJavaVM` function unloads the virtual machine instance denoted by the `JavaVM` interface pointer. The `AttachCurrentThread` function sets up the current native thread to run as part of a virtual machine instance. Once a thread is attached to the virtual machine instance, it can then make JNI function calls to perform such tasks as accessing objects and invoking methods. The `Detach-CurrentThread` function informs a virtual machine instance that the current thread no longer needs to issue JNI function calls, allowing the virtual machine implementation to perform cleanups and free resources.

The GetEnv function is new in Java 2 SDK release 1.2. It can serve two purposes. First, it can be used to check whether the current thread is attached to a virtual machine instance. Second, it can be used to obtain other interfaces, such as the JNIEnv interface, from the JavaVM interface pointer.

13.1.3 Functions Defined in Native Libraries

Java 2 SDK release 1.2 allows the programmer to export additional handler functions to be invoked when a virtual machine implementation loads and unloads a native library. When the virtual machine implementation loads a native library, it searches for and invokes the exported function entry JNI_OnLoad. When the virtual machine implementation unloads a native library, it searches for and invokes the exported function entry JNI_OnUnload.

13.1.4 The JNIEnv Interface

The JNIEnv interface supports the core features of the JNI. Virtual machine implementations pass a JNIEnv interface pointer as the first argument to each native method. Native code may also obtain a JNIEnv interface pointer by calling the GetEnv function on a JavaVM interface pointer. Although a JNIEnv interface pointer is valid only in a particular thread, the JavaVM interface pointer is valid for all threads in a virtual machine instance.

A JNIEnv interface pointer is a pointer to a pointer to a function table. The first three entries in the function table are reserved for future compatibility with Microsoft COM interface and are set to NULL. The fourth entry in the function table is reserved for future use and is also set to NULL.

The remainder of this chapter will cover all the entries in the JNIEnv interface in detail. For now we give a high-level overview.

Version Information

- GetVersion returns the version of the JNIEnv interface.

Class and Interface Operations

- DefineClass defines a class or interface type from a native byte array representing the raw class file data.
- FindClass returns a reference to a class or interface type of a given name.
- GetSuperclass returns the superclass of a given class or interface.

- `IsAssignableFrom` checks if an instance of one class or interface can be assigned to an instance of another class or interface, and is useful for runtime type checking.

Exceptions

- `Throw` and `ThrowNew` raise an exception in the current thread.
- `ExceptionOccurred` and `ExceptionCheck` check for pending exceptions in the current thread. `ExceptionCheck` is new in Java 2 SDK release 1.2.
- `ExceptionDescribe` prints a diagnostic message about the pending exception.
- `ExceptionClear` clears the pending exception.
- `FatalError` prints a message and terminates the current virtual machine instance.

Global and Local References

- `NewGlobalRef` creates a global reference, `DeleteGlobalRef` deletes one.
- `NewWeakGlobalRef` and `DeleteWeakGlobalRef` manage weak global references. Both are new in Java 2 SDK release 1.2.
- `DeleteLocalRef` reclaims the virtual machine resource needed for a local reference.
- `NewLocalRef` is new in Java 2 SDK release 1.2.
- `EnsureLocalCapacity` reserves space in the current thread for a fixed number of local references to be created. `EnsureLocalCapacity` is new in Java 2 SDK release 1.2.
- `PushLocalFrame` and `PopLocalFrame` create a nested scope for local references. Both functions are new in Java 2 SDK release 1.2.

Object Operations

- `AllocObject` allocates an uninitialized object.
- `NewObject` allocates an object and runs one of its constructors.
- `GetObjectClass` returns the class of a given instance.
- `IsInstanceOf` checks if a given object is an instance of a given class or interface.
- `IsSameObject` checks if two references refer to the same object.

Instance Field Access

- GetFieldID performs a symbolic lookup on a given class and returns the field ID of a named instance field.

- Functions of the *Get<Type>Field* and *Set<Type>Field* families access instance fields.

Static Field Access

- GetStaticFieldID performs a symbolic lookup on a given class or interface and returns the field ID of a named static field.

- Functions of the *GetStatic<Type>Field* and *SetStatic<Type>Field* families access static fields.

Instance Method Calls

- GetMethodID performs a symbolic lookup on a given class or interface and returns the method ID of an instance method or a constructor.

- Functions of the *Call<Type>Method* family invoke instance methods.

- Functions of the *CallNonvirtual<Type>Method* family invoke either instance methods of a superclass or constructors.

Static Method Calls

- GetStaticMethodID performs a symbolic lookup on a given class and returns the method ID of a static method.

- Functions of the *CallStatic<Type>Method* family invoke static methods.

String Operations

- NewString creates a java.lang.String object representing a native Unicode string.

- NewStringUTF creates a java.lang.String object representing a native UTF-8 string.

- GetStringLength returns the number of Unicode characters in a string represented by a java.lang.String object.

- GetStringLengthUTF returns the number of UTF-8 bytes needed to encode all characters in a string represented by a given java.lang.String object.

- GetStringChars and ReleaseStringChars access the content of a java.lang.String object as a pointer to a Unicode string.

- `GetStringUTFChars` and `ReleaseStringUTFChars` access the content of a java.lang.String objectas a pointer to a UTF-8 string.
- `GetStringCritical` and `ReleaseStringCritical` access the content of a java.lang.String object with minimum overhead. Both functions are new in Java 2 SDK release 1.2.
- `GetStringRegion` and `GetStringUTFRegion` copy the contents of a java.lang.String object into a native buffer. Both functions are new in Java 2 SDK release 1.2.

Array Operations

- `GetArrayLength` returns the number of elements in an array.
- `NewObjectArray` creates an array of objects, whereas functions of the *New<Type>Array* family create arrays of primitive types.
- `GetObjectArrayElement` and `SetObjectArrayElement` allow native code to access arrays of reference types.
- Functions of the *Get<Type>ArrayElements* and *Release<Type>Array-Elements* families access all the elements in arrays of primitive types.
- Functions of the *Get<Type>ArrayRegion* and *Set<Type>ArrayRegion* families copy multiple elements in or out of arrays of primitive types.
- `GetPrimitiveArrayCritical` and `ReleasePrimitiveArrayCritical` access elements in an array of primitive types with minimum overhead. Both functions are new in Java 2 SDK release 1.2.

Native Method Registration

- `RegisterNatives` and `UnregisterNatives` allow native code to eagerly link and unlink native methods.

Monitor Operations

- `MonitorEnter` and `MonitorExit` synchronize on the monitor associated with objects.

JavaVM Interface

- `GetJavaVM` returns the `JavaVM` interface pointer for the current virtual machine instance.

Reflection Support

- FromReflectedField converts instances of java.lang.reflect.Field in the Java Core Reflection API into field IDs. FromReflectedField is new in Java 2 SDK release 1.2.

- FromReflectedMethod converts instances of java.lang.reflect.Method or instances of java.lang.reflect.Constructor into method IDs. FromReflectedMethod is new in Java 2 SDK release 1.2.

- ToReflectedField and ToReflectedMethod carry out the conversions in the opposite direction. Both functions are new in Java 2 SDK release 1.2.

The flexibility of an interface pointer makes it easy to evolve (§11.5.2) the JNIEnv interface. A future version of the JNI specification could introduce a new interface, say a JNIEnv2 interface, that is different from the current version of the JNIEnv. A future virtual machine implementation can maintain backward compatibility by simultaneously supporting both JNIEnv and JNIEnv2 interfaces. The return value of the JNI_OnLoad handler of a native library informs the virtual machine implementation about the version of the JNI interface expected by the native library. For example, a native library can presently implement a native method Foo.f using a native function Java_Foo_f as follows:

```
JNIEXPORT void JNICALL
Java_Foo_f(JNIEnv *env, jobject this, jint arg)
{
    ... (*env)->... /* some call to the JNIEnv interface */
}
```

In the future, the same native method may also be implemented as follows:

```
/* possible implementation of Foo.f using a hypothetical
 * future version (JNI_VERSION_2_0) of the JNI interface */
JNIEnv2 *g_env;

JNIEXPORT jint JNICALL
JNIOnLoad(JavaVM *vm, void *reserved)
{
    jint res;
    /* cache JNIEnv2 interface pointer in global variable */
    res = (*vm)->GetEnv(vm, (void **)&g_env, JNI_VERSION_2_0);
    if (res < 0) {
        return res;
    }
    return JNI_VERSION_2_0; /* the required JNI version */
}
```

```
JNIEXPORT void JNICALL
Java_Foo_f(jobject this, jint arg)
{
    ... (*g_env)->... /* some call to the JNIEnv2 interface */
}
```

To highlight interface evolution, we have made the hypothetical future JNIEnv2 interface different from the JNIEnv interface in a number of ways. The JNIEnv2 interface need not be thread-local, and thus can be cached in a global variable. The JNIEnv2 interface need not be passed as the first argument to the Java_Foo_f native function. The name encoding convention (§11.3) of native method implementation functions such as Java_Foo_f need not be changed. Virtual machine implementations rely on the return value of the JNI_OnLoad handler to determine the argument passing convention of native method implementation functions in a given native library.

13.2　Specification of JNI Functions

This section contains the complete specification of the JNI functions. For each function, we provide information on the following:

- function prototypes
- a detailed description, including the parameters, return values, and possible exceptions
- linkage information, including 0-based index for all entries in the JNIEnv and JavaVM interface function tables

AllocObject

Prototype　　　`jobject AllocObject(JNIEnv *env, jclass clazz);`

Description　　　Allocates a new object without invoking any of the constructors for the object. Returns a local reference to the object.

The `clazz` argument must not refer to an array class. Use the *New<Type>Array* family of functions to allocate array objects.

Use `NewObject`, `NewObjectV`, or `NewObjectA` to allocate an object and execute one of its contructors.

Linkage　　　Index 27 in the `JNIEnv` interface function table.

Parameters　　　env: the `JNIEnv` interface pointer.

`clazz`: a reference to the class of the object to be allocated.

Return Values　　Returns a local reference to the newly allocated object, or `NULL` if the object cannot be allocated. Returns `NULL` if and only if an invocation of this function has thrown an exception.

Exceptions　　　`InstantiationException`: if the class is an interface or an abstract class.

`OutOfMemoryError`: if the system runs out of memory.

AttachCurrentThread

Prototype   jint AttachCurrentThread(JavaVM *vm, void **penv,
                           void *args);

Description   Attaches the current thread to a given virtual machine instance.
                       Once attached to the virtual machine instance, a native thread
                       has an associated java.lang.Thread instance. An attached
                       native thread may issue JNI function calls. The native thread
                       remains attached to the virtual machine instance until it calls
                       DetachCurrentThread to detach itself.

                       Trying to attach a thread that is already attached simply sets the
                       value pointed to by penv to the JNIEnv of the current thread.

                       A native thread cannot be attached simultaneously to two Java
                       virtual machine instances.

                       In JDK release 1.1, the second argument receives a JNIEnv
                       interface pointer. The third argument is reserved, and should be
                       set to NULL. The default java.lang.Thread constructor auto-
                       matically generates a thread name (for example, "Thread-123")
                       for the associated   java.lang.Thread   instance.   The
                       java.lang.Thread instance belongs to the default thread
                       group "main" created by the virtual machine implementation.

                       In Java 2 SDK release 1.2, the third argument may be set to
                       NULL to preserve the release 1.1 behavior. Alternatively, the
                       third argument may point to the following structure:

```
typedef struct {
    jint version;
    char *name;
    jobject group;
} JavaVMAttachArgs;
```

                       The version field specifies the version of the JNIEnv interface
                       passed back through the second argument. The valid versions
                       accepted by Java 2 SDK release 1.2 are JNI_VERSION_1_1 and
                       JNI_VERSION_1_2.

                       If the name field is not NULL, it points to a UTF-8 string specify-
                       ing the name of the associated java.lang.Thread instance. If
                       the name field is NULL, the default java.lang.Thread construc-

tor generates a thread name (for example, "Thread-123") for the associated java.lang.Thread instance.

If the group field is not NULL, it specifies a global reference of a thread group to which the newly created java.lang.Thread instance is added. If the group field is NULL, the java.lang.Thread instance is added to the default thread group "main" created by the virtual machine implementation.

Linkage   Index 4 in the JavaVM interface function table.

Parameters   vm: the virtual machine instance to which the current thread will be attached.

                     penv: a pointer to the location in which the JNIEnv interface pointer for the current thread will be placed.

                     args: reserved (in JDK release 1.1) or a pointer to a JavaVM-AttachArgs structure (in Java 2 SDK release 1.2).

Return Values   Returns zero on success; otherwise, returns a negative number.

Exceptions   None.

Call<Type>Method

Prototype   *<NativeType> Call<Type>Method*(JNIEnv *env,
            jobject obj, jmethodID methodID, ...);

Forms   This family of functions consists of ten members.

Call<Type>Method	*<NativeType>*
CallVoidMethod	void
CallObjectMethod	jobject
CallBooleanMethod	jboolean
CallByteMethod	jbyte
CallCharMethod	jchar
CallShortMethod	jshort
CallIntMethod	jint
CallLongMethod	jlong
CallFloatMethod	jfloat
CallDoubleMethod	jdouble

Description   Invokes an instance method, specified using a method ID, on an object.

Programmers place all arguments that are to be passed to the method immediately following the methodID argument. The *Call<Type>Method* function accepts these arguments and passes them to the method that the programmer wishes to invoke.

Linkage   Indices in the JNIEnv interface function table.

Call<Type>Method	**Index**
CallVoidMethod	61
CallObjectMethod	34
CallBooleanMethod	37
CallByteMethod	40
CallCharMethod	43
CallShortMethod	46
CallIntMethod	49
CallLongMethod	52
CallFloatMethod	55
CallDoubleMethod	58

Parameters   env: the JNIEnv interface pointer.

obj: a reference to the object on which the method is invoked.

methodID: method ID denoting the method to be invoked.

Additional arguments: arguments to be passed to the method.

Return Values   The result of calling the method.

Exceptions   Any exception raised during the execution of the method.

Call<Type>MethodA

Prototype   <NativeType> Call<Type>MethodA(JNIEnv *env,
                          jobject obj, jmethodID methodID, jvalue *args);

Forms   This family of functions consists of ten members.

Call<Type>MethodA	*<NativeType>*
CallVoidMethodA	void
CallObjectMethodA	jobject
CallBooleanMethodA	jboolean
CallByteMethodA	jbyte
CallCharMethodA	jchar
CallShortMethodA	jshort
CallIntMethodA	jint
CallLongMethodA	jlong
CallFloatMethodA	jfloat
CallDoubleMethodA	jdouble

Description   Invokes an instance method, specified using a method ID, on an object.

Programmers place all arguments to the method in an array of jvalues that immediately follows the methodID argument. The *Call<Type>MethodA* routine accepts the arguments in this array, and, in turn, passes them to the method that the programmer wishes to invoke.

Linkage   Indices in the JNIEnv interface function table.

Call<Type>MethodA	**Index**
CallVoidMethodA	63
CallObjectMethodA	36
CallBooleanMethodA	39
CallByteMethodA	42
CallCharMethodA	45
CallShortMethodA	48
CallIntMethodA	51
CallLongMethodA	54
CallFloatMethodA	57
CallDoubleMethodA	60

Parameters   env: the JNIEnv interface pointer.

obj: a reference to the object on which the method is invoked.

methodID: method ID denoting the method to be invoked.

args: an array of arguments to be passed to the method.

Return Values   Returns the result of calling the method.

Exceptions   Any exception raised during the execution of the method.

Call<Type>MethodV

Prototype

```
<NativeType> Call<Type>MethodV(JNIEnv *env,
    jobject obj, jmethodID methodID, va_list args);
```

Forms

This family of functions consists of ten members.

Call<Type>MethodV	*<NativeType>*
CallVoidMethodV	void
CallObjectMethodV	jobject
CallBooleanMethodV	jboolean
CallByteMethodV	jbyte
CallCharMethodV	jchar
CallShortMethodV	jshort
CallIntMethodV	jint
CallLongMethodV	jlong
CallFloatMethodV	jfloat
CallDoubleMethodV	jdouble

Description

Invokes an instance method, specified using a method ID, on an object.

Programmers place all arguments to the method in an `args` argument of type `va_list` that immediately follows the `methodID` argument. The *Call<Type>MethodV* routine accepts the arguments, and, in turn, passes them to the method that the programmer wishes to invoke.

Linkage   Indices in the `JNIEnv` interface function table.

Call<Type>MethodV	Index
CallVoidMethodV	62
CallObjectMethodV	35
CallBooleanMethodV	38
CallByteMethodV	41
CallCharMethodV	44
CallShortMethodV	47
CallIntMethodV	50
CallLongMethodV	53
CallFloatMethodV	56
CallDoubleMethodV	59

Parameters   env: the `JNIEnv` interface pointer.

obj: a reference to an object on which the method is invoked.

methodID: method ID of the method to be invoked.

args: a `va_list` of arguments passed to the invoked method.

Return Values   Returns the result of calling the method.

Exceptions   Any exception raised during the execution of the method.

CallNonvirtual<Type>Method

Prototype

```
<NativeType> CallNonvirtual<Type>Method(
    JNIEnv *env, jobject obj, jclass clazz,
    jmethodID methodID, ...);
```

Forms   This family of functions consists of ten members.

CallNonvirtual<Type>Method	*<NativeType>*
CallNonvirtualVoidMethod	void
CallNonvirtualObjectMethod	jobject
CallNonvirtualBooleanMethod	jboolean
CallNonvirtualByteMethod	jbyte
CallNonvirtualCharMethod	jchar
CallNonvirtualShortMethod	jshort
CallNonvirtualIntMethod	jint
CallNonvirtualLongMethod	jlong
CallNonvirtualFloatMethod	jfloat
CallNonvirtualDoubleMethod	jdouble

Descriptions   Invokes an instance method, specified using a class and a method ID, on an object.

The *CallNonvirtual<Type>Method* family of functions and the *Call<Type>Method* family of functions are different. *Call<Type>Method* functions invoke the method based on the real class of the object, while *CallNonvirtual<Type>Method* routines invoke the method based on the class, designated by the clazz parameter, from which the method ID is obtained. The clazz parameter must refer to the real class of the object or from one of its superclasses.

Programmers place all arguments that are to be passed to the method immediately following the methodID argument. The *CallNonvirtual<Type>Method* routine accepts these arguments and passes them to the method that the programmer wishes to invoke.

Linkage   Indices in the `JNIEnv` interface function table.

CallNonvirtual<Type>Method	**Index**
CallNonvirtualVoidMethod	91
CallNonvirtualObjectMethod	64
CallNonvirtualBooleanMethod	67
CallNonvirtualByteMethod	70
CallNonvirtualCharMethod	73
CallNonvirtualShortMethod	76
CallNonvirtualIntMethod	79
CallNonvirtualLongMethod	82
CallNonvirtualFloatMethod	85
CallNonvirtualDoubleMethod	88

Parameters   env: the `JNIEnv` interface pointer.

`clazz`: a reference to the class from which the method ID is derived.

`obj`: a reference to the object on which the method is invoked.

`methodID`: a method ID that is valid with the class reference `clazz`.

Additional arguments: arguments to be passed to the method.

Return Values Returns the result of calling the method.

Exceptions   Any exception raised during the execution of the method.

CallNonvirtual<Type>MethodA

Prototype

```
<NativeType> CallNonvirtual<Type>MethodA(
    JNIEnv *env, jobject obj, jclass clazz,
    jmethodID methodID, jvalue *args);
```

Forms

This family of functions consists of ten members.

CallNonvirtual<Type>MethodA	*<NativeType>*
CallNonvirtualVoidMethodA	void
CallNonvirtualObjectMethodA	jobject
CallNonvirtualBooleanMethodA	jboolean
CallNonvirtualByteMethodA	jbyte
CallNonvirtualCharMethodA	jchar
CallNonvirtualShortMethodA	jshort
CallNonvirtualIntMethodA	jint
CallNonvirtualLongMethodA	jlong
CallNonvirtualFloatMethodA	jfloat
CallNonvirtualDoubleMethodA	jdouble

Description

Invokes an instance method, specified using a class and a method ID, on an object.

The *CallNonvirtual<Type>MethodA* families of functions and the *Call<Type>MethodA* families of functions are different. *Call<Type>MethodA* functions invoke the method based on the real class of the object, while *CallNonvirtual<Type>MethodA* routines invoke the method based on the class, designated by the clazz parameter, from which the method ID is obtained. The clazz parameter must refer to the real class of the object or from one of its superclasses.

Programmers place all arguments to the method in an args array of jvalues that immediately follows the methodID argument. The *CallNonvirtual<Type>MethodA* routine accepts the arguments in this array, and, in turn, passes them to the method that the programmer wishes to invoke.

Linkage   Indices in the JNIEnv interface function table.

CallNonvirtual<Type>MethodA	Index
CallNonvirtualVoidMethodA	93
CallNonvirtualObjectMethodA	66
CallNonvirtualBooleanMethodA	69
CallNonvirtualByteMethodA	72
CallNonvirtualCharMethodA	75
CallNonvirtualShortMethodA	78
CallNonvirtualIntMethodA	81
CallNonvirtualLongMethodA	84
CallNonvirtualFloatMethodA	87
CallNonvirtualDoubleMethodA	90

Parameters   env: the JNIEnv interface pointer.

clazz: a reference to the class from which the method ID is derived.

obj: a reference to the object on which the method is invoked.

methodID: a method ID that is valid with the class reference clazz.

args: an array of arguments to be passed to the method.

Return Values   Returns the result of calling the method.

Exceptions   Any exception raised during the execution of the method.

CallNonvirtual<Type>MethodV

Prototype

```
<NativeType> CallNonvirtual<Type>MethodV(
    JNIEnv *env, jobject obj, jclass clazz,
    jmethodID methodID, va_list args);
```

Forms

This family of functions consists of ten members.

CallNonvirtual<Type>MethodV	*<NativeType>*
CallNonvirtualVoidMethodV	void
CallNonvirtualObjectMethodV	jobject
CallNonvirtualBooleanMethodV	jboolean
CallNonvirtualByteMethodV	jbyte
CallNonvirtualCharMethodV	jchar
CallNonvirtualShortMethodV	jshort
CallNonvirtualIntMethodV	jint
CallNonvirtualLongMethodV	jlong
CallNonvirtualFloatMethodV	jfloat
CallNonvirtualDoubleMethodV	jdouble

Description

Invokes an instance method, specified using a class and a method ID, on an object. The methodID argument must be obtained by calling GetMethodID on the class clazz.

The *CallNonvirtual<Type>MethodV* families of functions and the *Call<Type>MethodV* families of functions are different. *Call<Type>MethodV* functions invoke the method based on the real class of the object, while *CallNonvirtual<Type>MethodV* routines invoke the method based on the class, designated by the clazz parameter, from which the method ID is obtained. The clazz parameter must refer to the real class of the object or from one of its superclasses.

Programmers place all arguments to the method in an args argument of type va_list that immediately follows the methodID argument. The *CallNonvirtual<Type>MethodV* routine accepts the arguments, and, in turn, passes them to the method that the programmer wishes to invoke.

Linkage   Indices in the `JNIEnv` interface function table.

CallNonvirtual<Type>MethodV	Index
CallNonvirtualVoidMethodV	92
CallNonvirtualObjectMethodV	65
CallNonvirtualBooleanMethodV	68
CallNonvirtualByteMethodV	71
CallNonvirtualCharMethodV	74
CallNonvirtualShortMethodV	77
CallNonvirtualIntMethodV	80
CallNonvirtualLongMethodV	83
CallNonvirtualFloatMethodV	86
CallNonvirtualDoubleMethodV	89

Parameters   env: the `JNIEnv` interface pointer.

`clazz`: a reference to the class from which the method ID is derived.

`obj`: a reference to the object on which the method is invoked.

`methodID`: a method ID that is valid with the class reference `clazz`.

`args`: a `va_list` of arguments to be passed to the method.

Return Values   Returns the result of calling the method.

Exceptions   Any exception raised during the execution of the method.

CallStatic<Type>Method

Prototype

```
<NativeType> CallStatic<Type>Method(
    JNIEnv *env, jclass clazz,
    jmethodID methodID, ...);
```

Forms   This family of functions consists of ten members.

CallStatic<Type>Method	<NativeType>
CallStaticVoidMethod	void
CallStaticObjectMethod	jobject
CallStaticBooleanMethod	jboolean
CallStaticByteMethod	jbyte
CallStaticCharMethod	jchar
CallStaticShortMethod	jshort
CallStaticIntMethod	jint
CallStaticLongMethod	jlong
CallStaticFloatMethod	jfloat
CallStaticDoubleMethod	jdouble

Description   Invokes a static method, specified using a method ID, on a class. The method must be accessible in clazz, although it may be defined in one of the superclasses of clazz.

Programmers should place all arguments that are to be passed to the method immediately following the methodID argument. The *CallStatic<Type>Method* routine accepts these arguments and passes them to the static method that the programmer wishes to invoke.

Linkage   Indices in the JNIEnv interface function table.

CallStatic<Type>Method	**Index**
CallStaticVoidMethod	141
CallStaticObjectMethod	114
CallStaticBooleanMethod	117
CallStaticByteMethod	120
CallStaticCharMethod	123
CallStaticShortMethod	126
CallStaticIntMethod	129
CallStaticLongMethod	132
CallStaticFloatMethod	135
CallStaticDoubleMethod	138

Parameters   env: the JNIEnv interface pointer.

clazz: a reference to the class object on which the static method is called.

methodID: the static method ID of the method to be called.

Additional arguments: arguments to be passed to the static method.

Return Values Returns the result of calling the static method.

Exceptions   Any exception raised during the execution of the method.

CallStatic<Type>MethodA

Prototype

```
<NativeType> CallStatic<Type>MethodA(
    JNIEnv *env, jclass clazz,
    jmethodID methodID, jvalue *args);
```

Forms

This family of functions consists of ten members.

CallStatic<Type>MethodA	*<NativeType>*
CallStaticVoidMethodA	void
CallStaticObjectMethodA	jobject
CallStaticBooleanMethodA	jboolean
CallStaticByteMethodA	jbyte
CallStaticCharMethodA	jchar
CallStaticShortMethodA	jshort
CallStaticIntMethodA	jint
CallStaticLongMethodA	jlong
CallStaticFloatMethodA	jfloat
CallStaticDoubleMethodA	jdouble

Description

Invokes a static method, specified using a method ID, on a class. The method must be accessible in clazz, although it may be defined in one of the superclasses of clazz.

Programmers should place all arguments to the method in an args array of jvalues that immediately follows the methodID argument. The *CallStatic<Type>MethodA* routine accepts the arguments in this array, and, in turn, passes them to the static method that the programmer wishes to invoke.

Linkage   Indices in the JNIEnv interface function table.

CallStatic<Type>MethodA	Index
CallStaticVoidMethodA	143
CallStaticObjectMethodA	116
CallStaticBooleanMethodA	119
CallStaticByteMethodA	122
CallStaticCharMethodA	125
CallStaticShortMethodA	128
CallStaticIntMethodA	131
CallStaticLongMethodA	134
CallStaticFloatMethodA	137
CallStaticDoubleMethodA	140

Parameters   env: the JNIEnv interface pointer.

clazz: a reference to the class object on which the static method is called.

methodID: the static method ID of the method to be called.

args: an array of arguments to be passed to the static method.

Return Values   Returns the result of calling the static method.

Exceptions   Any exception raised during the execution of the method.

CallStatic<Type>MethodV

Prototype

```
<NativeType> CallStatic<Type>MethodV(
    JNIEnv *env, jclass clazz,
    jmethodID methodID, va_list args);
```

Forms This family of functions consists of ten members.

CallStatic<Type>MethodV	*<NativeType>*
CallStaticVoidMethodV	void
CallStaticObjectMethodV	jobject
CallStaticBooleanMethodV	jboolean
CallStaticByteMethodV	jbyte
CallStaticCharMethodV	jchar
CallStaticShortMethodV	jshort
CallStaticIntMethodV	jint
CallStaticLongMethodV	jlong
CallStaticFloatMethodV	jfloat
CallStaticDoubleMethodV	jdouble

Description Invokes a static method, specified using a method ID, on a class. The method must be accessible in clazz, although it may be defined in one of the superclasses of clazz.

Programmers should place all arguments to the method in an args argument of type va_list that immediately follows the methodID argument. The *CallStatic<Type>MethodV* routine accepts the arguments, and, in turn, passes them to the static method that the programmer wishes to invoke.

Linkage   Indices in the JNIEnv interface function table.

CallStatic<Type>MethodV	Index
CallStaticVoidMethodV	142
CallStaticObjectMethodV	115
CallStaticBooleanMethodV	118
CallStaticByteMethodV	121
CallStaticCharMethodV	124
CallStaticShortMethodV	127
CallStaticIntMethodV	130
CallStaticLongMethodV	133
CallStaticFloatMethodV	136
CallStaticDoubleMethodV	139

Parameters   env: the JNIEnv interface pointer.

clazz: a reference to the class object on which the static method is called.

methodID: the static method ID of the method to be called.

args: a va_list of arguments to be passed to the static method.

Return Values   Returns the result of calling the static method.

Exceptions   Any exception raised during the execution of the method.

DefineClass

Prototype
```
jclass DefineClass(JNIEnv *env, const char *name,
     jobject loader, const jbyte *buf,
     jsize bufLen);
```

Description   Creates a java.lang.Class instance from a buffer of raw class data representing a class or interface. The format of the raw class data is specified by *The Java™ Virtual Machine Specification*.

This function is slightly more general than the java.lang.ClassLoader.defineClass method. This function can define classes or interfaces with the null class loader. The java.lang.ClassLoader.defineClass method is an instance method and thus requires a java.lang.ClassLoader instance.

Linkage   Index 5 in the JNIEnv interface function table.

Parameters   env: the JNIEnv interface pointer.

name: the name of the class or interface to be defined.

loader: a class loader assigned to the defined class or interface.

buf: buffer containing the raw class file data.

bufLen: buffer length.

Return Values   Returns a local reference to the newly defined class or interface object, or NULL if an exception occurs. Returns NULL if and only if an invocation of this function has thrown an exception.

Exceptions   ClassFormatError: if the class data does not specify a valid class or interface.

NoClassDefFoundError: if the class data does not specify the named class or interface to be defined.

ClassCircularityError: if a class or interface would be its own superclass or superinterface.

OutOfMemoryError: if the system runs out of memory.

DeleteGlobalRef

Prototype　　　　void DeleteGlobalRef(JNIEnv *env, jobject gref);

Description　　　Deletes the global reference pointed to by gref. The gref argument must be a global reference, or NULL. The same non-NULL global reference must not be deleted more than once. Deleting a NULL global reference is a no-op.

Linkage　　　　　Index 22 in the JNIEnv interface function table.

Parameters　　　env: the JNIEnv interface pointer.

　　　　　　　　　gref: the global reference to be deleted.

Exceptions　　　None.

DeleteLocalRef

Prototype   void DeleteLocalRef(JNIEnv *env, jobject lref);

Description   Deletes the local reference pointed to by lref. The lref argu-
                     ment must be a local reference, or NULL. The same non-NULL
                     local reference must not be deleted more than once. Deleting a
                     NULL local reference is a no-op.

                     Deleting a local reference that does not belong to the topmost
                     local reference frame is a no-op. Each native method invocation
                     creates a new local reference frame. The PushLocalFrame
                     function (added in Java 2 SDK release 1.2) also creates a new
                     local reference frame.

Linkage   Index 23 in the JNIEnv interface function table.

Parameters   env: the JNIEnv interface pointer.

                     lref: the local reference to be deleted.

Exceptions   None.

DeleteWeakGlobalRef

Prototype

```
void DeleteWeakGlobalRef(JNIEnv *env,
    jobject wref);
```

Description

Deletes a weak global reference. The `wref` argument must be a weak global reference. The same weak global reference must not be deleted more than once.

This function was introduced in Java 2 SDK release 1.2.

Linkage

Index 227 in the `JNIEnv` interface function table.

Parameters

`env`: the `JNIEnv` interface pointer.

`wref`: the weak global reference to be deleted.

Exceptions

None.

DestroyJavaVM

Prototype   `jint DestroyJavaVM(JavaVM *vm);`

Description   Unloads a virtual machine instance and reclaims its resources. The system blocks until the current thread is the only remaining user thread before it attempts to unload the virtual machine instance. This restriction exists because an attached thread may be holding system resources such as locks, windows, and so on. Virtual machine implementations cannot automatically free these resources. By restricting the main thread to be the only running thread when the virtual machine instance is unloaded, the burden of releasing system resources held by arbitrary threads is on the programmer.

The support for `DestroyJavaVM` was not complete in JDK release 1.1; only the main thread may call `DestroyJavaVM`. The virtual machine implementation blocks until the main thread is the only user-level thread and returns a negative error code.

Java 2 SDK release 1.2 still does not support unloading virtual machine instances. There is a slight relaxation to the use of `DestroyJavaVM`, however; any thread may call `DestroyJavaVM`. The virtual machine implementation blocks until the current thread is the only user thread before it returns an error code.

Linkage   Index 3 in the `JavaVM` interface function table.

Parameters   vm: the virtual machine instance that will be destroyed.

Return Values Returns zero on success; otherwise, returns a negative number.

Exceptions   None.

DetachCurrentThread

Prototype   `jint DetachCurrentThread(JavaVM *vm);`

Description   Detaches the current thread from a virtual machine instance. All
monitors held by this thread are released. All threads waiting
for this thread to die (i.e., performing a `Thread.join` on this
thread) are notified.

In JDK release 1.1, the main thread cannot be detached from a
virtual machine instance. Instead, it must call `DestroyJavaVM`
to unload the entire virtual machine instance.

In Java 2 SDK release 1.2, the main thread may be detached
from a virtual machine instance.

Linkage   Index 5 in the `JavaVM` interface function table.

Parameters   vm: the virtual machine instance from which the current thread
will be detached.

Return Values   Returns zero on success; otherwise, returns a negative number.

Exceptions   None.

EnsureLocalCapacity

Prototype

```
jint EnsureLocalCapacity(JNIEnv *env,
    jint capacity);
```

Description

Ensures that at least a given number of local references can be created in the current thread.

Before it enters a native method, the virtual machine implementation ensures that at least **sixteen** local references can be created in the current thread.

Allocating more local references than the ensured capacity may or may not lead to an immediate failure depending on whether the virtual machine implementation has enough memory available. The virtual machine implementation calls FatalError if it is unable to provide the memory for additional local references beyond the ensured capacity.

For debugging support, a virtual machine implementation may give the user warnings when the user creates more local references than the ensured capacity. In Java 2 SDK release 1.2, the programmer can supply the -verbose:jni command line option to turn on these warning messages.

This function was introduced in Java 2 SDK release 1.2.

Linkage

Index 26 in the JNIEnv interface function table.

Parameters

env: the JNIEnv interface pointer.

capacity: the number of local references that will be created.

Return Values

Returns zero on success; otherwise, returns a negative number and throws an exception.

Exceptions

OutOfMemoryError: if the system runs out of memory.

ExceptionCheck

Prototype   jboolean ExceptionCheck(JNIEnv *env);

Description   Determines if an exception has been thrown. The exception stays thrown until either the native code calls ExceptionClear, or the caller of the native method handles the exception.

The difference between this function and ExceptionOccurred is that this function returns a jboolean to indicate whether there is a pending exception, whereas ExceptionOccurred returns a local reference to the pending exception, or returns NULL if there is no pending exception.

This function was introduced in Java 2 SDK release 1.2.

Linkage   Index 228 in the JNIEnv interface function table.

Parameters   env: the JNIEnv interface pointer.

Return Values Returns the JNI_TRUE if there is a pending exception, or JNI_FALSE if there is no pending exception.

Exceptions   None.

ExceptionClear

Prototype   `void ExceptionClear(JNIEnv *env);`

Description   Clears any pending exception that is currently being thrown in the current thread. If no exception is currently being thrown, this function has no effect. This function has no effect on exceptions pending on other threads.

`ExceptionDescribe` also has the side effect of clearing the pending exception.

Linkage   Index 17 in the `JNIEnv` interface function table.

Parameters   env: the `JNIEnv` interface pointer.

Exceptions   None.

ExceptionDescribe

Prototype   `void ExceptionDescribe(JNIEnv *env);`

Description   Prints the pending exception and a backtrace of the stack to the system error-reporting channel `System.out.err`. This is a convenience routine provided for debugging.

This function has the side effect of clearing the pending exception.

Linkage   Index 16 in the `JNIEnv` interface function table.

Parameters   env: the `JNIEnv` interface pointer.

Exceptions   None.

ExceptionOccurred

Prototype   `jthrowable ExceptionOccurred(JNIEnv *env);`

Description   Determines if an exception is pending in the current thread. The exception stays pending until either the native code calls `ExceptionClear`, or the caller of the native method handles the exception.

The difference between this function and `ExceptionCheck` (added in Java 2 SDK release 1.2) is that `ExceptionCheck` returns a `jboolean` to indicate whether there is a pending exception, whereas this function returns a local reference to the pending exception, or returns NULL if there is no pending exception.

Linkage   Index 15 in the `JNIEnv` interface function table.

Parameters   env: the `JNIEnv` interface pointer.

Return Values Returns the exception object that is pending in the current thread, or NULL if no exception is pending.

Exceptions   None.

FatalError

Prototype	`void FatalError(JNIEnv *env, const char *msg);`

Description   Raises a fatal error and does not expect the virtual machine implementation to recover. Prints the message in a system debugging channel, such as `stderr`, and terminates the virtual machine instance.

This function does not return.

Linkage   Index 18 in the `JNIEnv` interface function table.

Parameters   env: the `JNIEnv` interface pointer.

msg: an error message.

Exceptions   None.

FindClass

Prototype   `jclass FindClass(JNIEnv *env, const char *name);`

Description   Returns a reference to the named class or interface. This function was introduced in JDK release 1.1, and has been extended in Java 2 SDK release 1.2. In JDK release 1.1, this function loads a locally defined class or interface. It searches the directories and zip files specified by the CLASSPATH environment variable for the class or interface with the specified name.

In Java 2 SDK release 1.2, `FindClass` locates the class loader associated with the current native method. If the native code belongs to the `null` loader, then it uses the bootstrap class loader to load the named class or interface. Otherwise, it invokes the `ClassLoader.loadClass` method in the corresponding class loader to load the named class or interface.

`FindClass` initializes the class or interface it returns.

The `name` argument is a class descriptor (§12.3.2). For example, the descriptor for the `java.lang.String` class is:

       `"java/lang/String"`

The descriptor of the array class `java.lang.Object[]` is:

       `"[Ljava/lang/Object;"`

Linkage   Index 6 in the `JNIEnv` interface function table.

Parameters   `env`: the `JNIEnv` interface pointer.

`name`: the descriptor of the class or interface to be returned.

Return Values   Returns a local reference to the named class or interface, or `NULL` if the class or interface cannot be loaded. Returns `NULL` if and only if an invocation of this function has thrown an exception.

Exceptions   ClassFormatError: if the class data does not specify a valid class or interface.

ClassCircularityError: if a class or interface would be its own superclass or superinterface.

NoClassDefFoundError: if no definition for a requested class or interface can be found.

OutOfMemoryError: if the system runs out of memory.

ExceptionInInitializerError: if class or interface initialization fails.

FromReflectedField

Prototype   jfieldID FromReflectedField(JNIEnv *env,
                      jobject field);

Description   Converts a java.lang.reflect.Field instance to a field ID.

                  This function was introduced in Java 2 SDK release 1.2.

Linkage   Index 8 in the JNIEnv interface function table.

Parameters   env: the JNIEnv interface pointer.

                  field: a reference to a java.lang.reflect.Field instance.

Return Values Returns the field ID corresponding to the given instance of
                  java.lang.reflect.Field, or NULL if an exception occurs.
                  Returns NULL if and only if an invocation of this function has
                  thrown an exception.

Exceptions   OutOfMemoryError: if the system runs out of memory.

FromReflectedMethod

Prototype   jmethodID FromReflectedMethod(JNIEnv *env,
                         jobject method);

Description   Converts a java.lang.reflect.Method instance or a
                     java.lang.reflect.Constructor instance to a method ID.

                     This function was introduced in Java 2 SDK release 1.2.

Linkage   Index 7 in the JNIEnv interface function table.

Parameters   env: the JNIEnv interface pointer.

                     method: a reference to a java.lang.reflect.Method object or
                     a reference to a java.lang.reflect.Constructor object.

Return Values   Returns a method ID that corresponds to a given instance of the
                     java.lang.reflect.Method class or a given instance of the
                     java.lang.reflect.Constructor class, or NULL if an excep-
                     tion occurs. Returns NULL if and only if an invocation of this
                     function has thrown an exception.

Exceptions   OutOfMemoryError: if the system runs out of memory.

GetArrayLength

Prototype   `jsize GetArrayLength(JNIEnv *env, jarray array);`

Description   Returns the number of elements in a given array. The array argument may denote an array of any element types, including primitive types such as `int` or `double`, or referencs types such as the subclasses of `java.lang.Object` or other array types.

Linkage   Index 171 in the `JNIEnv` interface function table.

Parameters   env: the `JNIEnv` interface pointer.

                   `array`: a reference to the array object whose length is to be determined.

Return Values Returns the length of the array.

Exceptions   None.

Get<Type>ArrayElements

Prototype

```
<NativeType> *Get<Type>ArrayElements(JNIEnv *env,
    <ArrayType> array, jboolean *isCopy);
```

Forms

This family of functions consists of eight members.

Get<Type>ArrayElements	<ArrayType>	<NativeType>
GetBooleanArrayElements	jbooleanArray	jboolean
GetByteArrayElements	jbyteArray	jbyte
GetCharArrayElements	jcharArray	jchar
GetShortArrayElements	jshortArray	jshort
GetIntArrayElements	jintArray	jint
GetLongArrayElements	jlongArray	jlong
GetFloatArrayElements	jfloatArray	jfloat
GetDoubleArrayElements	jdoubleArray	jdouble

Description

Returns the body of the primitive array. The result is valid until the corresponding *Release<Type>ArrayElements* function is called. *Since the returned array may be a copy of the original array, changes made to the returned array will not necessarily be reflected in the original array until a corresponding Release<Type>ArrayElements is called.*

If isCopy is not NULL, then *isCopy is set to JNI_TRUE if a copy is made; if no copy is made, it is set to JNI_FALSE.

Linkage

Indices in the JNIEnv interface function table.

Get<Type>ArrayElements	Index
GetBooleanArrayElements	183
GetByteArrayElements	184
GetCharArrayElements	185
GetShortArrayElements	186
GetIntArrayElements	187
GetLongArrayElements	188
GetFloatArrayElements	189
GetDoubleArrayElements	190

Parameters   env: the JNIEnv interface pointer.

array: a reference to the primitive array whose elements are to be accessed.

isCopy: a pointer to a jboolean indicating whether a function returned a pointer to a copy of the array elements or a direct pointer to the original array elements.

Return Values   Returns a pointer to the array elements, or NULL if an exception occurs. Returns NULL if and only if an invocation of this function has thrown an exception.

Exceptions   OutOfMemoryError: if the system runs out of memory.

Get\<Type\>ArrayRegion

Prototype

```
void Get<Type>ArrayRegion(JNIEnv *env,
    <ArrayType> array, jsize start,
    jsize len, <NativeType> *buf);
```

Forms

This family of functions consists of eight members.

Get\<Type\>ArrayRegion	\<ArrayType\>	\<NativeType\>
GetBooleanArrayRegion	jbooleanArray	jboolean
GetByteArrayRegion	jbyteArray	jbyte
GetCharArrayRegion	jcharArray	jchar
GetShortArrayRegion	jshortArray	jhort
GetIntArrayRegion	jintArray	jint
GetLongArrayRegion	jlongArray	jlong
GetFloatArrayRegion	jfloatArray	jloat
GetDoubleArrayRegion	jdoubleArray	jdouble

Description

Copies a region of a primitive array into a buffer. The `array` reference and `buf` buffer must not be NULL.

Linkage

Indices in the `JNIEnv` interface function table.

Get\<Type\>ArrayRegion	Index
GetBooleanArrayRegion	199
GetByteArrayRegion	200
GetCharArrayRegion	201
GetShortArrayRegion	202
GetIntArrayRegion	203
GetLongArrayRegion	204
GetFloatArrayRegion	205
GetDoubleArrayRegion	206

Parameters   env: the JNIEnv interface pointer.

array: a reference to an array whose elements are to be copied.

start: the starting index of the array elements to be copied.

len: the number of elements to be copied.

buf: the destination buffer.

Exceptions   ArrayIndexOutOfBoundsException: if one of the indices in the region is not valid.

Get<Type>Field

Prototype   `<NativeType> Get<Type>Field(JNIEnv *env,`
                `    jobject obj, jfieldID fieldID);`

Forms   This family of functions consists of nine members.

Get<Type>Field	<NativeType>
GetObjectField	jobject
GetBooleanField	jboolean
GetByteField	jbyte
GetCharField	jchar
GetShortField	jshort
GetIntField	jint
GetLongField	jlong
GetFloatField	jfloat
GetDoubleField	jdouble

Description   Returns the value of a field of an instance. The field to access is specified by a field ID. The field ID must be valid in the class of the obj reference. The obj reference must not be NULL.

Linkage   Indices in the JNIEnv interface function table.

Get<Type>Field	Index
GetObjectField	95
GetBooleanField	96
GetByteField	97
GetCharField	98
GetShortField	99
GetIntField	100
GetLongField	101
GetFloatField	102
GetDoubleField	103

Parameters   env: the JNIEnv interface pointer.

obj: a reference to the instance whose field are to be accessed.

fieldID: a field ID of the given instance.

Return Values   Returns the value of the field.

Exceptions   None.

GetEnv

Prototype

```
jint GetEnv(JavaVM *vm, void **penv,
    jint interface_id);
```

Description

If the current thread is not attached to the given virtual machine instance, sets *penv to NULL, and returns JNI_EDETACHED. If the specified interface is not supported, sets *penv to NULL, and returns JNI_EVERSION. Otherwise, sets *env to the appropriate interface, and returns JNI_OK.

Java 2 SDK release 1.2 supports two valid interface versions: JNI_VERSION_1_1 and JNI_VERSION_1_2. In both cases, GetEnv sets *penv to a 1.2 version of the JNIEnv interface pointer.

This function is added in Java 2 SDK release 1.2.

Linkage

Index 6 in the JavaVM interface function table.

Parameters

vm: a virtual machine instance.

penv: a location for storing an interface pointer.

interface_id: an interface version number.

Return Values

Returns JNI_OK on success, JNI_EDETACHED when the current thread is not attached, and JNI_EVERSION when the specified interface is not supported.

Exceptions

None.

225

GetFieldID

Prototype

```
jfieldID GetFieldID(JNIEnv *env, jclass clazz,
        const char *name, const char *sig);
```

Description

Returns the field ID for an instance field of a class. The field is specified by its name and descriptor. The *Get<Type>Field* and *Set<Type>Field* families of accessor functions use field IDs to retrieve instance fields. The field must be accessible from the class referred to by clazz. The actual field, however, may be defined in one of clazz's superclasses. The clazz reference must not be NULL.

GetFieldID causes an uninitialized class to be initialized.

GetFieldID cannot be used to obtain the length of an array. Use GetArrayLength instead.

Linkage

Index 94 in the JNIEnv interface function table.

Parameters

env: the JNIEnv interface pointer.

clazz: a reference to the class object from which the field ID will be derived.

name: the field name in a 0-terminated UTF-8 string.

sig: the field descriptor in a 0-terminated UTF-8 string.

Return Values

Returns a field ID, or NULL if the operation fails. Returns NULL if and only if an invocation of this function has thrown an exception.

Exceptions

NoSuchFieldError: if the specified field cannot be found.

ExceptionInInitializerError: if the class initializer fails due to an exception.

OutOfMemoryError: if the system runs out of memory.

GetJavaVM

Prototype

```
jint GetJavaVM(JNIEnv *env, JavaVM **vm);
```

Description

Returns the `JavaVM` interface pointer to which the current thread is attached. The result is placed at the location pointed to by the second argument.

Linkage

Index 219 in the `JNIEnv` interface function table.

Parameters

env: the `JNIEnv` interface pointer.

vm: a pointer to where the result should be placed.

Return Values

Returns zero on success; otherwise, returns a negative value. Returns a negative number if and only if an invocation of this function has thrown an exception.

Exceptions

None.

GetMethodID

Prototype   jmethodID GetMethodID(JNIEnv *env, jclass clazz,
                       const char *name, const char *sig);

Description   Returns the method ID for an instance method of a class or
                    interface. The method may be defined in one of the clazz's
                    superclasses or superinterfaces and inherited by clazz. The
                    method is determined by its name and descriptor. The clazz
                    reference must not be NULL.

                    GetMethodID causes an uninitialized class or interface to be ini-
                    tialized.

                    To obtain the method ID of a constructor, supply "<init>" as
                    the method name and "V" as the return type. For example, the
                    following code segment obtains the method ID for the
                    String(char []) constructor:

                        jmethodID cid = (*env)->GetMethodID(env,
                          Class_java_lang_String, "<init>", "([C)V");

Linkage   Index 33 in the JNIEnv interface function table.

Parameters   env: the JNIEnv interface pointer.

                    clazz: a reference to the class or interface object from which
                    the method ID will be derived.

                    name: the method name in a 0-terminated UTF-8 string.

                    sig: the method descriptor in a 0-terminated UTF-8 string.

Return Values   Returns a method ID, or NULL if the operation fails. Returns
                    NULL if and only if an invocation of this function has thrown an
                    exception.

Exceptions   NoSuchMethodError: if the specified method cannot be found.

                    ExceptionInInitializerError: if the class or interface static
                    initializer fails due to an exception.

                    OutOfMemoryError: if the system runs out of memory.

GetObjectArrayElement

Prototype   jobject GetObjectArrayElement(JNIEnv *env,
                      jobjectArray array, jsize index);

Description   Returns an element of a java.lang.Object array. The array
                  reference must not be NULL.

Linkage   Index 173 in the JNIEnv interface function table.

Parameters   env: the JNIEnv interface pointer.

                  array: a reference to the java.lang.Object array from which
                  the element will be accessed.

                  index: the array index.

Return Values Returns a local reference to the element.

Exceptions   ArrayIndexOutOfBoundsException: if index does not specify
                  a valid index in the array.

GetObjectClass

Prototype jclass GetObjectClass(JNIEnv *env, jobject obj);

Description Returns the class of an object. The obj reference must not be NULL.

Linkage Index 31 in the JNIEnv interface function table.

Parameters env: the JNIEnv interface pointer.

obj: a reference to the object whose class will be obtained.

Return Values Returns a local reference to the class of the given object.

Exceptions None.

GetPrimitiveArrayCritical

Prototype   ```
void * GetPrimitiveArrayCritical(JNIEnv *env,
    jarray array, jboolean *isCopy);
```

**Description**        Returns a pointer to the body of a primitive array. The result is valid until the corresponding `ReleasePrimitiveArray-Critical` function is called.

It is important to treat the code inside this pair of functions as running in a "critical region." Inside a critical region, native code must not call other JNI functions, nor may the native code make any system call that may cause the current thread to block and wait for another thread in the virtual machine instance.

These restrictions make it more likely that native code will obtain an uncopied version of the array, even if the virtual machine implementation does not support pinning. For example, a virtual machine implementation may temporarily disable garbage collection when native code is holding a pointer to an array obtained via `GetPrimitiveArrayCritical`.

Multiple pairs of `Get/ReleasePrimitiveArrayCritical` calls may be overlapped:

```
jint len = (*env)->GetArrayLength(env, arr1);
jbyte *a1 = (*env)->
    GetPrimitiveArrayCritical(env, arr1 0);
if (a1 == NULL) {
    ... /* out of memory error */
}
jbyte *a2 = (*env)->
    GetPrimitiveArrayCritical(env, arr2, 0);
if (a2 == NULL) {
    ... /* out of memory error */
}
memcpy(a1, a2, len);
(*env)->ReleasePrimitiveArrayCritical(
    env, arr2, a2, 0);
(*env)->ReleasePrimitiveArrayCritical(
    env, arr1, a1, 0);
```

`GetPrimitiveArrayCritical` might still make a copy of the array if the virtual machine implementation internally represents arrays in a different format (noncontiguously, for exam-
```

ple). Therefore, it is important to check its return value against NULL for possible out-of-memory situations.

If isCopy is not NULL, then *isCopy is set to JNI_TRUE if a copy is made; or it is set to JNI_FALSE if no copy is made.

This function was introduced in Java 2 SDK release 1.2.

Linkage   Index 222 in the JNIEnv interface function table.

Parameters   env: the JNIEnv interface pointer.

array: a reference to the array whose elements are to be accessed.

isCopy: a pointer to a jboolean.

Return Values Returns a pointer to the array elements, or NULL if the operation fails. Returns NULL if and only if an invocation of this function has thrown an exception.

Exceptions   OutOfMemoryError: if the system runs out of memory.

GetStaticFieldID

Prototype

```
jfieldID GetStaticFieldID(JNIEnv *env,
    jclass clazz, const char *name,
    const char *sig);
```

Description

Returns the field ID for a static field of a class or interface. The field may be defined in the class or interface referred to by `clazz` or in one of its superclass or superinterfaces. The `clazz` reference must not be NULL. The field is specified by its name and descriptor. The *GetStatic<Type>Field* and *SetStatic<Type>Field* families of accessor functions use static field IDs to retrieve static fields.

`GetStaticFieldID` causes an uninitialized class or interface to be initialized.

Linkage

Index 144 in the JNIEnv interface function table.

Parameters

env: the JNIEnv interface pointer.

clazz: a reference to the class or interface object whose static field is to be accessed.

name: the static field name in a 0-terminated UTF-8 string.

sig: the field descriptor in a 0-terminated UTF-8 string.

Return Values

Returns a field ID, or NULL if the operation fails. Returns NULL if and only if an invocation of this function has thrown an exception.

Exceptions

NoSuchFieldError: if the specified static field cannot be found.

ExceptionInInitializerError: if the class or interface static initializer fails due to an exception.

OutOfMemoryError: if the system runs out of memory.

GetStatic<Type>Field

Prototype   *<NativeType>* GetStatic*<Type>*Field(JNIEnv *env,
                        jclass clazz, jfieldID fieldID);

Forms   This family of functions consists of nine members.

GetStatic<Type>Field	*<NativeType>*
GetStaticObjectField	jobject
GetStaticBooleanField	jboolean
GetStaticByteField	jbyte
GetStaticCharField	jchar
GetStaticShortField	jshort
GetStaticIntField	jint
GetStaticLongField	jlong
GetStaticFloatField	jfloat
GetStaticDoubleField	jdouble

Description   This family of accessor routines returns the value of a static
                    field of a class or interface. The clazz reference must not be
                    NULL. The field to access is specified by a field ID, which is
                    obtained by calling GetStaticFieldID.

Linkage   Indices in the JNIEnv interface function table.

GetStatic<Type>Field	**Index**
GetStaticObjectField	145
GetStaticBooleanField	146
GetStaticByteField	147
GetStaticCharField	148
GetStaticShortField	149
GetStaticIntField	150
GetStaticLongField	151
GetStaticFloatField	152
GetStaticDoubleField	153

Parameters   env: the JNIEnv interface pointer.

clazz: a reference to the class or interface object whose static field is to be accessed.

fieldID: the ID of the static field to be accessed.

Return Values   Returns the value of the static field.

Exceptions   None.

GetStaticMethodID

Prototype
```
jmethodID GetStaticMethodID(JNIEnv *env,
    jclass clazz, const char *name,
    const char *sig);
```

Description
Returns the method ID for a static method of a class. The method is specified by its name and descriptor. The method may be defined in the class referred to by clazz or in one of its superclasses. The clazz reference must not be NULL.

GetStaticMethodID causes an uninitialized class to be initialized.

Linkage
Index 113 in the JNIEnv interface function table.

Parameters
env: the JNIEnv interface pointer.

clazz: a reference to the class object whose static method is to be called.

name: the static method name in a 0-terminated UTF-8 string.

sig: the method descriptor in a 0-terminated UTF-8 string.

Return Values
Returns a method ID, or NULL if the operation fails. Returns NULL if and only if an invocation of this function has thrown an exception.

Exceptions
NoSuchMethodError: if the specified static method cannot be found.

ExceptionInInitializerError: if the class initializer fails due to an exception.

OutOfMemoryError: if the system runs out of memory.

GetStringChars

Prototype

```
const jchar * GetStringChars(JNIEnv *env,
    jstring string, jboolean *isCopy);
```

Description

Returns a pointer to the array of Unicode characters of the string. This pointer is valid until `ReleaseStringchars` is called.

If `isCopy` is not `NULL`, then `*isCopy` is set to `JNI_TRUE` if a copy is made; or it is set to `JNI_FALSE` if no copy is made.

Linkage

Index 165 in the `JNIEnv` interface function table.

Parameters

`env`: the `JNIEnv` interface pointer.

`string`: a reference to the string object whose elements are to be accessed.

`isCopy`: a pointer to a `jboolean` indicating whether a copy of the string is returned.

Return Values

Returns a pointer to a Unicode string, or `NULL` if the operation fails. Returns `NULL` if and only if an invocation of this function has thrown an exception.

Exceptions

`OutOfMemoryError`: if the system runs out of memory.

GetStringCritical

Prototype
```
const jchar * GetStringCritical(JNIEnv *env,
    jstring string, jboolean *isCopy);
```

Description
Returns a pointer to the contents of a jstring reference. The semantics of this function is similar to the GetStringChars function. If possible, the virtual machine implementation returns a pointer to the elements of the given string; otherwise, a copy is made. The pointer is valid until ReleaseStringCritical is called.

If isCopy is not NULL, then *isCopy is set to JNI_TRUE if a copy is made; if no copy is made, it is set to JNI_FALSE.

There are significant restrictions on how this function—and the corresponding ReleaseStringCritical function—can be used. In a code segment enclosed by GetStringCritical and ReleaseStringCritical calls, native code must not issue arbitrary JNI calls or cause the current thread to block and wait for another thread in the virtual machine instance.

The restrictions on GetStringCritical are the same as those on GetPrimitiveArrayCritical.

This function was introduced in Java 2 SDK release 1.2.

Linkage
Index 224 in the JNIEnv interface function table.

Parameters
env: the JNIEnv interface pointer.

string: a reference to the string object whose elements are to be accessed.

isCopy: a pointer to a jboolean indicating whether a copy has been made.

Return Values
Returns a pointer to a Unicode string, or NULL if the operation fails. Returns NULL if and only if an invocation of this function has thrown an exception.

Exceptions
OutOfMemoryError: if the system runs out of memory.

GetStringLength

Prototype   `jsize GetStringLength(JNIEnv *env, jstring string);`

Description   Returns the number of Unicode characters that constitute a string. The given string reference must not be NULL.

Linkage   Index 164 in the `JNIEnv` interface function table.

Parameters   env: the `JNIEnv` interface pointer.

string: a reference to the string object whose length is to be determined.

Return Values   Returns the length of the string.

Exceptions   None.

GetStringRegion

Prototype   `void GetStringRegion(JNIEnv *env, jstring str,`
                  `    jsize start, jsize len, jchar *buf);`

Description   Copies `len` number of Unicode characters, beginning at offset `start`. Copies the characters to the given buffer `buf`.

                  This function was introduced in Java 2 SDK release 1.2.

Linkage   Index 220 in the `JNIEnv` interface function table.

Parameters   `env`: the `JNIEnv` interface pointer.

                  `str`: a reference to the string object to be copied.

                  `start`: the offset within the string at which to start the copy.

                  `len`: the number of Unicode characters to copy.

                  `buf`: a pointer to a buffer to hold the Unicode characters.

Exceptions   `StringIndexOutOfBoundsException`: if an index overflow error occurs.

GetStringUTFChars

Prototype   `const jbyte * GetStringUTFChars(JNIEnv *env,`
                       `    jstring string, jboolean *isCopy);`

Description   Returns a pointer to an array of UTF-8 characters of the string.
                       This array is valid until it is released by `ReleaseStringUTF-`
                       `Chars`.

                       If `isCopy` is not `NULL`, then `*isCopy` is set to `JNI_TRUE` if a copy
                       is made; if no copy is made, it is set to `JNI_FALSE`.

Linkage   Index 169 in the `JNIEnv` interface function table.

Parameters   env: the `JNIEnv` interface pointer.

                       `string`: a reference to the string object whose elements are to
                       be accessed.

                       `isCopy`: a pointer to a `jboolean` indicating whether a copy has
                       been made.

Return Values   Returns a pointer to a UTF-8 string, or `NULL` if the operation
                       fails. Returns `NULL` if and only if an invocation of this function
                       has thrown an exception.

Exceptions   `OutOfMemoryError`: if the system runs out of memory.

GetStringUTFLength

Prototype

```
jsize GetStringUTFLength(JNIEnv *env,
        jstring string);
```

Description

Returns the number of bytes needed to represent a string in the UTF-8 format. The length does not include the trailing zero character. The given string reference must not be NULL.

Linkage

Index 168 in the JNIEnv interface function table.

Parameters

env: the JNIEnv interface pointer.

string: a reference to the string object whose UTF-8 length is to be determined.

Return Values

Returns the UTF-8 length of the string.

Exceptions

None.

GetStringUTFRegion

Prototype
```
void GetStringUTFRegion(JNIEnv *env, jstring str,
    jsize start, jsize len, char *buf);
```

Description   Translates len number of Unicode characters into UTF-8 format. The function begins the translation at offset start and places the result in the given buffer buf. The str reference and buf buffer must not be NULL.

Note that the len argument denotes the number to Unicode characters to be converted, not the number of UTF-8 characters to be copied.

This function was introduced in Java 2 SDK release 1.2.

Linkage   Index 221 in the JNIEnv interface function table.

Parameters   env: the JNIEnv interface pointer.

str: a reference to the string object to be copied.

start: the offset within the string at which to start the copy.

len: the number of Unicode characters to copy.

buf: a pointer to a buffer to hold the UTF-8 characters.

Exceptions   StringIndexOutOfBoundsException: if an index overflow error occurs.

GetSuperclass

Prototype   `jclass GetSuperclass(JNIEnv *env, jclass clazz);`

Description   Returns the superclass of the given class. If `clazz` represents any class other than the class `java.lang.Object`, then this function returns a reference to the superclass of the class specified by `clazz`.

If `clazz` represents the class `java.lang.Object`, or if `clazz` represents an interface, this function returns NULL.

Linkage   Index 10 in the `JNIEnv` interface function table.

Parameters   env: the `JNIEnv` interface pointer.

clazz: a reference to a class object whose superclass is to be determined.

Return Values Returns the superclass of the class represented by `clazz`, or NULL.

Exceptions   None.

GetVersion

Prototype

```
jint GetVersion(JNIEnv *env);
```

Description

Returns the version of the JNIEnv interface. In JDK release 1.1, GetVersion returns 0x00010001. In Java 2 SDK release 1.2, GetVersion returns 0x00010002. A virtual machine implementation that supports both the 1.1 and 1.2 versions of the JNI provides only one JNIEnv interface whose version is 0x00010002.

Linkage

Index 4 in the JNIEnv interface function table.

Parameters

env: the JNIEnv interface pointer.

Return Values

Returns the version of the JNIEnv interface.

Exceptions

None.

IsAssignableFrom

Prototype

```
jboolean IsAssignableFrom(JNIEnv *env,
    jclass clazz1, jclass clazz2);
```

Description   Determines whether an object of class or interface `clazz1` can be safely cast to class or interface `clazz2`. Both `clazz1` and `clazz2` must not be NULL.

Linkage   Index 11 in the `JNIEnv` interface function table.

Parameters   env: the `JNIEnv` interface pointer.

clazz1: the first class or interface argument.

clazz2: the second class or interface argument.

Return Values   Returns `JNI_TRUE` if any of the following is true:

- The first and second arguments refer to the same class or interface.
- The first argument refer to a subclass of the second argument.
- The first argument refers to a class that has the second argument as one of its interfaces.
- The first and second arguments both refer to array classes with element types X and Y, and `IsAssignableFrom(env, X, Y)` is `JNI_TRUE`.

Otherwise, this function returns `JNI_FALSE`.

Exceptions   None.

IsInstanceOf

Prototype

```
jboolean IsInstanceOf(JNIEnv *env, jobject obj,
    jclass clazz);
```

Description   Tests whether an object is an instance of a class or interface. The clazz reference must not be NULL.

Linkage   Index 32 in the JNIEnv interface function table.

Parameters   env: the JNIEnv interface pointer.

obj: a reference to an object.

clazz: a reference to a class or interface.

Return Values   Returns JNI_TRUE if obj can be cast to clazz, if obj denotes a null object, or if obj is a weak global reference to an already-collected object; otherwise, returns JNI_FALSE.

Exceptions   None.

IsSameObject

Prototype

```
jboolean IsSameObject(JNIEnv *env, jobject ref1,
    jobject ref2);
```

Description

Tests whether two references refer to the same object. A NULL reference refers to the null object.

In Java 2 SDK release 1.2, this function can also be used to check whether the object referred to by a weak global reference is alive.

Linkage

Index 24 in the JNIEnv interface function table.

Parameters

env: the JNIEnv interface pointer.

ref1: a reference to an object.

ref2: a reference to an object.

Return Values

Returns JNI_TRUE if ref1 and ref2 refer to the same object; otherwise, returns JNI_FALSE.

In Java 2 SDK release 1.2, as long as a weak global reference wref refers to a live object, IsSameObject(env, wref, NULL) returns JNI_FALSE. After the object referred to by wref is garbage collected, the IsSameObject(env, wref, NULL) call returns JNI_TRUE.

Exceptions

None.

JNI_CreateJavaVM

Prototype

```
jint JNI_CreateJavaVM(JavaVM **pvm, void **penv,
    void *vm_args);
```

Description

Loads and initializes a virtual machine instance. Once the virtual machine instance is initialized, the current thread is called the main thread. In addition, this function sets the env argument to the JNIEnv interface pointer of the main thread.

JDK release 1.1 and Java 2 SDK release 1.2 do not support creating more than one virtual machine instance in a single process.

In JDK release 1.1, the second argument to JNI_CreateJavaVM is always an address of a JNIEnv pointer. The third argument is a pointer to an initialization structure, JDK1_1InitArgs, that is specific to the JDK release 1.1. The version field in vm_args must be set to 0x00010001.

The JDK1_1InitArgs structure is not designed to be portable on all virtual machine implementations. It reflects the requirements of the JDK release 1.1 implementation:

```
typedef struct JDK1_1InitArgs {
    /* Java VM version */
    jint version;

    /* System properties. */
    char **properties;

    /* whether to check the source files are
     * newer than compiled class files.
     */
    jint checkSource;

    /* maximum native stack size of
     * java.lang.Thread threads.
     */
    jint nativeStackSize;

    /* maximum java.lang.Thread stack size. */
    jint javaStackSize;

    /* initial heap size. */
```

```
    jint minHeapSize;

    /* maximum heap size. */
    jint maxHeapSize;

    /* which byte code should be verified:
     * 0 -- none,
     * 1 -- remotely loaded code,
     * 2 -- all code.
     */
    jint verifyMode;

    /* local directory path for class loading. */
    const char *classpath;

    /* a hook for a function that redirects
     * all VM messages.
     */
    jint (*vfprintf)(FILE *fp,
                     const char *format,
                     va_list args);

    /* a VM exit hook. */
    void (*exit)(jint code);

    /* a VM abort hook. */
    void (*abort)();

    /* whether to enable class GC. */
    jint enableClassGC;

    /* whether GC messages will appear. */
    jint enableVerboseGC;

    /* whether asynchronous GC is allowed. */
    jint disableAsyncGC;

    /* Three reserved fields. */
    jint reserved0;
    jint reserved1;
    jint reserved2;
} JDK1_1InitArgs;
```

Java 2 SDK release 1.2 preserves backward compatibility with JDK release 1.1. If the initialization argument points to a JDK1_1InitArgs structure, JNI_CreateJavaVM still works as it did in JDK release 1.1.

In addition, Java 2 SDK release 1.2 introduces a generic virtual machine initialization structure that will work with Java 2 SDK release 1.2 as well as future virtual machine implementations. The JNI_CreateJavaVM accepts as the third argument a Java-VMInitArgs structure. Unlike JDK1_1InitArgs, which contains a fixed set of options, JavaVMInitArgs uses symbolic name/value pairs to encode arbitrary virtual machine start-up options. JavaVMInitArgs is defined as follows:

```
typedef struct JavaVMInitArgs {
    jint version;
    jint nOptions;
    JavaVMOption *options;
    jboolean ignoreUnrecognized;
} JavaVMInitArgs;
```

The version field must be set to JNI_VERSION_1_2. (In contrast, the version field in JDK1_1InitArgs must be set to JNI_VERSION_1_1.) The options field is an array of the following type:

```
typedef struct JavaVMOption {
    char *optionString;
    void *extraInfo;
} JavaVMOption;
```

The size of the array is denoted by the nOptions field in JavaVMInitArgs. If ignoreUnrecognized is JNI_TRUE, JNI_CreateJavaVM ignores all unrecognized option strings that begin with "-X" or "_". If ignoreUnrecognized is JNI_FALSE, JNI_CreateJavaVM returns JNI_ERR as soon as it encounters any unrecognized option strings. All Java virtual machine implementations must recognize the following set of standard options:

`optionString`	**Meaning**
`-D<name>=<value>`	Set a system property
`-verbose`	Enable verbose output. The option can be followed by a colon and a comma-separated list of names indicating what kind of messages will be printed by the VM. For example, `-verbose:gc,class` instructs the VM to print GC and class-loading related messages. Standard names include: `gc`, `class`, and `jni`. Implementation-specific names must begin with "X".
`vfprintf`	`extraInfo` is a pointer to the `vfprintf` hook.
`exit`	`extraInfo` is a pointer to the `exit` hook.
`abort`	`extraInfo` is a pointer to the `abort` hook.

In addition, virtual machine implementations may support their own set of implementation-dependent option strings. Implementation-dependent option strings must begin with "-X" or an underscore ("_"). For example, Java 2 SDK release 1.2 supports -Xms and -Xmx options to allow programmers to specify the initial and maximum heap size. Options that begin with "-X" can be specified at the "java" command line.

Here is the example code that creates a virtual machine instance in Java 2 SDK release 1.2:

```
JavaVMInitArgs vm_args;
JavaVMOption options[4];
/* disable JIT */
options[0].optionString =
    "-Djava.compiler=NONE";
/* user classes */
options[1].optionString =
    "-Djava.class.path=c:\\myclasses";
/* native lib path */
options[2].optionString =
    "-Djava.library.path=c:\\mylibs";
/* print JNI msgs */
options[3].optionString = "-verbose:jni";
vm_args.version = JNI_VERSION_1_2;
vm_args.options = options;
vm_args.nOptions = 4;
vm_args.ignoreUnrecognized = TRUE;

res = JNI_CreateJavaVM(&vm, (void **)&env,
                        &vm_args);
if (res < 0) {
    ... /* error occurred
}
```

Linkage   Exported from the native library that implements the Java virtual machine.

Parameters   pvm: pointer to the location where the resulting JavaVM interface pointer will be placed.

penv: pointer to the location where the JNIEnv interface pointer for the main thread will be placed.

args: Java virtual machine initialization arguments.

Return Values Returns zero on success; otherwise, returns a negative number.

Exceptions   None.

JNI_GetCreatedJavaVMs

Prototype

```
jint JNI_GetCreatedJavaVMs(JavaVM **vmBuf,
    jsize bufLen, jsize *nVMs);
```

Description

Returns pointers to all the virtual machine instances that have been created. This function writes the pointers to the virtual machine instances into the buffer vmBuf in the order that they were created. At most, it writes bufLen number of entries. Finally, it returns the total number of created virtual machine instances in *nVMs.

JDK release 1.1 and Java 2 SDK release 1.2 do not support creating more than one virtual machine instance in a single process.

Linkage

Exported from the native library that implements the Java virtual machine.

Parameters

vmBuf: pointer to the buffer where the pointer to virtual machine instance will be placed.

bufLen: the length of the buffer.

nVMs: a pointer to an integer.

Return Values

Returns zero on success; otherwise, returns a negative number.

Exceptions

None.

JNI_GetDefaultJavaVMInitArgs

Prototype   `jint JNI_GetDefaultJavaVMInitArgs(void *vm_args);`

Description   Returns a default configuration for the Java virtual machine implementation. Before calling this function, native code must set the `version` field in `vm_args` to `0x00010001`.

In JDK release 1.1, this function takes as argument a pointer to the `JDK1_1InitArgs` structure and upon successful return initializes that structure. You must set the `version` field in `JDK1_1InitArgs` to `0x00010001` before calling this function. The specification for the `JNI_CreateJavaVM` function describes the internals of the `JDK1_1InitArgs` structure.

The new virtual machine initialization structure in Java 2 SDK release 1.2 no longer requires programmers to call `JNI_GetDefaultJavaVMInitArgs`. This function is still supported but no longer useful in Java 2 SDK release 1.2.

Linkage   Exported from the native library that implements the Java virtual machine.

Parameters   `vm_args`: a pointer to a VM-specific initialization structure into which the default arguments are filled.

Return Values   Returns zero if the requested version is supported; otherwise, returns a negative number if the requested version is not supported.

Exceptions   None.

JNI_OnLoad

Prototype   `jint JNI_OnLoad(JavaVM *vm, void *reserved);`

Description   Performs initialization operations for a given native library and returns the JNI version required by the native library. The virtual machine implementation calls `JNI_OnLoad` when the native library is loaded, for example, through a call to `System.load-Library`. `JNI_OnLoad` must return the JNIEnv interface version required by the native library.

`System.loadLibrary` triggers the execution of this function. The `JNI_OnLoad` function returns the JNI version number required by the native library. If the native library does not export a `JNI_OnLoad` function, the virtual machine implementation assumes that the library only requires JNI version `JNI_VERSION_1_1`. If the virtual machine implementation does not recognize the version number returned by `JNI_OnLoad`, then the native library cannot be loaded.

Support for the `JNI_OnLoad` hook is added in Java 2 SDK 1.2.

Linkage   Exported from native libraries that contain native method implementation.

Parameters   `vm`: the pointer to the Java virtual machine instance that loaded the native library.

`reserved`: not currently used. This parameter is set to `NULL` and reserved for use in the future.

Return Values Returns the `JNIEnv` interface version number that the native library needs.

Exceptions   None.

JNI_OnUnload

Prototype   `void JNI_OnUnload(JavaVM *vm, void *reserved);`

Description   Performs cleanup operations for a native library. The virtual machine implementation calls `JNI_OnUnload` when the class loader containing the native library is garbage collected. This function can be used to perform cleanup operations. Because this function is called in an unknown context (such as from a finalizer), the programmer should be conservative when using Java virtual machine services and refrain from making arbitrary JNI function calls.

Support for the `JNI_OnUnload` hook is added in Java 2 SDK 1.2.

Linkage   Exported from native libraries that contain native method implementation.

Parameters   vm: the pointer to the Java virtual machine instance.

`reserved`: Not currently used. This parameter is set to `NULL` and reserved for possible use in the future.

Exceptions   None.

MonitorEnter

Prototype   `jint MonitorEnter(JNIEnv *env, jobject obj);`

Description   Enters the monitor associated with the object referred to by `obj`. The `obj` reference must not be `NULL`.

Each object has a monitor associated with it. If the current thread already owns the monitor associated with `obj`, it increments a counter in the monitor indicating the number of times this thread has entered the monitor. If the monitor associated with `obj` is not owned by any thread, the current thread becomes the owner of the monitor, setting the entry count of this monitor to 1. If another thread already owns the monitor associated with `obj`, the current thread waits until the monitor is released, then tries again to gain ownership.

A monitor entered through a `MonitorEnter` JNI function call cannot be exited using the `monitorexit` Java virtual machine instruction or a synchronized method return. A `MonitorEnter` JNI function call and a `monitorenter` Java virtual machine instruction may race to enter the monitor associated with the same object.

Linkage   Index 217 in the `JNIEnv` interface function table.

Parameters   env: the `JNIEnv` interface pointer.

obj: a reference to an object whose associated monitor will be entered.

Return Values Returns zero on success; otherwise, returns a negative value. Returns a negative number if and only if an invocation of this function has thrown an exception.

Exceptions   `OutOfMemoryError`: if the system runs out of memory.

MonitorExit

Prototype   `jint MonitorExit(JNIEnv *env, jobject obj);`

Description Exits the monitor associated with the given object. The current thread must be the owner of the monitor associated with the object referred to by `obj`. The `obj` reference must not be `NULL`.

The thread decrements the counter indicating the number of times it has entered this monitor. If the value of the counter becomes zero, the current thread releases the monitor.

Native code must not use `MonitorExit` to exit a monitor entered through a synchronized method or a `monitorenter` Java virtual machine instruction.

Linkage   Index 218 in the `JNIEnv` interface function table.

Parameters env: the `JNIEnv` interface pointer.

obj: a reference to an object whose associated monitor will be exited.

Return Values Returns zero on success; otherwise, returns a negative value. Returns a negative number if and only if an invocation of this function has thrown an exception.

Exceptions `OutOfMemoryError`: if the system runs out of memory.

`IllegalMonitorStateException`: if the current thread does not own the monitor.

259

NewGlobalRef

Prototype   `jobject NewGlobalRef(JNIEnv *env, jobject obj);`

Description   Creates a new global reference to the object referred to by the `obj` argument. The `obj` argument may be a global, weak global, or local reference. Global references must be explicitly disposed of by calling `DeleteGlobalRef`.

Linkage   Index 21 in the `JNIEnv` interface function table.

Parameters   env: the `JNIEnv` interface pointer.

                                        obj: a global or local reference.

Return Values   Returns a global reference. The result is NULL if the system runs out of memory, if the given argument is NULL, or if the given reference is a weak global reference referring to an object that has already been garbage collected.

Exceptions   None.

NewLocalRef

Prototype   `jobject NewLocalRef(JNIEnv *env, jobject ref);`

Description   Creates a new local reference that refers to the same object as `ref`. The given `ref` may be a global, weak global, or local reference.

This function was introduced in Java 2 SDK release 1.2.

Linkage   Index 25 in the `JNIEnv` interface function table.

Parameters   env: the `JNIEnv` interface pointer.

ref: a reference to the object for which the function creates a new local reference.

Return Values   Returns a local reference. The result is `NULL` if the system runs out of memory, if the given argument is `NULL`, or if the given reference is a weak global reference referring to an object that has already been garbage collected.

Exceptions   None.

NewObject

Prototype   `jobject NewObject(JNIEnv *env, jclass clazz,`
`                     jmethodID methodID, ...);`

Description   Constructs a new object. The method ID indicates which con-
                      structor method to invoke. This ID may be obtained by calling
                      `GetMethodID` with "`<init>`" as the method name and "V" as the
                      return type. The constructor must be defined in the class
                      referred to by `clazz`, not one of its superclasses.

                      The `clazz` argument must not refer to an array class.

                      Programmers place all arguments that are to be passed to the
                      constructor immediately following the `methodID` argument.
                      `NewObject` accepts these arguments and passes them to the con-
                      structor that the programmer wishes to invoke.

Linkage   Index 28 in the `JNIEnv` interface function table.

Parameters   env: the `JNIEnv` interface pointer.

                      `clazz`: a reference to the class object whose instance is to be
                      created.

                      `methodID`: the method ID of the constructor to be executed in
                      the newly created instance.

                      Additional arguments: arguments to be passed to the construc-
                      tor.

Return Values   Returns a local reference to an object, or NULL if the object can-
                      not be constructed. Returns NULL if and only if an invocation of
                      this function has thrown an exception.

Exceptions   `InstantiationException`: if the class is an interface or an
                      abstract class.

                      `OutOfMemoryError`: if the system runs out of memory.

                      Any exceptions thrown by the constructor.

NewObjectA

Prototype

```
jobject NewObjectA(JNIEnv *env, jclass clazz,
      jmethodID methodID, jvalue *args);
```

Description

Constructs a new object. The method ID indicates which constructor method to invoke. This ID may be obtained by calling GetMethodID with "<init>" as the method name and "V" as the return type. The constructor must be defined in the class referred to by clazz, not one of its superclasses.

The clazz argument must not refer to an array class.

Programmers place all arguments that are to be passed to the constructor in an args array of jvalues that immediately follows the methodID argument. NewObjectA accepts the arguments in this array, and, in turn, passes them to the constructor that the programmer wishes to invoke.

Linkage

Index 30 in the JNIEnv interface function table.

Parameters

env: the JNIEnv interface pointer.

clazz: a reference to the class object whose instance is to be created.

methodID: the method ID of the constructor to be executed in the newly created instance.

args: an array of arguments to be passed to the constructor.

Return Values

Returns a local reference to an object, or NULL if the object cannot be constructed. Returns NULL if and only if an invocation of this function has thrown an exception.

Exceptions

InstantiationException: if the class is an interface or an abstract class.

OutOfMemoryError: if the system runs out of memory.

Any exceptions thrown by the constructor.

NewObjectV

Prototype   jobject NewObjectV(JNIEnv *env, jclass clazz,
                       jmethodID methodID, va_list args);

Description   Constructs a new object. The method ID indicates which con-
                  structor method to invoke. This ID may be obtained by calling
                  GetMethodID with "<init>" as the method name and "V" as the
                  return type. The constructor must be defined in the class
                  referred to by clazz, not one of its superclasses.

                  The clazz argument must not refer to an array class.

                  Programmers place all arguments that are to be passed to the
                  constructor in an args argument of type va_list that immedi-
                  ately follows the methodID argument. NewObjectV accepts
                  these arguments, and, in turn, passes them to the constructor
                  that the programmer wishes to invoke.

Linkage   Index 29 in the JNIEnv interface function table.

Parameters   env: the JNIEnv interface pointer.

                  clazz: a reference to the class object whose instance is to be
                  created.

                  methodID: the method ID of the constructor to be executed in
                  the newly created instance.

                  args: a va_list of arguments to be passed to the constructor.

Return Values Returns a local reference to an object, or NULL if the object can-
                  not be constructed. Returns NULL if and only if an invocation of
                  this function has thrown an exception.

Exceptions   InstantiationException: if the class is an interface or an
                  abstract class.

                  OutOfMemoryError: if the system runs out of memory.

                  Any exceptions thrown by the constructor.

NewObjectArray

Prototype   jarray NewObjectArray(JNIEnv *env, jsize length,
             jclass elementType, jobject initialElement);

Description   Constructs a new array holding objects in class or interface
            elementType. All elements are initially set to initialEle-
            ment. The length argument can be zero. The elementType ref-
            erence must not be NULL.

Linkage   Index 172 in the JNIEnv interface function table.

Parameters   env: the JNIEnv interface pointer.

            length: the number of elements in the array to be created.

            elementType: class or interface of the elements in the array.

            initialElement: a reference to initialization value object. This
            value can be NULL.

Return Values   Returns a local reference to an array object, or NULL if the array
            cannot be constructed. Returns NULL if and only if an invocation
            of this function has thrown an exception.

Exceptions   OutOfMemoryError: if the system runs out of memory.

New<Type>Array

Prototype   `<ArrayType> New<Type>Array(JNIEnv *env,`
                      `jsize length);`

Forms   This family of functions consists of eight members.

New<Type>Array	<ArrayType>
NewBooleanArray	jbooleanArray
NewByteArray	jbyteArray
NewCharArray	jcharArray
NewShortArray	jshortArray
NewIntArray	jintArray
NewLongArray	jlongArray
NewFloatArray	jfloatArray
NewDoubleArray	jdoubleArray

Description   Constructs a new array of primitive element types. All elements
                  in the newly constructed array are initialized to zero.

Linkage   Indices in the JNIEnv interface function table.

New<Type>Array	Index
NewBooleanArray	175
NewByteArray	176
NewCharArray	177
NewShortArray	178
NewIntArray	179
NewLongArray	180
NewFloatArray	181
NewDoubleArray	182

Parameters   env: the JNIEnv interface pointer.

                  length: the number of elements in the array to be created.

Return Values   Returns a local reference to a primitive array, or NULL if the array cannot be constructed. Returns NULL if and only if an invocation of this function has thrown an exception.

Exceptions   OutOfMemoryError: if the system runs out of memory.

NewString

Prototype

```
jstring NewString(JNIEnv *env,
        const jchar *uchars, jsize len);
```

Description   Constructs a java.lang.String object from the given Unicode characters.

Linkage   Index 163 in the JNIEnv interface function table.

Parameters   env: the JNIEnv interface pointer.

uchars: pointer to the Unicode sequence that makes up the string.

len: length of the Unicode string.

Return Values   Returns a local reference to a string object, or NULL if the string cannot be constructed. Returns NULL if and only if an invocation of this function has thrown an exception.

Exceptions   OutOfMemoryError: if the system runs out of memory.

NewStringUTF

Prototype	```jstring NewStringUTF(JNIEnv *env, const char *bytes);```

Description Constructs a new java.lang.String object from an array of UTF-8 characters. The UTF-8 characters pointed to by bytes are 0-terminated.

Linkage Index 167 in the JNIEnv interface function table.

Parameters env: the JNIEnv interface pointer, or NULL if the string cannot be constructed.

bytes: the pointer to the sequence of UTF-8 characters that makes up the string.

Return Values Returns a local reference to a string object, or NULL if the string cannot be constructed. Returns NULL if and only if an invocation of this function has thrown an exception.

Exceptions OutOfMemoryError: if the system runs out of memory.

NewWeakGlobalRef

Prototype	jweak NewWeakGlobalRef(JNIEnv *env, jobject obj);

Description   Creates a new weak global reference to the object referenced to by obj. Weak global references are a special kind of global reference. Unlike normal global references, a weak global reference allows the underlying object to be garbage collected. You can use weak global references in any situation where you would otherwise use global or local references. When the garbage collector runs, it frees the underlying object if the object is only referred to by weak references. A weak global reference pointing to a freed object is functionally equivalent to the NULL reference. Programmers can detect whether a weak global reference points to a freed object by using the function IsSame-Object to compare the weak reference against NULL.

Weak global references in JNI are a simplified version of the Java weak references (java.lang.ref) API, available as part of Java 2 SDK release 1.2. The JNI weak global references are weaker than all four types of weak references in the Java weak references API.

This function was introduced in Java 2 SDK release 1.2.

Linkage   Index 226 in the JNIEnv interface function table.

Parameters   env: the JNIEnv interface pointer.

obj: the object for which the weak global reference will be created.

Return Values   Returns NULL if obj refers to null, if obj is a weak global reference to a garbage-collected object, or if the virtual machine implementation runs out of memory.

Exceptions   OutOfMemoryError: if the system runs out of memory.

PopLocalFrame

Prototype   `jobject PopLocalFrame(JNIEnv *env, jobject result);`

Description   Pops the current (top-most) local reference frame from the stack. In addition, this function frees all the local references contained in the frame and returns a local reference in the previous local reference frame for the given `result` object.

Pass `NULL` in the `result` parameter if you do not need to return a reference to the previous frame.

This function was introduced in Java 2 SDK release 1.2.

Linkage   Index 20 in the `JNIEnv` interface function table.

Parameters   env: the `JNIEnv` interface pointer.

result: an object to be passed to the previous local reference frame.

Return Values   Returns a local reference in the previous local reference frame that refers to the same object as the second argument.

Exceptions   None.

PushLocalFrame

Prototype　　　`jint PushLocalFrame(JNIEnv *env, jint capacity);`

Description　　Creates a new local reference frame in which at least the specified number of local references can be created. All the local references created in the new frame will be freed when `PopLocalFrame` is called.

This function was introduced in Java 2 SDK release 1.2.

Linkage　　　Index 19 in the `JNIEnv` interface function table.

Parameters　　env: the `JNIEnv` interface pointer.

`capacity`: the maximum number of local references that will be created in the local reference frame.

Return Values　Returns zero on success; otherwise, returns a negative number and throws `OutOfMemoryError`. Returns a negative number if and only if an invocation of this function has thrown an exception.

Exceptions　　`OutOfMemoryError`: if the system runs out of memory.

RegisterNatives

Prototype
```
jint RegisterNatives(JNIEnv *env, jclass clazz,
    const JNINativeMethod *methods, jint nMethods);
```

Description   Registers native methods with the class specified by the `clazz` argument. The `methods` parameter specifies an array of JNINativeMethod structures that contains the names, descriptors, and function pointers of the native methods. The `nMethods` parameter specifies the number of native methods in the array. The `JNINativeMethod` structure is defined as follows:

```
typedef struct {
    char *name;
    char *signature;
    void *fnPtr;
} JNINativeMethod;
```

The `fnPtr` fields in the `JNINativeMethod` structures must be valid function pointer that implements the native method.

Linkage   Index 215 in the JNIEnv interface function table.

Parameters   env: the JNIEnv interface pointer.

clazz: a reference to a class object in which the native methods will be registered.

methods: native methods to be registered.

nMethods: the number of native methods to be registered.

Return Values   Returns zero on success; otherwise, returns a negative value. Returns a negative number if and only if an invocation of this function has thrown an exception.

Exceptions   NoSuchMethodError: if a specified method cannot be found or if the method is not native.

Release<Type>ArrayElements

Prototype

```
void Release<Type>ArrayElements(JNIEnv *env,
    <ArrayType> array, <NativeType> *elems,
    jint mode);
```

Forms

This family of functions consists of eight members.

Release<Type>ArrayElements	<ArrayType>	<NativeType>
ReleaseBooleanArrayElements	jbooleanArray	jboolean
ReleaseByteArrayElements	jbyteArray	jbyte
ReleaseCharArrayElements	jcharArray	jchar
ReleaseShortArrayElements	jshortArray	jshort
ReleaseIntArrayElements	jintArray	jint
ReleaseLongArrayElements	jlongArray	jlong
ReleaseFloatArrayElements	jfloatArray	jfloat
ReleaseDoubleArrayElements	jdoubleArray	jdouble

Description

Informs the virtual machine implementation that native code no longer needs access to primitive array elements, derived using the corresponding *Get<Type>ArrayElements* function. If necessary, this function copies back all changes made to elems to the original array.

The mode argument provides information on how the array buffer should be released. The mode argument has no effect if elems is not a copy of the elements in array. Otherwise, mode has the following impact, as shown in the following table:

Mode	Actions
0	copy back and free the elems buffer
JNI_COMMIT	copy back but do not free the elems buffer
JNI_ABORT	free the buffer without copying back the possible changes in the elems buffer

In most cases, programmers pass 0 to the mode argument to ensure consistent behavior for both pinned and copied arrays. The other options give the programmer more control over memory management and should be used with extreme care.

274

Linkage   Indices in the `JNIEnv` interface function table.

Release<Type>ArrayElements	Index
ReleaseBooleanArrayElements	191
ReleaseByteArrayElements	192
ReleaseCharArrayElements	193
ReleaseShortArrayElements	194
ReleaseIntArrayElements	195
ReleaseLongArrayElements	196
ReleaseFloatArrayElements	197
ReleaseDoubleArrayElements	198

Parameters   `env`: the `JNIEnv` interface pointer.

                         `array`: a reference to an array object.

                         `elems`: a pointer to array elements.

                         `mode`: the release mode.

Exceptions   None.

275

ReleasePrimitiveArrayCritical

Prototype

```
void ReleasePrimitiveArrayCritical(JNIEnv *env,
    jarray array, void *carray, jint mode);
```

Description

Informs the virtual machine implementation that native code no longer needs access to carray, the result of a previous GetPrimitiveArrayCritical call. If necessary, this function copies back all changes made to carray to the original array.

The mode argument provides information on how the array buffer should be released. The mode argument has no effect if carray is not a copy of the elements in array. Otherwise, mode has the following impact, as shown in the following table:

Mode	Actions
0	copy back and free the carray buffer
JNI_COMMIT	copy back but do not free the carray buffer
JNI_ABORT	free the buffer without copying back the possible changes in the carray buffer

In most cases, programmers pass 0 to the mode argument to ensure consistent behavior for copied arrays. The other options give the programmer more control over memory management and should be used with extreme care.

This function was introduced in Java 2 SDK release 1.2.

Linkage

Index 223 in the JNIEnv interface function table.

Parameters

env: the JNIEnv interface pointer.

array: a reference to an array object.

carray: a pointer to array elements.

mode: the release mode.

Exceptions

None.

ReleaseStringChars

Prototype
```
void ReleaseStringChars(JNIEnv *env,
    jstring string, const jchar *chars);
```

Description   Informs the virtual machine implementation that native code no longer needs access to chars. The chars argument is a pointer obtained from string using GetStringChars.

Linkage   Index 166 in the JNIEnv interface function table.

Parameters   env: the JNIEnv interface pointer.

string: a reference to a string object.

chars: a pointer to a Unicode string.

Exceptions   None.

ReleaseStringCritical

Prototype

```
void ReleaseStringCritical(JNIEnv *env,
    jstring string, const jchar *carray);
```

Description

Informs the virtual machine implementation that native code no longer needs access to carray. The carray argument is a pointer obtained from string using GetStringCritical.

In a code segment enclosed by GetStringCritical and ReleaseStringCritical calls, native code must not issue arbitrary JNI calls or cause the current thread to block and wait for another thread in the virtual machine instance.

This function was introduced in Java 2 SDK release 1.2.

Linkage

Index 225 in the JNIEnv interface function table.

Parameters

env: the JNIEnv interface pointer.

string: a reference to a string object.

chars: a pointer to a Unicode string.

Exceptions

None.

ReleaseStringUTFChars

Prototype

```
void ReleaseStringUTFChars(JNIEnv *env,
        jstring string, const char *utf);
```

Description

Informs the virtual machine implementation that native code no longer needs access to the native string `utf`. The `utf` argument is a pointer derived from `string` using `GetStringUTFChars`.

Linkage

Index 169 in the `JNIEnv` interface function table.

Parameters

`env`: the `JNIEnv` interface pointer.

`string`: a reference to a string object.

`utf`: a pointer to a UTF-8 string.

Exceptions

None.

Set<Type>ArrayRegion

Prototype

```
void Set<Type>ArrayRegion(JNIEnv *env,
    <ArrayType> array, jsize start,
    jsize len, <NativeType> *buf);
```

Forms

This family of functions consists of eight members.

Set<Type>ArrayRegion	<ArrayType>	<NativeType>
SetBooleanArrayRegion	jbooleanArray	jboolean
SetByteArrayRegion	jbyteArray	jbyte
SetCharArrayRegion	jcharArray	jchar
SetShortArrayRegion	jshortArray	jshort
SetIntArrayRegion	jintArray	jint
SetLongArrayRegion	jlongArray	jlong
SetFloatArrayRegion	jfloatArray	jfloat
SetDoubleArrayRegion	jdoubleArray	jdouble

Description

Copies back a region of a primitive array from a buffer. The array reference and buf buffer must not be NULL.

Linkage

Indices in the JNIEnv interface function table.

Set<Type>ArrayRegion	Index
SetBooleanArrayRegion	207
SetByteArrayRegion	208
SetCharArrayRegion	209
SetShortArrayRegion	210
SetIntArrayRegion	211
SetLongArrayRegion	212
SetFloatArrayRegion	213
SetDoubleArrayRegion	214

Parameters   env: the JNIEnv interface pointer.

array: a reference to a primitive array to which the elements are copied.

start: the starting index in the primitive array.

len: the number of elements to be copied.

buf: the source buffer.

Exceptions   ArrayIndexOutOfBoundsException: if one of the indices in the region is not valid.

Set\<Type\>Field

Prototype   void *Set\<Type\>Field*(JNIEnv *env, jobject obj,
                  jfieldID fieldID, *\<NativeType\>* value);

Forms   This family of functions consists of nine members.

Set\<Type\>Field	\<NativeType\>
SetObjectField	jobject
SetBooleanField	jboolean
SetByteField	jbyte
SetCharField	jchar
SetShortField	jshort
SetIntField	jint
SetLongField	jlong
SetFloatField	jfloat
SetDoubleField	jdouble

Description   Sets the value of an instance field of an object. The obj refer-
                  ence must not be NULL.

Linkage   Indices in the JNIEnv interface function table.

Set\<Type\>Field	Index
SetObjectField	104
SetBooleanField	105
SetByteField	106
SetCharField	107
SetShortField	108
SetIntField	109
SetLongField	110
SetFloatField	111
SetDoubleField	112

Parameters   env: the JNIEnv interface pointer.

obj: a reference to an object.

fieldID: a field ID.

value: the new value of the field.

Exceptions   None.

SetObjectArrayElement

Prototype
```
void SetObjectArrayElement(JNIEnv *env,
      jobjectArray array, jsize index,
      jobject value);
```

Description
Sets an element of an Object array. The array reference must not be NULL.

Linkage
Index 174 in the JNIEnv interface function table.

Parameters
env: the JNIEnv interface pointer.

array: a reference to an array whose element will be accessed.

index: index of the array element to be accessed.

value: the new value of the array element.

Exceptions
ArrayIndexOutOfBoundsException: if index does not specify a valid index in the array.

ArrayStoreException: if the class of value is not a subclass of the element class of the array.

SetStatic<Type>Field

Prototype   void *SetStatic<Type>Field*(JNIEnv *env,
                           jclass clazz, jfieldID fieldID,
                           <NativeType> value);

Forms   This family of functions consists of nine members.

SetStatic<Type>Field	*<NativeType>*
SetStaticObjectField	jobject
SetStaticBooleanField	jboolean
SetStaticByteField	jbyte
SetStaticCharField	jchar
SetStaticShortField	jshort
SetStaticIntField	jint
SetStaticLongField	jlong
SetStaticFloatField	jfloat
SetStaticDoubleField	jdouble

Description   Sets the value of a static field of a class or interface. The field to
                       access is specified by a field ID.

Linkage   Indices in the JNIEnv interface function table.

SetStatic<Type>Field	**Index**
SetStaticObjectField	154
SetStaticBooleanField	155
SetStaticByteField	156
SetStaticCharField	157
SetStaticShortField	158
SetStaticIntField	159
SetStaticLongField	160
SetStaticFloatField	161
SetStaticDoubleField	162

Parameters   env: the JNIEnv interface pointer.

clazz: a reference to a class or interface whose static field will be accessed.

fieldID: an ID denoting the static field to be accessed.

value: the new value of the field.

Exceptions   None.

Throw

Prototype ·	`jint Throw(JNIEnv *env, jthrowable obj);`

Description   Causes a `java.lang.Throwable` object to be thrown. A thrown exception will be pending in the current thread, but does not immediately disrupt native code execution.

Linkage   Index 13 in the `JNIEnv` interface function table.

Parameters   env: the `JNIEnv` interface pointer.

obj: a `java.lang.Throwable` object.

Return Values   Returns zero on success; otherwise, returns a negative value.

Exceptions   The given `java.lang.Throwable` object.

ThrowNew

Prototype

```
jint ThrowNew(JNIEnv *env, jclass clazz,
        const char *message);
```

Description   Constructs an exception object from the specified class with the message specified by message and causes that exception to be thrown.

Linkage   Index 14 in the JNIEnv interface function table.

Parameters   env: the JNIEnv interface pointer.

clazz: a subclass of java.lang.Throwable.

message: the message used to construct the java.lang.Throwable object.

Return Values   Returns zero on success; otherwise, returns a negative value if the specified exception cannot be thrown.

Exceptions   The newly constructed java.lang.Throwable object, or any exception that occurs in constructing this object.

ToReflectedField

Prototype

```
jobject ToReflectedField(JNIEnv *env, jclass cls,
    jfieldID fieldID, jboolean isStatic);
```

Description

Converts a field ID derived from `cls` to an instance of the `java.lang.reflect.Field` class.

This function was introduced in Java 2 SDK release 1.2.

Linkage

Index 12 in the `JNIEnv` interface function table.

Parameters

`env`: the `JNIEnv` interface pointer.

`cls`: a reference to a class or interface.

`fieldID`: a JNI field ID.

`isStatic`: whether the field ID denotes a static field.

Return Values

Returns an instance of the `java.lang.reflect.Field` class; otherwise, returns `NULL`. Returns `NULL` if and only if an invocation of this function has thrown an exception.

Exceptions

`OutofMemoryError`: if the system runs out of memory.

ToReflectedMethod

Prototype	jobject ToReflectedMethod(JNIEnv *env, jclass cls, jmethodID methodID, jboolean isStatic);
Description	Converts a method ID derived from cls to an instance of the java.lang.reflect.Method class or to an instance of the java.lang.reflect.Constructor class. This function was introduced in Java 2 SDK release 1.2.
Linkage	Index 9 in the JNIEnv interface function table.
Parameters	env: the JNIEnv interface pointer. cls: a reference to a class or interface. methodID: a method ID. isStatic: whether the method ID refers to a static method.
Return Values	Returns an instance of the java.lang.reflect.Method class or an instance of the java.lang.reflect.Constructor class; otherwise, returns NULL. Returns NULL if and only if an invocation of this function has thrown an exception.
Exceptions	OutofMemoryError: if the system runs out of memory.

UnregisterNatives

Prototype   `jint UnregisterNatives(JNIEnv *env, jclass clazz);`

Description   Unregisters native methods of a class. The class goes back to the state before it was linked or registered with its native method functions.

This function should not be used in normal native code. Instead, it provides special programs a way to reload and relink native libraries.

Linkage   Index 216 in the `JNIEnv` interface function table.

Parameters   env: the `JNIEnv` interface pointer.

clazz: a reference to a class object whose native methods are to be unregistered.

Return Values Returns zero on success; otherwise, returns a negative value.

Exceptions   None.

Index

J

The Addison-Wesley Java™ Series

Ken Arnold · James Gosling
The Java™ Programming Language
Second Edition

ISBN 0-201-31006-6

Mary Campione · Kathy Walrath
The Java™ Tutorial
Second Edition
Object-Oriented Programming for the Internet

ISBN 0-201-31007-4

Campione · Walrath · Huml · Tutorial Team
The Java™ Tutorial
Continued
The Rest of the JDK™

ISBN 0-201-48558-3

Patrick Chan
The Java™ Developers
ALMANAC 1999

ISBN 0-201-43298-6

Patrick Chan · Rosanna Lee
The Java™ Class Libraries
Second Edition, Volume 2
java.applet java.awt java.beans

ISBN 0-201-31003-1

Patrick Chan · Rosanna Lee · Douglas Kramer
The Java™ Class Libraries
Second Edition, Volume 1
java.io java.lang java.math
java.net java.text java.util

ISBN 0-201-31002-3

Patrick Chan · Rosanna Lee · Douglas Kramer
The Java™ Class Libraries
Second Edition, Volume 1
Supplement for the Java 2 Platform
Standard Edition, v1.2

ISBN 0-201-48552-4

James Gosling · Bill Joy · Guy Steele
The Java™ Language
Specification

ISBN 0-201-63451-1

James Gosling · Frank Yellin · The Java Team
The Java™ Application
Programming
Interface, Volume 1
Core Packages

ISBN 0-201-63453-8

James Gosling · Frank Yellin · The Java Team
The Java™ Application
Programming
Interface, Volume 2
Window Toolkit and Applets

ISBN 0-201-63459-7

Li Gong
Inside Java™ 2
Platform Security
Architecture, API Design, and Implementation

ISBN 0-201-31000-7

Jonni Kanerva
The Java™
FAQ

ISBN 0-201-63456-2

Doug Lea
Concurrent
Programming in Java™
Second Edition
Design Principles and Patterns

ISBN 0-201-31009-0

Sheng Liang
The Java™
Native Interface
Programmer's Guide and Specification

ISBN 0-201-32577-2

Tim Lindholm · Frank Yellin
The Java™ Virtual
Machine Specification
Second Edition

ISBN 0-201-43294-3

Henry Sowizral · Kevin Rushforth · Michael Deering
The Java™ 3D
API Specification

ISBN 0-201-32576-4

Kathy Walrath · Mary Campione
The JFC
Swing Tutorial
A Guide to Constructing GUIs

ISBN 0-201-43321-4

White · Fisher · Cattell · Hamilton · Hapner
JDBC™ API Tutorial and
Reference, Second Edition
Universal Data Access for the Java™ 2 Platform

ISBN 0-201-43328-1

Please see our web site (http://www.awl.com/cseng/javaseries)
for more information on these titles.

Addison-Wesley Computer and Engineering Publishing Group

How to Interact with Us

1. Visit our Web site

http://www.awl.com/cseng

When you think you've read enough, there's always more content for you at Addison-Wesley's web site. Our web site contains a directory of complete product information including:

- Chapters
- Exclusive author interviews
- Links to authors' pages
- Tables of contents
- Source code

You can also discover what tradeshows and conferences Addison-Wesley will be attending, read what others are saying about our titles, and find out where and when you can meet our authors and have them sign your book.

2. Subscribe to Our Email Mailing Lists

Subscribe to our electronic mailing lists and be the first to know when new books are publishing. Here's how it works: Sign up for our electronic mailing at **http://www.awl.com/cseng/mailinglists.html**. Just select the subject areas that interest you and you will receive notification via email when we publish a book in that area.

3. Contact Us via Email

cepubprof@awl.com
Ask general questions about our books.
Sign up for our electronic mailing lists.
Submit corrections for our web site.

bexpress@awl.com
Request an Addison-Wesley catalog.
Get answers to questions regarding your order or our products.

innovations@awl.com
Request a current Innovations Newsletter.

webmaster@awl.com
Send comments about our web site.

mikeh@awl.com
Submit a book proposal.
Send errata for an Addison-Wesley book.

cepubpublicity@awl.com
Request a review copy for a member of the media interested in reviewing new Addison-Wesley titles.

We encourage you to patronize the many fine retailers who stock Addison-Wesley titles. Visit our online directory to find stores near you or visit our online store:
http://store.awl.com/ or call **800-824-7799**.

Addison Wesley Longman
Computer and Engineering Publishing Group
One Jacob Way, Reading, Massachusetts 01867 USA
TEL 781-944-3700 • FAX 781-942-3076